THE OSPREY GUIDE TO
ANTHONY TROLLOPE

THE
OSPREY GUIDE TO
Anthony Trollope

MICHAEL HARDWICK

OSPREY

FIRST PUBLISHED IN 1974 BY
OSPREY PUBLISHING LTD, P.O. BOX 25
707 OXFORD ROAD, READING, BERKSHIRE

ISBN 0 85045 158 2

Printed in Great Britain by
Cox & Wyman Ltd,
London, Fakenham and Reading

Contents

27946

N.B. The six titles to which the letter (*B*) is appended comprise the series known as *The Chronicles of Barsetshire*.

THE OSPREY GUIDE TO
ANTHONY TROLLOPE

Introduction

ANTHONY TROLLOPE'S popularity declined in the last years of his life and plummeted soon after his death when the publication of his *Autobiography*, with its revelation of his income and industrious (almost industri*al*) manner of working, scandalized a public who could not believe that a writer worthy of the name could approach his art in the manner of a tradesman. Even so, a few of his novels continued to be admired, and the number of titles reprinted has advanced slowly over the years. Today he is one of the most widely read Victorian novelists.

Much of his accelerated rehabilitation in recent years must be attributed to dramatizations of his work for the mass media of radio and television, which have lured many thousands of people who had never read a word of him into libraries and bookshops in search of his writings. Of course, there is a deal of difference between the compulsion of, say, a television version, with all its short cuts towards appreciation, its subtle modernization of dialogue, its sheer visual interest of 'period' setting, costume and manners, and the mass of reading needed to get through a lengthy novel written by a Victorian for Victorians. Often enough, watchers of television or listeners to radio who have been tempted to try the original have turned away again, disappointed. I doubt whether this has been so much the case with Trollope as with some others: there is a pace about his work which can appeal to many readers today who find his contemporaries stodgy and heavy going.

Again, I think it is the mass media – which render greater service to literature than is always acknowledged – that are partly responsible for the availability today of some of Trollope's novels which might not otherwise have been thought commercially eligible for inclusion in such series as the Oxford University Press's 'The World's Classics' and J. M. Dent's 'Everyman's Library', or, more recently, in paperback reprint. But even if these comparatively borderline cases were eliminated there would still be a number of 'Trollopes' constantly available: certainly the six novels which make up the Barchester sequence, the six 'Palliser' ones, and, perhaps, *The Belton Estate, The Claverings, The Way We Live Now, Dr Wortle's School*, and a handful more. At its most conservative this adds up to more than a third of his total of forty-seven novels, which is a record not many novelists have achieved and any in our century would envy. Charles Dickens, of course, takes the Eng. Lit. Prize with all his work perpetually in print; but Dickens, whom Trollope envied and affected somewhat to scorn, was a genius, and wrote far fewer novels than Trollope, who was a journeyman and wrote too many. Trollope is perhaps better compared with Thackeray, whom he admired for his qualities but censured for his comparative indolence, and beats easily in percentage terms. In one of the critical digressions in the *Autobiography* he places Thackeray first of all in his time, for his characterization, style and general technique; George Eliot, for her analytical penetration, second; and Dickens a grudging third – the place which I suspect only the required modesty prevented him awarding himself.

Trollope had many great qualities, but I do not believe that they included a sense of the ridiculous such as Dickens possessed and which, more than his sentiment and his 'teaching', made him idolized. Trollope said he found Dickens's humour 'very much below' that of Thackeray, but admitted that it had 'reached the intellect of all'. This comment, to my mind, is self-revelatory of a deficiency in Trollope as a writer that, had it not existed, might have put him shoulder to shoulder with Dickens. He was far from being a humourless man, or a humourless writer, but he did not see life as the comedy which, for all the pathos and iniquity he found in it, Dickens was always so aware of and instinctively portrayed. Trollope felt he ought to be plumbing depths and exploring areas of behaviour and the mind. Interestingly, perceptively and often amusingly though he often succeeded in doing so, I feel we have lost something remarkable that he might have given us if he had *tried* a little less hard and laughed a little more.

His writings are typical of himself. He was energetic, opinionated and highly observant, and certainly did not allow social delicacy to make him pull his punches to the extent that Dickens did. He had more to say about the sexual dilemmas and materialistically-motivated behaviour of his time, and instinctively knew that handsome villains and cads are as fascinating to readers as they prove to be to a number of his heroines. Bigamy, illegitimacy and matrimonial manoeuvring are prominent amongst his themes. He generally describes his characters in much detail, and then lets them get on and tell their stories through their actions and what they say to one another, rather than rely upon long narrative, which is no doubt the reason why his stories tend to dramatize so satisfyingly. His sometimes exasperating digressions and asides to the reader can be skipped without loss, and if many of his people and places are given names which are irritatingly facetious, they are often made memorable by their very aptness.

Anthony Trollope was a hard-working, hard-riding, peppery old buffer – not always old, of course, though that is how I for one always see him – who lashed about in many directions and landed many a point-scoring blow. He was, above all things, a tremendous professional, and proud of it, which eventually damned him in the eyes of the 'Art for Art's sake' coteries, who, enthroned in Chelsea and Bloomsbury, appointed themselves arbiters of what constituted worth-while literature in following decades. To today's more realistic audience, hungry for good story-telling and fed up with obliquity and obscurity, he has much to offer.

Because he wrote so much, Trollope created a vast number of characters. To keep this present volume within the permissible bounds of size and price I have had to restrict the section *The Characters* to principals and other significant figures only: even so, there are nearly five hundred entries. Many of his descriptions of a single character extend to two, three and even four pages, whereas I can afford only a few lines. I have tried to find quotations for all the more important figures which convey something of character or manner, rather than of appearance: Trollope tends to standardize the looks of his heroines, heroes and villains. In the case of those of his works generally acknowledged to be of least quality or interest I have merely given identifications without supporting quotes. In the belief that the character-quotes convey enough of Trollope's writing style I have dispensed with a Quotations section as such. This means that his dialogue is not represented, but perhaps the reader who is not yet acquainted with him will accept an assurance that it is generally excellent. He knew the essential rules of dialogue-writing which too many writers even today have never grasped. He did not always practise what he preached about the writer's craft, but in the case of dialogue he most often did. This is what he had to say about it in the *Autobiography*:

The writer may tell much of his story in conversations, but he may only do so by putting such words into the mouths of his personages as persons so situated would probably use. He is not allowed for the sake of his tale to make his characters give utterance to long speeches, such as are not customarily heard from men and women. The ordinary talk of ordinary people is carried on in short sharp expressive sentences, which very frequently are never completed, – the language of which even among educated people is often incorrect. The novel-writer in constructing his dialogue must so steer between absolute accuracy of language – which would give to his conversation an air of pedantry, and the slovenly inaccuracy of ordinary talkers, which if closely followed would offend by an appearance of grimace – as to produce upon the ear of his readers a sense of reality. If he be quite real he will seem to attempt to be funny. If he be quite correct he will seem to be unreal. And above all, let the speeches be short. No character should utter much above a dozen words at a breath, – unless the writer can justify to himself a longer flood of speech by the speciality of the occasion.

As to the rest of this book: *The Works*, being so many in number, have had to be summarized very briefly, but I hope adequately; and in writing the short life I have confined myself to what I believe to be the essentials. The introductions to the respective plots, giving details of writing and publication, serve as additions to the *Life*. (They are arranged, incidentally, in order of the works' composition, not publication.)

The most modern full-length biography is James Pope Hennessy's highly readable *Anthony Trollope* (Jonathan Cape, 1971). Michael Sadleir's *Trollope: A Commentary* (first published by Constable in 1927 and revised in 1945) combines valuably arranged facts and authoritative opinion. Other important studies are *Anthony Trollope: His Work, Associates and Originals* (The Bodley Head, 1913) by Thomas Sweet Escott, his close friend, and Hugh Walpole's *Anthony Trollope* (Macmillan, 1928). These works will be found to point the way to others, notably the long memoir *What I Remember* by Trollope's brother Tom, first published in 1887 and now abridged for modern reading and introduced by Herbert van Thal (Kimber, 1973). Eileen Bigland's *The Indomitable Mrs Trollope* (Barrie & Jenkins, 1970) is revelatory about her family as well as absorbing in its own right. There is a volume devoted to Trollope, edited by Donald Smalley (1969) in Routledge & Kegan Paul's *Critical Heritage* series; and his *Collected Letters*, edited by Bradford A. Booth, were published by the Oxford University Press in 1951, though Trollope, as a letter-writer, is disappointing.

Many other works on him, or of associated interest, exist; but without doubt the most fascinating of all is his own *Autobiography*, written in 1875-6 and published in 1883, the year following his death, with a preface by his son Henry M. Trollope. It is a splendid reflection of his character and attitudes of mind, and contains a great deal that is pertinent to the writer's craft and trade today. There is no standard edition of all Trollope's works, and it is extremely difficult to amass a complete set, however heterogeneous.

Finally, I should add that this present volume deals only with his novels, merely noting in passing the writing and publication of the short stories and other works.

MICHAEL HARDWICK

Anthony Trollope

My boyhood was, I think, as unhappy as that of a young gentleman could well be, my misfortune arising from a mixture of poverty and gentle standing on the part of my father, and from an utter want on my own part of that juvenile manhood which enables some boys to hold up their heads even among the distresses which such a position is sure to produce.

THUS, after a brief apologia for writing about himself at all, Anthony Trollope plunges forthrightly into that revealing and lively *Autobiography* which is to be so often mentioned and quoted in this present work. To judge of his boyhood as recorded in it, 'unhappy' seems to have been an understatement.

He was born in Keppel Street, Russell Square, in the Bloomsbury district of London on 24 April 1815. His father, Thomas Anthony Trollope (1774–1835), was a Chancery barrister who, through rash enterprises, Micawberish ineffectuality, and a temper so vile that attorneys preferred to take their briefs elsewhere, soon brought his family down to financial ruin. The ambitions of that man, who, in Anthony's words, 'was never destined to have an ambition gratified', condemned his sons to the unmatchable humiliation of poor boys amongst rich ones at the great public schools of Winchester and Harrow, where Anthony suffered the best part of twelve years' persecution from fellow-pupils and masters alike for his shabbiness, dirtiness, ungainliness, ugliness, and stupidity. In addition, for some of the time, he was denied credit even for necessary clothing and received no pocket-money, for his fees had not been paid.

This latter circumstance was due to his having been virtually deserted by his family, all of whom had gone to America in the wake of Anthony's resolute mother, Frances Milton Trollope

(1780–1863). She had set forth with the notion of establishing what proved to be an unneeded fancy-goods emporium, but returned at length with the infinitely more valuable stock-in-trade of observation and experience from which, in her fifty-second year, she proceeded to fashion her best-selling controversial book *Domestic Manners of the Americans*, 1832; it proved to be the foundation-stone of a literary career which was to result in some fifty works of travel and fiction and saved her family from the penury to which her husband had reduced it. But the money she earned was quickly spent and in April 1834 the family fled to Bruges, in Belgium, carrying with them the few belongings they had managed to snatch from under the bailiffs' noses.

Anthony went with them this time, and so his education ended when he was nineteen; for all it had brought him in the way of knowledge or prospects it might well never have begun. His exaggerated recollection in the *Autobiography* was of having been taught nothing but Latin and Greek, and of having absorbed little of either; yet he began his working life briefly as classical usher in a private school in Bruges. He lasted six weeks in the post. Then a close friend of his mother, whose father, Sir Francis Freeling, was Secretary of the General Post Office in London, heard of his plight and secured him an interview there. Although he knew nothing of arithmetic and could not even copy some lines from *The Times* accurately or without blots (the only examination he had to undergo), he was given a desk and a chair and so began the Civil Service career which was to last for thirty-three years.

The first years at the Post Office were almost as replete with misery and discomfort as his school life had been. He often came close to being dismissed for slovenly work, unpunctuality and misbehaviour. He was hard put to make ends meet on his £90 a year and fell into the clutches of moneylenders. He also almost fell into the clutches of one of various young women who flitted through his life at this period: her mother turned up in the office he shared with several other clerks and demanded, for all to hear,

'Anthony Trollope, when are you going to marry my daughter?'
He managed to resist.

Yet he tried hard to please, though apparently with much of
the unfortunate capacity of his father (now dead) for failing at
almost everything he tried. One hilarious example he recounts
in the *Autobiography* concerned another Secretary of the G.P.O.,
Colonel William Leader Maberly:

On one occasion, in the performance of my duty, I had to put a
private letter containing bank-notes on the secretary's table, – which
letter I had duly opened, as it was not marked private. The letter was
seen by the Colonel, but had not been moved by him when he left the
room. On his return it was gone. In the meantime I had returned to the
room, again in the performance of some duty. When the letter was missed
I was sent for, and there I found the Colonel much moved about his
letter, and a certain chief clerk, who, with a long face, was making
suggestions as to the probable fate of the money. The letter has been
taken, said the Colonel, turning to me angrily, and, by G —! there has
been nobody in the room but you and I. As he spoke, he thundered his
fist down upon the table. 'Then,' said I, 'by G— ! you have taken it.'
And I also thundered my fist down; – but, accidentally, not upon the
table. There was a standing movable desk, at which, I presume, it was
the Colonel's habit to write, and on this movable desk was a large bottle
full of ink. My fist unfortunately came on the desk, and the ink at once
flew up, covering the Colonel's face and shirt-front. Then it was a sight
to see that senior clerk, as he seized a quire of blotting-paper, and rushed
to the aid of his superior officer, striving to mop up the ink; and a sight
also to see the Colonel, in his agony, hit right out through the blotting-
paper at that senior clerk's unoffending stomach. At that moment there
came in the Colonel's private secretary, with the letter and the money,
and I was desired to go back to my own room. This was an incident not
much in my favour, though I do not know that it did me special harm.

He faced life very much alone. His brother Henry had died in
his early twenties at Bruges in 1834, the year before their father
had died there. In 1836 his sister Emily had succumbed to con-
sumption, aged sixteen, at the home at Hadley, Hertfordshire,
which she shared with Mrs Trollope after their return from
Belgium. The remaining sister, Cecilia, lived on with Mrs

Trollope at Hadley and her succession of other homes; and Tom took teaching jobs in various parts of the country, eventually moving with Mrs Trollope to permanent residence in Florence in 1844, shortly before the death of Cecilia, who had married one of Anthony's Post Office colleagues, John Tilley. There are many links between events and people in Anthony Trollope's novels and his own early years of seedy lodgings, short commons, and yearning for love – or at least acceptance – and some real sense of direction. There is no space to discuss them here, but *The Three Clerks* may be mentioned for its reflection of the young Anthony and his troubles in the character and escapades of Charley Tudor.

His fortunes changed dramatically in 1841, when he was twenty-six. A report from Ireland upon the incompetence of a Post Office surveyor's clerk there reached Anthony's hands before anyone else's. More than usually troubled at that moment by debts and the disapproval of Colonel Maberly, he volunteered to replace the man. Such posts were usually filled by appointment, but the Secretary assented with relief.

The income was not great, but there was a daily subsistence allowance of fifteen shillings, and sixpence a mile for travelling on duty. Anthony calculated that, after paying his expenses, it amounted to over £400 a year, to him a small fortune. He landed in Dublin in September 1841 with little conception of Ireland except as 'a land flowing with fun and whisky, in which irregularity was the rule of life, and where broken heads were looked upon as honourable badges'. Presenting himself to the Secretary of the Irish Post Office he was aggrieved to learn that Colonel Maberly had reported very adversely on him, but encouraged to be told that he would be judged on his performance: 'From that time to the day on which I left the service, I never heard a word of censure, nor had many months passed before I found that my services were valued. Before a year was over, I had acquired the character of a thoroughly good public servant.'

He also acquired an interest that would provide his principal relaxation until old age, and would become as much a feature of his fiction as his clergymen – hunting. His own words convey best what it came to mean to him:

I found that the surveyor to whom I had been sent kept a pack of hounds, and therefore I bought a hunter. I do not think he liked it, but he could not well complain. He never rode to hounds himself, but I did; and then and thus began one of the great joys of my life. I have ever since been constant to the sport, having learned to love it with an affection which I cannot myself fathom or understand. Surely no man has laboured at it as I have done, or hunted under such drawbacks as to distances, money, and natural disadvantages. I am very heavy, very blind, have been – in reference to hunting – a poor man, and am now an old man. I have often had to travel all night outside a mailcoach, in order that I might hunt the next day. Nor have I ever been in truth a good horseman. And I have passed the greater part of my hunting life under the discipline of the Civil Service. But it has been for more than thirty years a duty for me to ride to hounds; and I have performed that duty with a persistent energy. Nothing has ever been allowed to stand in the way of hunting, – neither the writing of books, nor the work of the Post Office, nor other pleasures. As regarded the Post Office, it soon seemed to be understood that I was to hunt; and when my services were re-transferred to England, no word of difficulty ever reached me about it. I have written on very many subjects, and on most of them with pleasure; but on no subject with such delight as that on hunting. I have dragged it into many novels, – into too many no doubt, – but I have always felt myself deprived of a legitimate joy when the nature of the tale has not allowed me a hunting chapter.

Well might he add that the life he led in Ireland was altogether 'very jolly'. It became more so when, at a fashionable watering-place near Dublin, he met Rose Heseltine, the daughter of the manager of a small bank at Rotherham, Yorkshire. They were soon engaged. Her father had no money to offer with her, and Anthony, who still had a number of debts to settle, set back their marriage plans further by buying his horse; but they were married on 11 June 1844 at Rotherham. She was seven years his junior, and survived him by thirty-four, dying in 1917 aged ninety-five. They had two sons, Henry Merivale Trollope, born in 1846, and Frederick James Anthony Trollope, born 1847.

The marriage was a placid, harmonious relationship, with Rose doing what she could to ease her husband's burden of work by copying his manuscripts, and keeping him content by putting up with his preference for the male companionship of the hunting field and the club over mixed social entertainment, which he disliked. She also had the great good sense not to oppose his one romantic attachment outside their marriage, which, perhaps partly due to her tolerance of it, never developed into anything more than love-at-a-distance. The lady involved was a Bostonian, Kate Field, whom Anthony and Rose Trollope met in Florence in 1860 when he was forty-five and Kate twenty-one. She was pretty and vivacious, and the possessor of multifarious talents of an artistic kind, none of which, however, she succeeded in mastering to a professional degree, although she did make an international name for herself at length as a lecturer in the cause of women's rights. Anthony Trollope's platonic love for her lasted for the rest of his life. They met quite often, generally in Rose's company, and corresponded warmly; but that was all. Kate Field died in 1896.

There is now little more to add to this brief *Life*. The course of Trollope's professional activities, as Civil Servant and writer, is charted in the introductions to the summaries of his novels. One inevitably asks, though, how any writer became a writer in the first place, and this curiosity is intensified in the case of Anthony Trollope, who, for all his early lack of any kind of learning, discipline or advantage, transformed himself into one of the most widely read Victorian novelists and one of the most disciplined, hard-working and prolific of all time.

His motive in trying to write was to find a means of escape from the drudgery and boredom of his early Post Office service: there seemed no prospect of achieving this other than through writing. He had acquired some literary background through his own reading; and there was the example of his mother, who had leaped so sensationally to celebrity with her first book in middle age. He took stock of the possibilities.

Poetry I did not believe to be within my grasp. The drama, too, which I would fain have chosen, I believed to be above me. For history, biography, or essay writing I had not sufficient erudition. But I thought it possible that I might write a novel. I had resolved very early that in that shape must the attempt be made. But the months and years ran on, and no attempt was made. And yet no day was passed without thoughts of attempting, and a mental acknowledgment of the disgrace of post-poning it. What reader will not understand the agony of remorse produced by such a condition of mind?

The attempt remained postponed until after his engagement to Rose Heseltine, and how it was made, and what were its results, are the subject of the following pages, which cover his life's work.

Death, when it came looking for Anthony Trollope in his sixty-eighth year, found him in London, where he had moved into Garlant's Hotel, Suffolk Street, in the belief that the climate on the Sussex–Hampshire border, where he had been living for some years, was unsympathetic to his declining health. On 3 November 1882 he collapsed with a stroke during a jolly gathering at the Pimlico house of his brother-in-law, Sir John Tilley, that same John Tilley who had been a clerk with him many years before and had married his sister Cecilia. He was moved to a nursing home in Welbeck Street, where he died on 6 December, never having regained his speech. He was buried on 8 December at Kensal Green Cemetery, not far from the writer whom he had placed first in his table of admiration, William Makepeace Thackeray.

We have cause to be immensely grateful to his son Henry for exercising his discretion in favour of publishing, rather than suppressing, the *Autobiography*. Ironically, the act did Anthony Trollope's reputation immense disservice. Literary pundits were offended by the revelation of his frank attitude towards writing as a trade, practised for *money*, even to the extent of listing his receipts: they totalled, incidentally, nearly £70,000, and that with seven years of writing still to go from the time he finished the *Autobiography* – the equivalent of perhaps a million pounds today.

His popularity, which had been on the wane for some time, consequently went into full eclipse, from which it gradually emerged after the First World War, to rise to heights of similarly undeserved adulation before settling into that steady and enduring regard which, surely, is precisely the plane it deserves to occupy.

I have said nothing about Anthony Trollope's personal attitude towards either religion or politics, which play so important a part in many of his stories and whose professional practitioners are major figures in his two most famous series. In fact, he was neither a 'religious' nor a 'political' man in the passionate or active sense – his candidature for Parliament at Beverley, Yorkshire, in 1868 was a half-hearted gesture which would have done nothing much for him, and less for his country, had he succeeded. He held – or at least professed – certain idealistic notions of the qualities an English Statesman should possess, and did possess in comparison with his foreign counterparts. His view of churchmen varies from admiration to contempt, depending upon the individual's personality and the sincerity of his actions. In other words, Trollope's view was typical of that of most Englishmen then as now: the Church and politics, like most other elements of 'The Establishment', represented much that was to be respected and a great deal that was suspect, to the mind of the ordinary citizen. It is all there in his stories, and we approve or reject according to the prejudices we ourselves hold.

The Works

THE MACDERMOTS OF BALLYCLORAN

AT some time between his arrival in Ireland in September 1841 and his sitting down with pen, ink and paper in September 1843, Anthony Trollope took a stroll with a fellow Englishman at Drumsna, County Leitrim, where they came across a ruined house approached by a weed-choked drive. He recalled later:

It was one of the most melancholy spots I ever visited. I will not describe it here because I have done so in the first chapter of my first novel. We wandered about the place, suggesting to each other causes for the misery we saw there, and while I was still among the ruined walls and decayed beams I fabricated the plot of *The Macdermots of Ballycloran*.

He began this first novel in September 1843, proceeded slowly until after his marriage to Rose Heseltine in June 1844, and then with gathering momentum up to its completion in June 1845. Trollope's mother patronizingly offered to submit it to a publisher for him, but declined to read it before doing so. It was issued in three volumes by Thomas Newby, London, in May 1847. This first edition brought him no money, and he dismisses the work in the *Autobiography* as the failure he had anticipated it would be; yet it was widely and sympathetically reviewed.

The Macdermots is a drama of hatred, seduction, murder and wholesale retribution, against a background of the desperate life of the rural Ireland Trollope had observed so widely and, as the book proves, so perceptively. Ballycloran – based on the ruined house which had given him the germ of the plot – is the dilapidated home of the Macdermots: Lawrence ('Larry'), the feckless, despondent widower, and his son and daughter, Thady and

Euphemia ('Feemy'). The house is a 'gentleman's' residence, but they inhabit it in grubby poverty, for Macdermot is no longer able to meet his mortgage payments and is beyond caring about his environment.

Before Larry's decline, his mortgager, Joe Flannelly, who had built the house, had wanted a match between him and his daughter Sally, in order to raise her social status. Larry had refused her, which Flannelly had taken as an insult, marrying her off instead to his agent, Hyacinth Keegan, whom he is now using in his endeavours to dispossess the Macdermots, so that Hyacinth and Sally may have Ballycloran for their own.

Matters are resolved by a dramatic sequence of misfortunes. The most detested man in the neighbourhood is a British police officer, Captain Myles Ussher, whose mission is to seek out and destroy the many illegal potheen (whiskey) stills. The distillers, led by Joe Reynolds, are waiting their opportunity to kill Myles, who has had Reynolds's brother Tim unjustly imprisoned. Thady Macdermot's servant, Pat Brady, is enlisted as spy within Ballycloran and is able to report that Feemy is in love with Myles, which in local eyes is tantamount to treason on her part.

Myles's love, moreover, has already taken tangible form: he has seduced Feemy. When he is notified of his promotion and transfer he agrees to take her with him, though not as wife. Thady catches them leaving and jumps to the conclusion that Myles, whom he hates as much as anyone, is taking his sister away against her will. He strikes Myles and kills him, with the result that he is tried and hanged, Feemy dies giving birth to a child, and Larry lapses into insanity, so that there are no longer any Macdermots at Ballycloran.

THE KELLYS AND THE O'KELLYS:
or LANDLORDS AND TENANTS

THE failure of *The Macdermots* to sell proved no deterrent to Trollope, who later recorded: 'I do not remember that I felt in any way disappointed or hurt. I am quite sure that no word of complaint passed my lips. I think I may say that after the publication I never said a word about the book, even to my wife.' He was already writing another, *The Kellys and the O'Kellys*, to be published the following year, July 1848, by Henry Colburn, on a profit-sharing basis. In the event, there were no profits. In its author's words: 'The book was not only not read, but was never heard of . . . And yet it is a good Irish story, much inferior to *The Macdermots* as to plot, but superior in the mode of telling.' He quotes with evident relish the words of a review in *The Times* – obtained, to his annoyance, by a friend's influence, instead of by the work on its own behalf: 'Of *The Kellys and the O'Kellys* we may say what the master said to his footman, when the man complained of the constant supply of legs of mutton on the kitchen table. "Well, John, legs of mutton are good substantial food"; and we may say also what John replied: "Substantial, sir; – yes, they are substantial, but a little coarse."'

'Even that,' Trollope adds wryly, 'did not sell the book!'

Its sub-title is 'Landlords and Tenants'. The principal landlord is Lord Ballindine (Frank O'Kelly), the horse-fancying young head of the Kelly and O'Kelly clans. He wishes to marry Fanny Wyndham, the heiress ward of the Earl of Cashel, who has compelled them to break their engagement, on the grounds that he disapproves of Frank's propensities for the turf. He would prefer her to marry his own son, Lord Kilcullen, who could well do with Fanny's personal fortune to enable him to pay his gambling debts, but she refuses.

An heiress of a lesser degree, is Anastasia ('Anty') Lynch, daughter of Simeon Lynch who had managed the Ballindine estates; in fact, had managed them so well to his own advantage that he had been able to send his son Barry to Eton with the present Lord Ballindine. Anty is entitled to half this ill-gotten fortune, and in order to get his hands on it Barry attempts to murder her. She takes refuge with a tenant of Frank, Mrs Kelly, who runs an inn and shop. Even now there is danger to Anty's inheritance, for Mrs Kelly's son Martin, though ten years Anty's

junior, would not scruple to get her to marry him if it would
bring him the money.

Out of this sordid motive, however, emerges true affection,
for Martin falls genuinely in love with Anty and she with him.
Fanny Wyndham and Frank are reunited; Lord Kilcullen is
hounded by his creditors to France; and the debauched Barry
Lynch, having failed in his attempts to bring ruin to the Kellys
for succouring his sister, also deems it wiser to make his home
abroad.

An important additional character who keeps appearing in the
tale is Walter ('Dot') Blake, a crafty squire, ostensibly Lord
Ballindine's friend, but, in truth, wholly devoted to his own
interests.

LA VENDÉE: AN HISTORICAL ROMANCE

WITH two failures to his name, and an understandable tendency
to believe that he had always been ill-used by life, Trollope might
well have been sympathized with if he had given up his attempts
to be a novelist in 1848, when Henry Colburn told him, in a
letter about the loss he had sustained over *The Kellys*: 'It is
evident that readers do not like novels on Irish subjects as well
as on others. Thus you will perceive it is impossible for me to
give any encouragement to you to proceed in novel-writing.'
He took it philosophically, however, and pressed on with the
new book he had nearly finished, and which Colburn had agreed
to read. It was the historical romance *La Vendée*.

Trollope confesses in his *Autobiography* that the £20 advance
Colburn at length agreed to pay him on this work had been
'talked out of' the publisher by Tom Trollope, Anthony's
brother, who by now was established as an author and journalist
of repute. Neither publisher nor author had cause to congratulate
himself upon the outcome. The three-volume work, which
appeared in 1850, did not sell and received almost no critical

attention. Trollope's later comment is: 'The story is certainly inferior to those which had gone before; – chiefly because I knew accurately the life of the people in Ireland, and knew, in truth, nothing of life in the La Vendée country, and also because the facts of the present time came more within the limits of my powers of story-telling than those of past years. But,' he reassured himself, 'I read the book the other day, and am not ashamed of it. The conception as to the feeling of the people is, I think, true; the characters are distinct; and the tale is not dull.'

In fact, most of the characters in *La Vendée* are taken from real life: Robespierre, his fiancée Eleanor Duplay and her cabinet-maker father Simon, the revolutionary Bertrand Barère, the ruthless soldier Westermann; and, above all, the members of the Larochejaquelin (as Trollope spelt it) family, whose part in the Vendéan counter-Revolutionary insurrection of 1793 is a central theme. Trollope's story, for the most part, faithfully reflects the true events of the uprising, which need not be retraced here. Where the demands of story-telling need to prevail he departs from or 'bends' the facts a little, and finds some facets of character which suit the novelist's purpose, in defiance of the historian. His principal modification is the introduction of a fictional member of the Larochejaquelins, Agatha, a 'sister' of the Vendéan leader Henri, through whom he introduces a personal conflict within the movement by making her reject the hand of one of its real leaders, Adolphe Denot, for which he exacts fierce revenge.

(*Note*: With the exception of Agatha Larochejaquelin, the many characters in this insignificant novel, being drawn from real life, are not dealt with in *The Characters* section of this present work.)

THE WARDEN

When my historical novel failed, as completely as had its predecessors, the two Irish novels, I began to ask myself whether, after all, that was my proper line. I have never thought of questioning the justice of the verdict expressed against me. The idea that I was the unfortunate owner of unappreciated genius never troubled me. I did not look at the books after they were published, feeling sure that they had been, as it were, damned with good reason. But still I was clear in my mind that I would not lay down my pen. Then and therefore I determined to change my hand, and to attempt a play. – (*Autobiography*)

THE play he wrote in 1850 was a comedy-drama in five acts, *The Noble Jilt*, set in Bruges in the same period as *La Vendée*. Trollope sent it to his mother's friend George Bartley, who had recently retired after a successful career as actor-manager, and received a frank verdict: 'Had I still been a manager, *The Noble Jilt* is not a play I could have recommended for production.' Nor was it produced – it was published as a curiosity, in a limited edition, in 1923. Trollope later re-worked many of its elements into the first of the 'Palliser' novels, *Can You Forgive Her?* (1864). (Its *dramatis personae* do not appear in The Characters in this present work, except in references to their equivalents in the novel.)

After this further setback, Trollope set himself at a literary venture of yet another type. He had met John Murray, who, besides publishing many of the most eminent authors of the time, had made something of a speciality of guide-books. Trollope proposed one on Ireland, a country, as he explained, about whose topography he knew more at first hand than most people, if not, indeed, anyone at all. Murray invited him to submit some specimen material, at which Trollope threw himself into a frenzy of riding about Dublin, Killarney and the routes between them, labouring eagerly and earnestly at writing up his observations. He sent the roll of manuscript to Albemarle Street, and busied himself with his official duties to pass the time until Murray's decision, which he had understood him to promise within a fortnight of receiving the material. It did not come until nine months later, in response to an angry inquiry from Trollope: the roll of paper was returned, obviously never having been opened.

Thus far, Anthony Trollope had failed as novelist and as playwright, and had seen his one incursion into non-fiction treated with, to say the least, indifference. Fortunately for his livelihood and his self-esteem, he still had his official duties, which he took very seriously and performed conscientiously, and it happened at this juncture that a change in them intervened to demand so much of his time and energy that writing was put out of the question, anyway, and to provide him with what he termed two of the happiest years of his life. He was recalled to England to organize a rational and efficient system of rural mail deliveries in the south-western and western counties, such as he had done in Ireland. It involved riding an average of forty miles a day on horseback, visiting post offices, stately homes, parsonages, remote farmhouses and all other manner of dwellings, to inquire into the postal arrangements. And, among other places, it took him to Salisbury.

He had, he tells us, often turned over in his head fragments of plot he might use, if only he could find the time to write; but it was not until he chanced to wander into Salisbury cathedral close one midsummer evening, and paused on the little bridge spanning the stream, that there suddenly came to him the conception of the work that would earn him fame and would lead to a series of sequels which were to bring him immortality.

It was more than a year before he was able to begin writing *The Warden* (he intended at first to call it *The Precentor*) in July 1852 at Tenbury, Worcestershire, taking for the first time the settings of Barchester close and the parish of Plumstead Episcopi, and introducing his readers to those latterly beloved men, Archdeacon Grantly and the Reverend Septimus Harding. Its writing was slowed down by the demands of his Post Office work, causing him to comment in the *Autobiography* that in later days it would have been completed in six weeks. As James Pope Hennessy no doubt rightly comments, *The Warden* must owe much of its quality to its leisurely gestation, and might well have turned out as flimsy as some of the last works, had it been written in such haste.

It was finished in the autumn of 1853 and published by Longman, Brown, Green, and Longmans, as the house of Longman was then known, in January 1855. It was tolerably well received by reviewers, but virtually ignored by the public at large, several years being needed to sell out the printing of 1,000 copies, about a third of which had to be sold at reduced price. If a parallel with an instance of some thirty years later involving another author might be permitted, the initial failure of the book which had introduced characters who would subsequently carry Trollope to fame could be matched with that of Arthur Conan Doyle's *A Study in Scarlet*, which its author had to sell outright for £25 to the only publisher who would show an interest in it; which was ignored by the public when published in 1887; yet which had introduced into literature two figures who would become immortal, Sherlock Holmes and Dr Watson.

As Trollope remarked of his receipts from *The Warden*, 'stone-breaking would have done better'. Yet he was able to console himself that this was the first money he had earned by his pen – 'that £20 which poor Mr Colburn had been made to pay certainly never having been earned at all'. He also recognized that he had found through it where his strength as a writer lay, in the creation of characters real enough and warm enough to attract interest and sympathy. And, for the first time, his work had been given the substance of a 'message', rather than a mere plot.

The warden of the title is the Revd Septimus Harding, precentor of Barchester cathedral, who, through a centuries-old foundation, is also warden of Hiram's Hospital, an almshouse for twelve old men of the city. The sinecure carries with it an emolument of several hundred pounds a year, which the warden has accepted without thought for the contrast between it and the tiny allowance meted out each week to his dozen 'bedesmen', who are content enough with their lot and with him, and especially appreciative of the 'cello solos with which he entertains them.

His younger daughter, Eleanor, however, is loved by a young surgeon, John Bold, whose other passion is for the righting of what he considers to be social abuses. Becoming convinced that the accounts of the hospital are being mismanaged, Bold takes out a writ, demanding a public inquiry. The archdeacon, Dr Theophilus Grantly, who is married to Septimus Harding's other daughter, Susan, is outraged – 'impious demagogue' is his epithet for John Bold; but kindly old Septimus Harding's complacency has been shaken, and he has begun to question his right to receive a comfortable income for doing very little. Against general urging he insists on resigning.

Eleanor makes John see the error of his ways. He withdraws his suit and they later marry. But the damage has been done: Mr Harding takes the appointment of rector of St Cuthbert's, the bishop fails to appoint a new warden, and the twelve old pensioners in the neglected almshouse are the chief sufferers from this bout of cathedral close squabbling.

BARCHESTER TOWERS

Before he had finished *The Warden* Trollope had been posted back to Ireland: first to the North, for a year which began late in 1853; then, shortly after being promoted to surveyor, to Dublin, where he remained five years. Before leaving Belfast he had begun a sequel to *The Warden*, but a discouraging letter from William Longman caused him to lay it aside and write instead a pseudo-Carlylean diatribe entitled *The New Zealander*, setting forth his views upon the faults of the British State, with his proposals for rectifying them. Longman dutifully sent it to the reader who had advised acceptance of the previous work. The latter replied, virtually by return of post: 'If you had not told me that this work was by the author of *The Warden* I could not have believed it. Such a contrast between two works by the same pen was hardly ever before witnessed . . . I regret to say I would advise you not to publish the work on any terms.' Longman returned the manuscript (it has never been published to this day), and, no doubt questioning to himself whether he was ever going to succeed, Trollope celebrated his fortieth birthday and returned to the suspended novel, *Barchester Towers*.

His Post Office duties were keeping him as busy as ever, but he now hit upon an agreeable means of combining business with pleasure. Where he had once done all his travelling on horseback, he began using the railway. Then it occurred to him that, rather than waste time like his fellow-passengers in staring out of the windows or reading, he could be writing: 'I made for myself therefore a little tablet, and found after a few days' exercise that I could write as quickly in a railway-carriage as I could at my desk. I worked with a pencil, and what I wrote my wife copied afterwards. In this way was composed the greater part of *Barchester Towers* and of the novel which succeeded it, and much also of others subsequent to them. My only objection to the practice came from the appearance of literary ostentation, to which I felt myself to be subject when going to work before four or five fellow-passengers. But I got used to it . . .'

Thus, *Barchester Towers*, resumed in April 1855, was finished by the beginning of November 1856 and in the hands of Long-man, who passed it on to that same reader. The report this time was cautiously favourable: 'It is very difficult for me to convey to you a distinct impression of my opinion of this work, since my own impressions of it are themselves very indistinct. And no wonder; for the execution is so unequal, that while there are parts of it that I would be disposed to place on a level with the best morsels by contemporary novelists, there are others – and unfortunately these preponderate – the vulgarity and exaggera-tion of which, if they do not unfit them for publication, are at least likely to be repulsive to the reader . . . But in noticing these defects I am far from saying that it is uninteresting. On the contrary, there is a fatal facility in the execution that makes you fancy that the author is playing with his reader, showing how easy it is to write a novel in three volumes . . .'

His conclusion was that the work would be publishable if condensed to a single volume. Longman transmitted the opinion in full to Trollope, softening the impact a little by suggesting a splitting of the difference in the shape of two volumes. Trollope answered that, while he would have no objection to expunging anything which might prove distasteful – indeed, would be pained to gain the reputation of being a distasteful writer – he could not countenance reducing a work conceived and written in three volumes into two. His *Autobiography* records: 'I am at a loss to know how such a task could be performed. I could burn the MS., no doubt, and write another book on the same story; but how two words out of six are to be withdrawn from a written novel I cannot conceive.'

Mr Longman, as Trollope put it, was 'too gracious to insist on his critic's terms', and agreed to publish in three volumes if the author would make certain changes. A long list of these was provided by the reader, some on the grounds of ineffectiveness, others where certain passages or expressions were 'too warm'. The manuscript of the unamended work no longer exists, but Michael Sadleir, who printed the exchange of letters between author, publisher and reader in their interesting detail in his *Trollope: A Commentary*, remarks, '... it reveals to an almost horrific degree the perturbations of the squeamish 'fifties ... Let us be thankful, however, that the author's submissiveness did not extend to the elimination of the Signora Neroni. To save her from suppression we gleefully accept the sacrifice of "foul breathing" and of "fat stomach", although the former would have invigorated the first presentment of the revolting Slope and the latter is but poorly substituted by "deep chest".'

In addition to this series of literary obstacles a financial hurdle had to be cleared. With new-found confidence, Trollope had demanded £100 as an advance on royalties. Longman had demurred, to be lectured firmly that if a three-volume novel were worth anything at all, it was worth £100, and warned that if he would not pay the work would be taken elsewhere. The publisher capitulated, and so acquired what was to become one of the most celebrated English novels. Looking back nearly twenty years, as he wrote the *Autobiography*, its author ventured to declare, 'Perhaps I may be assuming upon myself more than I have a right to do in saying now that *Barchester Towers* has become one of those novels which do not die quite at once, which live and are read for perhaps a quarter of a century.' Time has proved that to be a magnificent understatement. However, he was right to add that, should it endure, it would be in part attributable to 'the vitality of some of its younger brothers'. *Barchester Towers* would hardly be so well known as it is had there been no *Framley Parsonage* and no *Last Chronicle of Barsetshire*.

It was published in May 1857. Again, no sensation ensued, but the critics were generally pleased and 'it was one of the novels which novel readers were called upon to read'. – (*Autobiography*)

Somewhere in the brief limbo between the end of *The Warden* and the start of *Barchester Towers* John Bold has died, leaving Eleanor a pregnant widow. The story begins with the approach of another death in the city – that of Bishop Grantly himself. This sad event sets the cat amongst the cathedral pigeons, for the re-election or fall of the Government is in the balance at this moment, and the outcome is of vital importance to the bishop's son and archdeacon of Barchester, the Venerable Dr Theophilus Grantly. If the Government is unchanged he may expect to succeed his father as bishop. If it loses office, his chance is virtually nil. This splendid, vigorous churchman is not above hoping that the old man might slip away without delay, before the threatened change of administration can occur; though he immediately repents the unworthy wish and prays beside the deathbed that his father might be spared. He is, for a few days, but the archdeacon's repentance does not earn its reward: the Government falls.

The newly-appointed bishop is Thomas Proudie, an insignificant little man, totally dominated by his disagreeable, aggressive wife, with the assistance of her husband's domestic chaplain, the Revd Obadiah Slope. Mrs Proudie and Slope are not long in making their influence felt. Ecclesiastical and lay sympathizers of the Revd Septimus Harding over the unnecessary scandalmongering which had made him resign from the wardenship of Hiram's

Hospital wish him to be restored. Mrs Proudie and Slope deter-
mine that he shall not, though Slope shows signs of making a
bid for supremacy in cathedral matters by taking it upon himself
to offer the post to the vicar of Puddingdale, the Revd Quiverful,
who has a wife and fourteen children to support.

Slope soon has cause to realize that he has acted precipitately,
when he learns that the widowed Eleanor Bold, who is the dis-
placed warden's daughter, has a tidy income in her own right.
He begins to take a keen interest in her, and seeks to ease his
way by switching his sympathy to her father. Unwittingly, however, he provides himself with a rival for Eleanor's favour. He
wishes Bishop Proudie to recognize in him a potentially efficient
dean. One of his meddlesome actions is to persuade the bishop
that the rector of Crabtree Canonicorum and of Stoke Pinquium,
the Hon. and Revd Dr Vesey Stanhope, who is a prebendary of
Barchester cathedral, has no business to be living in Italy on his
stipends from his neglected parishes, and should be recalled.
This is, no doubt, justifiable enough, and Dr Stanhope duly
arrives; but besides his wife he brings his two daughters and one
son, Bertie, something of a ne'er-do-well, who has been living
off his father but has no objection to being supported by a wife
if he can acquire one without undue effort. Eleanor becomes the
object of this lethargic quest.

Worse is to come Slope's way. One of Dr Stanhope's daughters
is the somewhat exotic Signora Madeline Neroni, the possessor
of a dramatic past which has left her a cripple, confined to her
couch but by no means averse to receiving gentlemen visitors.
The ill-treatment by her departed Italian husband which has
reduced her to invalidism has also left her with a desire for
revenge upon the whole male sex, which she exacts by bewitching them while keeping them at arm's length. The susceptible
Slope is soon one of their number, which enables Mrs Proudie
to get him dismissed from his chaplaincy and sent away. He
finishes up with a London living and a rich widow; the Revd
Quiverful is installed as warden of Hiram's Hospital, with his
wife as matron; Eleanor Bold marries again, this time with the

Revd Francis Arabin, who is appointed dean of Barchester; and Mrs Proudie is left unchallenged ruler of the cathedral close.

THE THREE CLERKS

As will be found in her entry in *The Characters*, Trollope was in later life to write of the domineering Mrs Proudie, of *Barchester Towers*, that although other characters had subsequently 'grown up equally dear to me', he had never managed to dissever himself from her 'and still live much in company with her ghost'. One might perhaps have expected that, having created this immortal character and established the interlocking and conflicting relationships of the residents of Barchester cathedral close, he would have been eager to exploit the rich potential which he must have recognized there. Instead, he turned his back on Barsetshire and looked to London and an entirely different theme, from which there was to emerge another female character – albeit the antithesis of Mrs Proudie – for whom he would conceive an affection capable of bringing tears to his eyes in later years whenever he re-read her story. She is Kate Woodward, in *The Three Clerks*: and side by side with her he created yet another Trollope immortal, the barrister, Chaffanbrass.

He began writing his novel in the spring of 1857 and had finished it by mid-August. He must have been in buoyant spirits as he worked, for although he drew heavily upon personal memories of monotonous toil in his early Post Office career and of the pecuniary and emotional difficulties of his early clerkship, he wrote of it all with a strength and detachment which, had he not had the stimulus of some success within him, might have sagged into self-pity. Instead, it was with self-assurance that he addressed himself to Longman about its sale, rejecting indignantly the latter's proposal of £100 advance. He declared that he would not contemplate anything less than double that figure and threatened to take his work elsewhere; at which, Trollope recalls in the

Autobiography, 'he endeavoured to convince me that I might lose more than I gained, even though I should get more money by going elsewhere. "It is for you," said he, "to think whether our names on your title-page are not worth more to you than the increased payment." This seemed to me to savour of that high-flown doctrine of the contempt of money which I have never admired. I did think much of Messrs Longman's name, but I liked it best at the bottom of a cheque.'

He did take the manuscript elsewhere, and what befell it makes an interesting comparison with our own time, when publishing tends to be effected by committee and computer, and the processes of transforming an accepted work from a manuscript to a book in a shop seldom require less than six months and more often take the best part of a year.

An obvious alternative to Longman was Colburn, the publisher of Trollope's second two novels. The firm had by this time become Hurst & Blackett, and it was to this office that he went one day by appointment to offer *The Three Clerks*. When, after an hour's waiting, the man he had engaged to meet had failed to turn up, Trollope left and went straight to Richard Bentley, who had founded the journal *Bentley's Miscellany* in 1837, with Charles Dickens as its editor. Bentley bought *The Three Clerks* on the spot for £250 outright, and it was on the bookstalls six weeks later – 30 November 1857. The *Autobiography* records: 'His son still possesses it, and the firm has, I believe, done very well with the purchase. It was certainly the best novel I had as yet written. The plot is not so good as that of the *Macdermots*; nor are there any characters in the book equal to those of Mrs Proudie and the Warden; but the work has a more continued interest, and contains the first well-described love-scene that I ever wrote.'

The three government clerks of the title are Henry Norman, the eldest of the trio and younger brother to the heir to property. He works in the Weights and Measures Office, as does his friend Alaric Tudor. Alaric's cousin Charley (the character said to have been based by Trollope on himself when young, and certainly reflecting many of his experiences) works elsewhere in the Civil Service, in the Internal Navigation Office. The three friends are regular callers at the homely cottage of Henry's cousin, Mrs Woodward, a clergyman's widow in the Thames-side suburb of Hampton. The fact that this lady has three daughters does not, however, imply neat and immediate pairing-off for all concerned. Henry loves one of them, Gertrude; but her fancy is taken by Alaric. A further misfortune for Henry is that, recalling the farcical ease with which he himself had got into the Post Office with no qualifications at all, Trollope happened to hold strong views about the necessity for abolishing patronage in granting jobs in the Civil Service, advocating competitive examination open to all. He proceeds through his story to show the process in action, letting Alaric sit such an examination and, through it, win a post to which Henry had been aspiring.

A form of consolation is not long in coming to Henry, though, for his elder brother dies and Henry succeeds to the family estates. He also discovers enough to attract him in Mrs Woodward's second daughter, Linda, who accepts his proposal of marriage. Meanwhile, it is Alaric, for whom all had seemed set so fair, who is foundering. Wanting urgently to raise the money that will enable him to live up to his new status, he has listened too eagerly to the proposals of a financial manipulator of noble family, 'Undy' Scott, M.P. for the Tillietudlum district of Scotland, and succumbed to the temptation to invest money that is not his own. The gamble fails to come off and Alaric is sent for trial to the Old Bailey, where, despite the defence of that skilled barrister Chaffanbrass, he is sentenced to six months' imprisonment. Upon his release his former rival, Henry, generously helps him and Gertrude, the wife Henry had originally wanted for himself, to emigrate to New Zealand. Henry himself is by now married to Linda.

For the third clerk, Charley, life has brought little fulfilment. His work is boring and without prospects; he is in debt to moneylenders; and the good Mrs Woodward disapproves of him as a prospect for her youngest daughter, Katie, who loves him. In despairing reaction he is on the verge of marrying a barmaid, Norah Geraghty; but Katie influences him to see the error of his ways, cast off his undesirable friends, and make something of his career. Katie herself appears to be mortally ill, and, in the passage which its author tells us never ceased to move him, she tries to set him free from her love in order that he shall not feel her death so keenly. Fortunately for them both, as the *Autobiography* tells us: 'I had not the heart to kill her. I never could do that. And I do not doubt but that they are living happily together to this day.'

In short, Katie recovers, Mrs Woodward withdraws her objection to the reformed swain, and so the three clerks and the three Woodward girls have been paired off, after all.

DOCTOR THORNE

BETWEEN finishing *The Three Clerks*, in August 1857, and seeing it published that November, Trollope and his wife went to Florence to visit his mother. His mind was busy as they travelled, not only recording all he saw and experienced, but seeking anxiously for a new plot. None would come, and, for the only time in his life, he requested someone else to provide him with one. That person was his brother Tom; and it has proved a happy chance for posterity that the story he outlined should have been that of *Doctor Thorne*.

The novel was begun in October, when Trollope was back home again, but was interrupted by the demands of official duty. Early in 1858 Trollope was dispatched by his Post Office chiefs to Egypt, to negotiate a new treaty for the carriage of mail there. Interrupted; but not seriously, for throughout the long and extremely rough sea voyage to Alexandria he worked steadily at his daily writing stint, despite, on more than one occasion, having to leave his papers on the general cabin table while he dashed off to be sick in the privacy of his own.

He was travelling alone this time, and sent batches of the manuscript back to his wife for copying. Apart from the self-disciplined routine by which he was now accustomed to work, he had every incentive to keep the tale moving, for he had succeeded in selling it before leaving London to Chapman & Hall for £400, after Richard Bentley had first agreed to that figure and then backed down. Once more, this proved to be a case of a publisher missing out on a lucrative prospect for want of a little more initiative. Chapman & Hall were to publish many more works by their newly-acquired author, but none more popular than that conceived in Italy, largely written at sea and in Egypt, but set squarely in the utterly Englishness of Barsetshire. *Doctor Thorne* was finished on 1 April 1858 and published in three volumes in June.

There had once been two brothers, Thomas and Henry Thorne, sons of one of Barchester's many clergymen. Thomas had studied medicine and qualified as a doctor; but the younger son, intended for the bar, had progressed no farther than Oxford, from which he had been expelled for his dissolute behaviour. One of his drinking companions at Barchester had been a young, recently-married stonemason, Roger Scatcherd, who had a beautiful sister, Mary. On the strength of promises of marriage, and perhaps assisted by the administration of drugs, Henry Thorne had succeeded in seducing Mary Scatcherd. Her brother, determined to teach her betrayer a lesson, had struck too hard with some blunt instrument, with the consequence that he had found himself charged with murder but sentenced to only six months' imprisonment, leaving Mary alone in the world to bear Henry Thorne's child. Dr Thorne, who had tried in vain to reform his brother, now felt it his personal duty to redeem Henry's great wrong. He attended Mary in childbirth, and was looking for other ways to help her when he was approached by a former sweetheart of hers, who offered to marry her and take her to America, but could not bring himself at the same time to adopt another man's unwanted child.

Dr Thorne had persuaded Mary to accept this offer, volunteering to take charge himself of his late brother's baby, now his nearest relative. So Mary Scatcherd had become Mary Tomlinson and crossed the Atlantic; her baby, also Mary, had been named Thorne, and Scatcherd, still in prison, given to understand that the infant had died at birth. Dr Thorne, abandoning his own matrimonial hopes, had at length set himself up in a village practice at Greshambury, near Barchester, where his house was shared by his 'daughter', whose origins no one knew.

Greshambury is named after its squires, the Greshams of Greshambury Park. They live in the style befitting the principal family of commoners in the county; but despite the advantages of one of their number, Francis Newbold Gresham, having married into the great De Courcy clan, the financial status of the family has declined to a point at which, as the story proper begins, parts of the estates are mortgaged to no less a person than the former gaolbird Roger Scatcherd, now a railway millionaire, baronet and chronic alcoholic, who has set himself up in a fine mansion on Boxall Hill, part of the property. His medical attendant is Dr Thorne, whose 'daughter', Scatcherd has no reason to suspect, is his own sister Mary's child. To make the situation trebly fraught, Dr Thorne is also the intimate friend of the Greshams – and Frank Gresham, the Cambridge-graduate heir to the estates, is in love with Mary.

Much of the novel concerns the varying degrees of dilemma faced by Dr Thorne in his role of catalyst between these factions: between Frank and his parents, Francis Newbold Gresham and Lady Arabella; between those parents themselves, the husband preoccupied with financial difficulties and the need to restore the family fortunes by marrying Frank off well, and Lady Arabella with her unbending pride and growing mistrust of the doctor himself; and between Frank and Mary, the latter having her own kind of pride, which will not let her accept the advances of the man she loves, because of their inequality of station.

Over all these things hangs an extra cloud of tension: Sir Roger Scatcherd must soon drink himself to death, and then his ineffectual son Louis will inherit his estate and the mortgages on the Greshams' property; but if this does not happen before Louis reaches the age of twenty-five – and there are four years to go before then – Boxall Hill and the fortune attached to it will become the Greshams' once again. To tauten the situation further, Louis is also drinking heavily and may kill himself before he reaches twenty-five; in which case Mary, as daughter of Sir Roger Scatcherd's sister Mary, will inherit the estate and will become an eligible choice for Frank Gresham.

After a brandy too many, Sir Roger suffers a violent attack of delirium tremens and dies, knowing by now that his niece is alive somewhere, but not suspecting her to be Mary. The dissipated Louis becomes master of Boxall Hill in his place, and Dr Thorne wrestles with his conscience, asking himself whether he should ease Mary's and Frank's path by disclosing her identity and potential inheritance to the Greshams, and to what extent he would be morally justified in neglecting to save the life of a worthless young man, upon whose inevitable death depends the happiness of the girl the doctor loves as if she had been his true daughter.

The brandy bottle solves all, carrying off Sir Louis Scatcherd only months after his father had downed his fatal glass. Mary inherits; Lady Arabella, who has treated her throughout with contempt and determinedly undermined her relationship with Frank, is confounded; the marriage which will prove the saving of the Gresham estates and fulfil the yearnings of two young people can take place; Dr Thorne can extend his practice, to the dismay of his rival, Dr Fillgrave, and, whenever his duties allow, saunter over to Boxall Hill to drink tea with the young couple and box Mary's ears whenever she ventures to suggest he has reached the time for retirement.

THE BERTRAMS

My novels, whether good or bad, have been as good as I could make them. Had I taken three months of idleness between each they would have been no better. Feeling convinced of that, I finished *Doctor Thorne* on one day, and began *The Bertrams* on the next.

IF much of its predecessor had been composed in several places other than the England of its setting, this was to be even more so. It was begun in Egypt, continued in the Holy Land, Malta, Gibraltar, Spain, Scotland, England and Ireland, and completed in the West Indies in December 1858, just over nine months after its commencement. For all Trollope's obsession with professionalism for professionalism's sake, and his contempt for those fellow-writers who needed special conditions under which to advance their leisured progress, his new novel might perhaps have turned out better than it did had he permitted himself a little more reflection before starting it and a little more ease during the writing. However, Chapman & Hall had given him £400 advance for it, and his professionalism, unlike some of his fellows', included a strong sense of responsibility.

In the *Autobiography* he admits of *The Bertrams*: 'I do not know that I have ever heard it well spoken of even by my friends, and I cannot remember that there is any character in it that has dwelt in the minds of novel-readers ... A novel should give a picture of common life enlivened by humour and sweetened by pathos. To make that picture worthy of attention, the canvas should be crowded with real portraits, not of individuals known to the world or to the author, but of created personages impregnated with traits of character which are well known. To my thinking, the plot is but the vehicle for all this; and when you have the vehicle without the passengers, a story of mystery in which the agents never spring to life, you have but a wooden show. There must, however, be a story. You must provide a vehicle of some sort. That of *The Bertrams* was more than ordinarily bad; and as the book was relieved by no special character, it failed. Its failure never surprised me.'

'But,' he adds, 'I have been surprised by the success of *Doctor Thorne*'; and he insisted, defiant to the judgement of most others of his time and since, that *The Bertrams* and *Doctor Thorne* were of about equal merit, neither of them good, and both inferior to *The Three Clerks*.

The Bertrams was published by Chapman & Hall, in three volumes, in March 1859.

George Bertram's father, Colonel Sir Lionel Bertram, is idling away his life in an undemanding quasi-military post in Persia, leaving his son's upbringing and education to George Bertram senior, the boy's wealthy uncle. George has worked hard and emerged from Oxford with an excellent degree, but no definite sense of direction. His uncle, a merchant, is pressing him to go into business, but his inclinations, such as they are, are of a more spiritual nature, and he decides to visit the Holy Land, there to take the decision whether or not to enter the Church.

In Jerusalem he chances to meet his uncle's granddaughter, Caroline Waddington, who is touring with her guardian, Miss Baker. They fall in love, but Caroline makes it clear that she will not marry him until he is well settled in a sound career with a good income attached to it. He agrees to read for the Bar. This is a slow process, but George will not meanwhile go to his uncle for the financial help that would enable him to marry. After waiting with increasing impatience for three years Caroline marries a man who has already scaled the heights which George has scarcely begun to climb, Sir Henry Harcourt, M.P., the Solicitor-General, who had been a friend of George's at Oxford.

Sir Henry has his own ambitions, however, mostly centred upon acquiring a fortune. It is in pursuit of this that he has married Caroline, whom he believes erroneously to be her grandfather's heiress. He acquires an expensive home and commences a series of grand entertainments designed to impress his guests; but when he tries to make Caroline persuade old Mr Bertram to advance her money to pay for it all she refuses and leaves him, preferring the gloomy house of her difficult grandfather to the luxurious one of her self-seeking husband. Unable to pay the bills he has accumulated through his false expectations, Sir Henry loses his office when the Government changes. Deserted by his wife and friends, he commits suicide.

Sir Lionel Bertram has retired and returned to England to live at a fashionable watering place, Littlebath. He, too, is in pursuit of a wealthy female, Miss Sally Todd, a gregarious party-giving spinster whom he had met in the Middle East; but she refuses him, and, having already decided against proposing marriage to Miss Baker, who has no fortune, he falls back upon sponging on his son for money. The latter has by now been reconciled with the widowed Caroline, and they are married.

A sub-plot concerns another of George's friends, the Revd Arthur Wilkinson, whose father has left him his living at Hurst Staple on condition that he make do with a curate's salary and support his mother with the rest of his income. Arthur wishes to marry Miss Adela Gauntlet and take over the vicarage in its entirety for their home, and this secondary story is of the resultant conflict with his mother, until she finally gives way.

CASTLE RICHMOND

The Bertrams was finished in the West Indies: Trollope was there from the early winter of 1858 until the following summer, reorganizing the lax postal services, which were, of course, administered from London at that time. As soon as he had learned of this assignment he had hurried along to Chapman & Hall to propose a book about the territory he would soon be investigating thoroughly, and had had no difficulty in getting Edward Chapman to pay £250 for a single volume. He wrote the bulk of it in the West Indies and added the finishing touches during the voyage home, so that he was able to place the complete manuscript on Chapman's desk immediately upon returning to London in 1859. It was published as *The West Indies and the Spanish Main* that October and was very well received. Happily for Trollope, his view of the relative position of black and white men in the West Indies coincided with that of the writer of three much-discussed articles to *The Times* which closely drew wide attention to the book, resulting in good sales and a growth in critical respect for its author, who later termed it 'the best book that has come from my pen'.

Its consequence for his novel-writing was that he was enabled to demand higher terms for the new Irish tale he had already begun, *Castle Richmond*. Chapman agreed to pay him £600, and by the end of October the new novel was half written. There then intervened one of those exciting, yet alarming offers which to this day occasionally lift up the hearts of authors with the knowledge that they are actually *wanted*, and which, therefore, are almost impossible to refuse, however much they must inevitably add to existing pressures of time and stress. In Trollope's case, it was a request from Messrs Smith, Elder & Co., who were preparing to launch the *Cornhill Magazine*, under the editorship of W. M. Thackeray, that he provide them with a three-volume novel to run in serial form in the first and subsequent issues. The fee of £1,000 was offered, with the stipulation that the first portion of the manuscript must be in the editor's hands in six weeks' time.

A flattering letter followed from Thackeray, whose own novels Trollope admired above all others, and after a brief struggle with himself Trollope overcame the belief he had hitherto entertained that no part of any of his works should be published until the whole was completed. He accepted the commission, suspecting, he tells us in the *Autobiography*, that the true reason for this last-minute approach was that Thackeray himself had originally undertaken to supply the opening serial, but had simply not got down to writing it. 'There was still,' he reflected a trifle smugly in later years, 'as much time for him as for me. I think there was, – for though he had his magazine to look after, I had the Post Office. But he thought, when unable to trust his own energy, that he might rely upon that of a new recruit. He was but four years my senior in life, but he was at the top of the tree, while I was still at the bottom.'

Trollope did the obvious thing: he went to Chapman and asked if he might use the already half-finished *Castle Richmond* for the purpose. The publisher assented, and Trollope hastened to his first meeting with George Smith, of Smith, Elder, to outline his tale. To his dismay, Smith shook his head over the idea of launching the new magazine with a story set in Ireland: 'and he suggested the Church, as though it were my peculiar subject ... He wanted an English tale, on English life, with a clerical flavour.' There was nothing to be done but start from scratch and create a long work, for which he had no immediate idea, deliver a substantial part of it in less than six weeks' time, while continuing to fulfil his full-time duties with the Post Office, and keep *Castle Richmond* moving in order to meet Chapman & Hall's deadline of 31 March. He succeeded in both literary tasks; but while, as will be seen, the serial, *Framley Parsonage*, turned out to be one of his biggest successes, *Castle Richmond* failed. As George Smith had rightly discerned, the English public at the time did not want stories about Ireland; but, its setting aside, *Castle Richmond* has been found too mannered in style and lacking in too many qualities to gain posthumous popularity. Its first publication was in three volumes in May 1860.

The story concerns two neighbouring families in County Cork during the famine of the 1840s. The Fitzgeralds of Richmond Castle are living under a personal blight: the supposedly dead husband of Lady Fitzgerald had turned up again some years before and has been blackmailing her husband, Sir Thomas, ever since, with the threat to disclose the invalidity of his marriage and the illegitimacy of his three children, Herbert, Emmeline and Mary. If the illegitimacy were to emerge, the Castle Richmond estates would pass to a relative of the family, Owen Fitzgerald, of Hap House, a handsome bachelor of dubious reputation, in love with Clara, the daughter of the other principal family of the story, the Desmonds, of Desmond Court.

Unfortunately for this association, Clara's mother, the Dowager Countess of Desmond, is herself in love with Owen; while – although Trollope was probably unconscious of the implications which might be read into some of his scenes – Owen also entertains an affection bordering on the passionate for the young Patrick, Earl of Desmond, aged sixteen and just out of Eton.

The story, then, is largely of the jealousy of a mother for her daughter's handsome young lover; and of a family on the brink of ruin at the hands of a blackmailer. The stress of the latter situation kills Sir Thomas Fitzgerald when his lawyer, Prendergast, advises that the blackmailer's bluff be called. When all seems to be up for the family, Prendergast discovers that Lady Fitzgerald's former 'husband', Matthew Mollett, had been married before going through the ceremony of marriage with her, and that, therefore, her only legal marriage had been that to Sir Thomas. Herbert Fitzgerald marries Clara Desmond, and Owen Fitzgerald goes off to foreign parts for two years with the young earl, before continuing his wanderings alone.

FRAMLEY PARSONAGE

WE have seen, under *Castle Richmond*, in what circumstances Anthony Trollope was activated into writing *Framley Parsonage*. How, precisely, he rose to the challenge is described in the *Autobiography* in a way that is characteristic both of him and of that lively self-portrait of a writing man:

On my journey back to Ireland, in the railway carriage, I wrote the first few pages of that story. I had got into my head an idea of what I meant to write, – a morsel of the biography of an English clergyman who should not be a bad man, but one led into temptation by his own youth and by the unclerical accidents of those around him. The love of his sister for the young lord was an adjunct necessary, because there must be love in a novel. And then by placing Framley Parsonage near Barchester, I was able to fall back upon my old friends Mrs Proudie and the archdeacon. Out of these slight elements I fabricated a hodge-podge in which the real plot consisted at last simply of a girl refusing to marry the man she loved till the man's friends agreed to accept her lovingly. Nothing could be less efficient or artistic. But the characters were so well handled, that the work from the first to the last was popular, – and was received as it went on with still increasing favour by both editor and proprietor of the magazine. There was a little fox-hunting and a little tuft-hunting, some Christian virtue and some Christian cant. There was no heroism and no villainy. There was much Church, but more love-making. And it was downright honest love, in which there was no pretence on the part of the lady that she was too ethereal to be fond of a man, no half-and-half inclination on the part of the man to pay a certain price and no more for a pretty toy. Each of them longed for the other, and they were not ashamed to say so. Consequently, they in England who were living, or had lived, the same sort of life, liked *Framley Parsonage*.

Writing it, he stated in the *Autobiography*, had taught him two things: that the demands of serial publication forbade tediousness on any page – a lesson, however, which did not save him from perpetrating much tedium in his later novels; and that his imaginary county of Barsetshire had assumed a reality for him which, he did not know as he created it, would remain equally vivid for generations of readers:

I had it all in my mind, – its roads and railroads, its towns and parishes, its members of Parliament, and the different hunts which rode over it. I knew all the great lords and their castles, the squires and their parks, the rectors and their churches. This was the fourth novel of which I had placed the scene in Barsetshire, and as I wrote it, I made a map of the dear county. Throughout these stories there has been no name given to a fictitious site which does not represent to me a spot of which I know all the accessories, as though I had lived and wandered there.

This, of course, is by no means the same thing as saying that all his fictional places had their origins in real ones, any more than all his characters had their counterparts in life. The 'Trollope Game' of deductive identification, like the Shakespeare, Dickens and Sherlock Holmes Games, has been much played by enthusiasts, but this present volume is not the place for it.

Framley Parsonage was published in the *Cornhill* from January 1860 – April 1861, and in book form (three volumes) by Smith,

D

Elder in May 1861. It was the first of Trollope's novels to be
illustrated by John Everett Millais.

As a young boy, being tutored in the home of a clergyman,
Mark Robarts has struck up a close friendship with a fellow pupil,
Ludovic, Lord Lufton, of Framley Court, Barsetshire. The two
had gone on together to Harrow and then Oxford, their friendship deepening with the years; and when it became apparent that
Mark was destined for Holy Orders, he had been invited by his
friend's mother, the widowed Lady Lufton, to accept the vacant
living of Framley, with its comfortable income. In due course
he had moved into the desirable Framley Parsonage, but he had
not been alone there for long: Lady Lufton, who had strong
views about the desirability of a clergyman's being married, had
introduced him to the beautiful and thoroughly eligible Fanny
Monsell, with whom he had dutifully – and enthusiastically –
fallen in love. Now, married to her and comfortably ensconced
at Framley, he seems justified in feeling that the luck which has
attended him throughout life will go on holding.

If anything, his luck appears to be on the increase when he is
invited to hobnob in influential society at Chaldicotes, the home
of Nathaniel Sowerby, M.P., where he is to preach a charity
sermon and meet Sowerby's brother-in-law, Harold Smith, who
is tipped for eventual office in the Government. Fanny has mis-
givings about his accepting the invitation, which will not please
Lady Lufton, who disapproves of the Chaldicotes circle. Mark,
too, recognizes that he will be compromising himself a little in
mixing with people of dubious reputation; but, determining
that a man is entitled to live his own life, and that advantage
must be seized when it offers itself, he goes to Chaldicotes.
There he is further flattered to receive an invitation with the
rest to dine at Gatherum Castle with the old Duke of Omnium,
whose diehard Whig principles go much against the grain of the
predominantly Tory society of Barsetshire, but whose command
to his haughty presence is eagerly obeyed by ambitious men.

The flattery of all this attention rubs off heavily on to the
impressionable Mark, who, although he realizes that his friend

Sowerby is something of a shady character, feels indebted to him. Having carefully established this frame of mind in the young clergyman, Sowerby confides in him his wish to marry the heiress Martha Dunstable, in order to redeem the fortunes he has lost through gambling and buy back the title-deeds to Chaldicotes, which have passed into the Duke of Omnium's hands. But to court Miss Dunstable in a proper fashion Sowerby needs money immediately, and he first hints, then forthrightly suggests, that Mark Robarts help him to it. Mark has no money of his own, so Sowerby persuades him to sign a promissory note for several hundred pounds as a form of guarantee for Sowerby to use – though he assures his young friend that by the time the three-month term of the promissory note is run he will have captured Miss Dunstable anyway, and will have no need to present it.

Things do not eventuate so simply, and the note, together with a further one Mark has signed, fall into the hands of money-lenders. The duke presses for payment; Martha Dunstable refuses Sowerby and marries Dr Thomas Thorne, the Barchester physician, taking possession of Chaldicotes, whose mortgages she has bought, and setting him up there as a country gentleman; and Mark Robarts's luck appears to have run out at last.

Mark's father has by now been dead for some time, and his dazzling young sister Lucy has been living with him and Fanny at the parsonage. Much as she approves of Lucy, Lady Lufton is annoyed at length to hear her son expressing a wish to marry the girl: Lady Lufton's plan is that he shall marry Grizzell Grantly, one of the archdeacon of Barchester's two daughters. He refuses to comply, and Grizzell soon after marries Lord Dumbello. Lufton is incensed to hear his mother describe Lucy as too 'insignificant' to be his wife, and proposes to her; but Lucy, not wishing to compromise her brother's standing with his patroness, answers that she will only consent if the request comes from Lady Lufton. There seems little likelihood of this, especially as the promissory notes Mark had so rashly given Sowerby have now come home to roost, and the broker's men are making an inventory of the contents of the parsonage, preparatory to seizing them.

All works out for the best, though. Lord Lufton buys in the notes and Mark is saved. Mrs Crawley, the wife of the over-worked and needy perpetual curate of Hogglestock parish, falls seriously ill and is nursed by Lucy Robarts, whose devotion moves Lady Lufton to recognize that the girl's qualities far out-weigh her lack of rank. Lady Lufton makes the request Lucy had stipulated, and the marriage takes place, Lady Lufton graciously moving from her place at the top of the table in favour of the new mistress of Framley Court.

ORLEY FARM

FOUR days after completing *Framley Parsonage* Trollope took up his pen again and commenced *Orley Farm*. Its writing took him from July 1860 until June 1861. This unusually long period – by his standards of performance – is largely accounted for by his having spent several of the months writing seventeen short stories, some of which first appeared in periodicals, which he would collect into two bound series of *Tales of All Countries*, published by Chapman & Hall in 1861 and 1863. He also paid another visit to his mother and brother in Florence – not that this would have stemmed his literary flow. Most of the new novel was written at Waltham House, Waltham Cross, Hertfordshire, into which he had moved in the winter of 1859, and which was to be his home for eleven years. This location enabled him to hobnob for the first time with London literary society, into which, thanks to the success of *Framley Parsonage* and the con-sequent public demand for the earlier Barsetshire novels, he was able to step on terms of full equality.

For *Orley Farm*, though, he again turned away from Barset-shire, and recalled memories of a run-down farm at Harrow Weald where he had lived unhappily, alone with his father, for some time in his youth, though he injected into the story a good deal of his most puckish humour. Looking back, he would be reservedly pleased with the result: 'Most of those among my friends who talk to me now about my novels, and are competent to form an opinion on the subject, say that this is the best I have written. In this opinion I do not coincide ... The plot of *Orley Farm* is probably the best I have ever made; but it has the fault of declaring itself, and thus coming to an end too early in the book. When Lady Mason tells her ancient lover that she did forge the will, the plot of *Orley Farm* has unravelled itself; – and this she does in the middle of the tale. Independently, however, of this the novel is good. Sir Peregrine Orme, his grandson, Madeline Staveley, Mr Furnival, Mr Chaffanbrass, and the commercial gentlemen are all good. The hunting is good. The lawyer's talk is good. Mr Moulder carves his turkey admirably, and Mr Kantwise sells his tables and chairs with spirit. I am fond of *Orley Farm*; – and am especially fond of its illustrations by Millais, which are the best I have seen in any novel in the language.'

It appeared in twenty shilling numbers from March 1861 and in two volumes (Chapman & Hall) in 1862.

It is not true that a rose by any other name will smell as sweet. Were it true, I should call this story 'The Great Orley Farm Case'. But who would ask for the ninth number of a serial work burthened with so very uncouth an appellation? Thence, and therefore, – Orley Farm.

So the tale commences; and, indeed, its elements and events all proceed towards a Court of Assize, where Lady Mason will stand in the dock for the second time in her life. Her first trial, at which she had been acquitted, had been for forgery. The charge this second time is perjury; and although her plea is 'Not guilty' she well knows, and the reader well knows, that the truth is otherwise.

The sequence of events had begun many years earlier with the death of her aged husband, Sir Joseph Mason. Besides a widow, he had left behind a grown-up son and three daughters from an earlier marriage, and one infant son, Lucius, by his second wife, Lady Mason, forty-five years his junior, whom he had married with the disapproval of his existing family. The daughters had been handsomely remembered; the elder son, Joseph, had been left his father's landed estate in Yorkshire, Groby Park; his widow had been moderately provided for; and a codicil to the will had left his youngest son a small farm and house some twenty-five miles from London. The name of this property is Orley Farm, and it and the validity of the codicil concerning it are the contentious elements upon which the story hinges, for Joseph Mason had always understood that, on his father's death, Orley Farm would come to him. Accordingly, Joseph challenges the codicil, and his counsel does not fail to draw the court's attention to the curious circumstance that the codicil, which is in Lady Mason's writing, also provides a legacy of £2,000 to a girl named Miriam Usbech, who had been one of the witnesses to its signing. It had been drafted by her late father, a penniless lawyer. It is, of course, Joseph Mason's contention that the codicil had been devised by Lady Mason for the benefit of Lucius, and that she had forged Sir Joseph's signature to it and made it financially worth the witnesses' while to attest to its authenticity. Contention being one thing and proof another, Lady Mason is acquitted.

Years pass and Lucius, having studied agricultural science on the Continent, returns to Orley Farm to manage it efficiently. In reappraising certain leases connected with the estate he makes the unwitting blunder of terminating one held by a lawyer named Samuel Dockwrath, thereby making a dangerous enemy; for Dockwrath is married to that very Miriam Usbech who had acted as a witness to the codicil. Without her son's knowledge, the horrified Lady Mason instructs her friend and counsel, Thomas Furnival, to buy off Dockwrath's animosity at almost any price. But it is too late: Dockwrath is already re-examining the evidence, and eventually comes up with enough dubious detail to warrant a charge of perjury against Lady Mason.

Defended by the redoubtable Chaffanbrass, whom we have already met in another court, unsuccessfully appearing for Alaric

Tudor in *The Three Clerks*, Lady Mason is again acquitted. But Lucius, having learned that his mother had indeed forged the codicil, hands over Orley Farm to Joseph and takes his mother to live with him in a small town in Germany, before himself going on to Australia to begin a new life.

'A novel can hardly be made interesting or successful without love,' Trollope was to affirm in his *Autobiography*, and there is plenty of love, or professed love, in *Orley Farm*. Lady Mason is loved by an old gentleman, Sir Peregrine Orme, whom she rejects but who continues to support her, even after she confesses her crime to him. Madeline Staveley, daughter of Lady Mason's neighbour Judge Staveley, who plays a prominent part in the story, is wooed by Sir Peregrine Orme's grandson, Peregrine, and by one of the trial lawyers, Felix Graham, to whom she at length becomes engaged, Graham having earlier unsuccessfully tried to educate a drunken engraver's daughter, Mary Snow, sufficiently to make her worthy to be his wife. Lucius Mason is engaged for a time to Thomas Furnival's daughter Sophia. But, through this labyrinth of side-issues, it is 'The Great Orley Farm Case' which forms the high-road of the tale.

THE STRUGGLES OF BROWN, JONES AND ROBINSON: BY ONE OF THE FIRM

'I THINK that *Brown, Jones and Robinson* was the hardest bargain I ever sold to a publisher.'

This was Anthony Trollope's summing-up of the brief history he gives of this book in the *Autobiography*. He meant that never had a publisher got so little value from him for his money; but his sentence could justifiably be read to mean that he never had a harder job to drive a bargain at all.

He had first put up the idea back in 1857, when Longman was still his publisher, and had it forthrightly declined, despite the fact that the firm had so recently published his classic-to-be,

Barchester Towers. William Longman could see what the eager author could not: the proposed skit on modern advertising methods, under a title almost identical to the artist Richard Doyle's *Foreign Tour of Messrs Brown, Jones and Robinson*, could not hope to sell. Nevertheless, Trollope sat down and wrote part of the short novel. In the summer of 1858, full of enthusiasm for his new and open-handed publishers, Chapman & Hall, he put forward the idea again, and again it was declined.

He laid it aside unfinished; but not for good. In 1861, his celebrity now established with *Framley Parsonage*, he pressed the idea upon the *Cornhill's* proprietor, George Smith. Whether or not Smith recognized that he was committing himself to an inferior purchase, he acted shrewdly in agreeing to serialize it and to pay its author £600; for although the story was condemned by critics and disliked by readers, its acceptance kept its author happy with Smith and subsequently brought the publisher several of Trollope's best works, which, had he been offended by the rejection of his nonsensical trifle, he might have taken elsewhere.

The facetious tale, 'By One of the Firm, Edited by Anthony Trollope', ran in the *Cornhill* from August 1861 – March 1862. Its publisher's truthful opinion of it, whether confirmed or prompted by its reception, is perhaps best deduced from his failure to produce it in book form (one volume) until 1870. Trollope's own comment on it in the *Autobiography* is: 'I attempted a style for which I certainly was not qualified, and to which I never had again recourse. It was meant to be funny, was full of slang, and was intended as a satire on the ways of trade. Still I think that there is some good fun in it, but I have heard no one else express such an opinion. I do not know that I have ever heard any opinion expressed on it, except by the publisher, who kindly remarked that he did not think it was equal to my usual work.'

Mr Brown, a retired butter dealer, is persuaded by his commercially ambitious son-in-law, Jones, to invest his savings in a haberdashery emporium, in partnership with Jones and Robinson, a keen advocate of modern advertising methods. The business fails and is sold up; but after briefly questioning himself as to the true value of advertising, and finding no reassuring answer, Robinson is impelled, by the example of rich men who had started with nothing, to try again.

The sub-plot concerns the pursuit of Brown's daughter, Mary-anne, by Robinson and William Brisket, a butcher. She rejects both and devotes herself to caring for her father, broken by his business failure.

RACHEL RAY

A NEW experience awaited Anthony Trollope in connection with his next novel, *Rachel Ray*, begun in the spring of 1863. He was more or less pressed into writing it by a Glaswegian friend, the Revd Dr Norman Macleod, a leading member of the Evangelical movement and editor of the weekly magazine, *Good Words*, whose pious stories and articles were, apart from the Bible, the only Sabbath reading permitted in many Victorian households, to the intense boredom of their servants and junior members of the family. Macleod asked Trollope to provide him with a novel to serialize, and would not listen to his friend's gentle protest that he was scarcely the man for the job. A commission being a commission, and the fee of £1,000 being agreed, Trollope set about the task and delivered the short novel by the end of June. The eager editor had its first portions set up in print before he read the whole, with mounting concern. Not only did it guy the Evangelists and their acidulated, kill-joy clergy, but its young hero was a partner in a brewery.

'A letter more full of wailing and repentance no man ever wrote,' Trollope recalled, in the *Autobiography*, of Macleod's next communication. 'It was, he said, all his own fault. He should have taken my advice. He should have known better. But the story, such as it was, he could not give to his readers in the pages of *Good Words*. Would I forgive him? Any pecuniary loss to which his decision might subject me the owner of the publication would willingly make.'

Trollope did forgive him – indeed, he and Dr Macleod remained as firm friends afterwards as before – but he felt justified in asking for half the promised fee. It was paid without demur, and Trollope published the novel that October, in two volumes, through Chapman & Hall.

The brewery of Bungall and Tappitt at Baslehurst in Devonshire produces an almost undrinkable liquor and enjoys little prosperity in that cider-drenched county. Old Thomas Tappitt, the surviving partner, has no wish to change things, living comfortably enough off the moderate income the firm provides him. But the late Bungall's widow dies and leaves her interest to a nephew, Luke Rowan, who is distantly related to Tappitt. Tappitt expects to be able to buy the young man out with £1,000, but Luke's lawyer demands ten times that sum. When Tappitt refuses, Luke comes to Baslehurst and sets about improving the brew by the application of modern scientific methods.

He stays in the Tappitt household, and is at least welcomed by Mrs Tappitt, who has three daughters and hopes Luke will marry the eldest, Augusta. He falls in love instead with Rachel Ray, who lives with her widowed mother and widowed elder sister, Dorothea Prime, whose embittered, anti-male outlook has infected their mother and causes her to oppose the association between Rachel and Luke. Mrs Ray is further influenced by an Evangelical clergyman, Mr Prong, a thrusting young man, intolerant of more easy-going clergy and somewhat interested in Mrs Prime, or, rather, in her property.

Luke quarrels with Tappitt and leaves Baslehurst, to return in time to make a speech which narrowly secures the Parliamentary seat for Mr Butler Cornbury, whose socially influential wife is the daughter of a kindly clergyman friend of Mrs Ray, the Revd Comfort. In his speech, Luke has avowed that he will settle in Baslehurst and brew better beer, a sentiment which has gained him popular support. It also provides the cue for Mrs Tappitt to persuade her stubborn husband to retire and take her to live in Torquay off the income Luke guarantees them. Through Mrs Cornbury's influence Mrs Ray and Mrs Prime also withdraw their opposition to Luke, and he and Rachel are married.

THE SMALL HOUSE AT ALLINGTON

In 1861 the War of Secession had broken out in America, and from the first I interested myself much in the question. My mother had thirty years previously written a very popular, but, as I thought, a somewhat unjust book about our cousins over the water. She had seen what was distasteful in the manners of a young people, but had hardly recognised their energy. I had entertained for many years an ambition to follow her footsteps there, and to write another book. – (*Autobiography*)

TROLLOPE'S first step was to consult Edward Chapman, who willingly commissioned the book on the author's terms. His second necessity was to apply for nine months' leave of absence to the Secretary of the Post Office, Sir Rowland Hill, the inaugurator, in 1840, of penny postage. There was no love lost between Trollope and Hill, so he went directly instead to the Postmaster-General, and gained somewhat grudging assent. He left for America in August and returned in April 1862 with the book finished. It was published the following month as *North America* (two volumes) and enjoyed wide popularity.

The work following it in volume form was again not a novel, but a second series of *Tales of All Countries*, published by Chapman & Hall in 1863. But by the time this appeared Trollope was thoroughly back in favour with the novel-reading public through the serialization in the *Cornhill* of what is regarded by many as his masterpiece, *The Small House at Allington*, which ran from September 1862 – April 1864. It appeared in book form in March 1864, in two volumes, published by Smith, Elder, and evidently provoked sighs of relief and sentiment all round:

The Small House at Allington redeemed my reputation with the spirited proprietor of the *Cornhill*, which must, I should think, have been damaged by *Brown, Jones and Robinson*. In it appeared Lily Dale, one of the characters which readers of my novels have liked the best. In the love with which she has been greeted I have hardly joined with much enthusiasm, feeling that she is somewhat of a French prig . . . Prig as she was, she made her way into the hearts of many readers, young and old; so that, from time to time, I have been continually honoured with letters, the purport of which has always been to beg me to marry Lily Dale to Johnny Eames. Had I done so, however, Lily would never have so endeared herself to these people as to induce them to write letters to the author concerning her fate. It was because she could not get over her troubles that they loved her.

Lily Dale lives with her widowed mother and her sister Isabella ('Bell') in the Small House at Allington. Up at the Great House lives Mrs Dale's brother-in-law, Christopher Dale, the local squire, who had not approved of her marriage to his late younger brother Philip, but has made the Small House available for the sake of her daughters' upbringing. Bell is earmarked by the Squire as the future wife of his nephew and heir, Captain Bernard Dale, but Bell loves Dr James Crofts, a physician in the near-by town of Guestwick, whom she eventually marries.

Lily falls in love with a friend of Bernard's, Adolphus Crosbie, a handsome and plausible young Civil Servant, living in comfortable bachelor ease in London, where he is assiduously climbing the social ladder. After a while he proposes marriage, and she accepts; but social advancement comes before romantic obligation in Adolphus's scale of priorities, and at a house party at Courcy Castle, the Barsetshire seat of the de Courcy family, he recognizes the susceptibility of Lady Alexandrina de Courcy, who is already past her prime of youth and has had one abortive engagement. He proposes to her and is accepted.

It is no consolation to Lily to know that, however untrue her betrothed may have proved, another man adores her; for her love for Adolphus is passionate. The other man is Johnny Eames, a poor Government clerk under the guardianship of Squire Dale.

Johnny lives in London in a boarding house kept by a Mrs Roper, whose daughter Amelia is hopeful that he might offer to marry her. He has always loved Lily Dale, but has not been above flirting with Amelia Roper, who gets him to write a proposal. It is never honoured: Johnny is promoted and changes his lodgings, Amelia later finding a husband in Johnny's fellow-boarder, Joseph Cradell.

Although he himself has behaved less than well towards Amelia, Johnny is overcome by righteous indignation on hearing that Adolphus Crosbie has jilted Lily and gives the latter a beating. Crosbie marries Lady Alexandrina in spite of this, but the union is an immediate disaster and she leaves him after a few weeks, to live abroad with her mother and soon dies. Johnny is taken up by Lord de Guest, brother-in-law of Squire Dale, whom he saves from an attack by a bull and who leaves him a handsome legacy. But Lily still will not marry him, preferring to devote her attention to her mother and old Squire Dale, and Johnny's great love for her, as Trollope's readers never ceased to complain to him, remains unrequited.

THE PALLISER NOVELS

Can You Forgive Her?, Phineas Finn, The Eustace Diamonds, Phineas Redux, The Prime Minister, The Duke's Children

I never could arrange a set of events before me. But the evil and the good of my puppets, and how the evil would always lead to evil, and the good produce good, – that was clear to me as the stars on a summer night.

BARSETSHIRE and its host of characters, which spread themselves over a 'canvas' of six novels, developed out of what had been conceived as a single story, *The Warden*. This was one of those cases known to every writer of good novels of characters insisting on dictating, to a large extent, their own relationships, actions and destinies: that almost mystical process which Arthur Conan Doyle expressed succinctly in a couplet:

> I feel a second finger lie
> Above mine on the pen.

The Barsetshire stories were written at sporadic intervals over a period of fourteen years; and because they were not planned sequentially they are being considered in this present work in their chronological context with the other novels. However, the 'Palliser', or 'Parliamentary' novels, though also six in number and spread in composition over a thirteen-year period (August 1863–October 1876), and interspersed with many other works, need to be considered *en bloc*: not because Trollope set out to write them with an exact plan of their development before him – he did no such thing – but because from the outset he knew that he was going to create a series in which the destinies of certain characters would be closely interwoven into a tapestry depicting 'the faults and frailties and vices, – as also the virtues, the graces, and the strength of our highest classes' in both the social and political spheres.

To judge from the *Autobiography* he seems deliberately to have spread the writing of the series over so long a period in accordance with his conviction that, to attain absolute reality, fictional characters must be allowed to mature and change in lifelike relationship to the supposed time-span of the story through which they move, rather than be grown forcibly in a literary hot-house:

> In conducting these characters from one story to another I realised the necessity, not only of consistency, – which had it been maintained by a hard exactitude, would have been untrue to nature, – but also of those changes which time always produces. There are, perhaps, but few of us who, after the lapse of ten years, will be found to have changed our chief characteristics. The selfish man will still be selfish, and the false man false. But our manner of showing or of hiding these characteristics will be changed, – as also our power of adding to or diminishing their

intensity. It was my study that these people, as they grew in years, should encounter the changes which come upon us all; and I think that I have succeeded. The Duchess of Omnium, when she is playing the part of Prime Minister's wife, is the same woman as that Lady Glencora who almost longs to go off with Burgo Fitzgerald, but yet knows that she will never do so; and the Prime Minister Duke, with his wounded pride and sore spirit, is he who, for his wife's sake, left power and place when they were first offered to him; – but they have undergone the changes which a life so stirring as theirs would naturally produce. To do all this thoroughly was in my heart from first to last; but I do not know that the game has been worth the candle. To carry out my scheme I have had to spread my picture over so wide a canvas that I cannot expect that any lover of such art should trouble himself to look at it as a whole. Who will read *Can You Forgive Her? Phineas Finn, Phineas Redux*, and *The Prime Minister* consecutively, in order that they may understand the characters of the Duke of Omnium, of Plantagenet Palliser, and of Lady Glencora? Who will ever know that they should be so read? But in the performance of the work I had much gratification, and was enabled from time to time to have in this way that fling at the political doings of the day which every man likes to take, if not in one fashion then in another. I look upon this string of characters, – carried sometimes into other novels than those just named, – as the best work of my life. Taking him altogether, I think that Plantagenet Palliser stands more firmly on the ground than any other personage I have created.

CAN YOU FORGIVE HER?

Actually, Plantagenet Palliser first appears in *The Small House at Allington*, as heir to the old Duke of Omnium and as prospective husband of Lady Glencora MacCluskie, an eighteen-year-old Scottish heiress of great fortune. The first true entrance of this couple, though, is in *Can You Forgive Her?*, when they immediately take over the story and invest it and its sequels with the brand-name 'Palliser'.

By the time they appear, *Can You Forgive Her?* is already telling the story of Alice Vavasor, hesitating whether to marry a worthy but possessive country gentleman, John Grey, to whom she is engaged, or to unleash her passion for her cousin, George

Vavasor, erratic in his nature and his ways but romantically manly and fascinatingly scarred about the face as a result of a childhood fight with a burglar, whom he had managed to kill. A somewhat parallel situation at once develops, with Lady Glencora, married to the dry, politically-preoccupied Plantagenet Palliser, yet unable to keep her imagination from dwelling on her first lover, Burgo Fitzgerald, gambler, drinker, but 'certainly among the handsomest of God's creatures'.

In the event, Alice does marry John Grey and Lady Glencora does resist the temptation to elope with Fitzgerald, leaving one to speculate, perhaps with some regret, what an Emily Brontë or a Thomas Hardy might have done that Trollope did not with such a dual situation of smouldering passions.

Can You Forgive Her?, which he derived from his unperformed play *The Noble Jilt*, was written between August 1863–April 1864 and first published by Chapman & Hall in twenty monthly numbers from January 1864–August 1865. It reappeared in two volumes, published respectively in October 1864 and June 1865.

PHINEAS FINN: THE IRISH MEMBER

In November 1866 Trollope began the second story in the sequence, *Phineas Finn*. The Pallisers themselves are at the side of the stage in this tale, Plantagenet having, at the end of its predecessor, declined the post of Chancellor of the Exchequer in order to secure his wife's fidelity and taken her on a European tour, an outcome of which had been the birth of his heir, the future Lord Silverbridge. Their place in the spotlight is now taken by Phineas Finn, a young Irishman in London, where he is reading for the Bar. He is subsequently elected to the House of Commons. It is not, however, any remarkable rise to parliamentary fame that is the theme of this 'political' novel, in which the Palace of Westminster is more the backdrop than the stage setting, but Phineas's meteoric ascendancy in fashionable society, and especially amongst the ladies who grace it. His engagement to a simple girl back home, Mary Flood Jones, makes him none the less susceptible to the statuesque, red-headed Lady Laura Standish, who constitutes herself his advisor and helps him into Parliament. She loves him, but will not marry him, for he has no fortune and hers had gone in paying the debts of her wild and violent-tempered brother, Lord Chiltern. Instead, she marries another Member of Parliament, Robert Kennedy, who has a great deal of money but proves to be the possessor of so sanctimonious a nature that he is intolerable as a husband. Laura leaves him, to go and live in Dresden with her father, the Earl of Brentford.

Having been rejected by Laura, Phineas has sought to marry her closest friend, Violet Effingham, whom Laura had intended for her brother, Lord Chiltern. The fiery Chiltern, finding Phineas to be his rival, challenges him to a duel, but no harm is done, the two men are reconciled, and Violet marries Chiltern.

Still wifeless after two attempts, Phineas is also deprived of his parliamentary seat after refusing to vote with his party. He is taken up by Marie Goesler, the clever and rich widow of a Viennese banker. A woman widely courted for her influence as well as for her wealth, she resolves to help Phineas find another seat. When he refuses her financial patronage she offers him it less directly through marriage with her, but he is too proud to accept, and, rather belatedly resolving to fulfil his responsibility to his childhood sweetheart, returns to Ireland and marriage with Mary Flood Jones.

Phineas Finn was written between November 1866 and May 1867. It was serialized from October 1867–May 1869 in a new periodical, *St Paul's Magazine*, edited by Trollope himself and founded by a printer and publisher, James Virtue, who also published the novel in two-volume form in March 1869.

THE EUSTACE DIAMONDS

The Pallisers themselves – Lady Glencora in particular – are onlookers in the third novel of the canon. The 'star' of *The Eustace Diamonds*, almost constantly on stage, is making (to continue the theatrical simile) a sensational début. Her name is Lizzie

Eustace; or, to begin with, Lizzie Greystock, though it takes very few pages for this cunning, pretty little orphan, aided by her aunt, Lady Linlithgow, to get a proposal of marriage out of Sir Florian Eustace, Bt., who is young, wealthy – and dying. Within a year he is dead, and yet another rich widow is added to the many who populate Anthony Trollope's works.

Eustace has left his widow a handsome income and a life interest in his Scottish castle, Portray. According to her he had also, while alive, made her a gift of the Eustace Diamonds; but this is now disputed by the family lawyer, Samuel Camperdown, who contends that the jewels constitute a family heirloom and cannot be made an individual gift, even if there were any proof that they had been. Lizzie refuses to part with the diamonds, and while she is staying in a Carlisle hotel, *en route* from Portray to London, thieves break into her room and steal the safe in which she keeps them.

The subject of the Eustace Diamonds becomes one for heated debate in many quarters. There are those who believe them genuinely stolen – among these are Lizzie's cousin Frank Greystock, a young Member of Parliament who has resisted her matrimonial overtures because he is engaged to Lucy Morris, governess in the household of Lady Fawn; those who fancy that the robbery had been an 'inside job', arranged by one of Lizzie's admirers, Lord George Carruthers; and others who suspect that the jewels are still in Lizzie's possession. The latter are correct. The robbery had been real enough – the safe had been stolen, but not the diamonds, which had not been in it at the time; a detail Lizzie had not seen fit to mention to the police. Thus, when she is robbed yet again, this time in London, and the diamonds really are taken, she can only go on insisting that they had been stolen on the first occasion.

Even when the diamonds are found on the Continent – 'adorning the bosom of a certain enormously rich Russian princess' – and a well-known thief, Smiler, and a fence, Benjamin, are in the dock, there remains a doubt as to Lizzie Eustace's precise degree of involvement in the matter, for she has sent a message from Scotland that she is too ill to attend the trial, and counsel for the accused has some aspersions to cast, despite which the two men are found guilty and sentenced heavily.

Plantagenet Palliser's uncle, the old Duke of Omnium, has been following the whole affair in fascination, kept abreast of its developments by Lady Glencora. His concluding remark, having heard that Lizzie Eustace has married Joseph Emilius, a fashionable preacher of Bohemian–Jewish origins who is known to be a mere fortune-hunter is: 'I'm afraid, you know, that your friend hasn't what I call a good time before her.' How true this prophecy proves to be is revealed in the next novel in the series, *Phineas Redux*. Trollope did not keep his readers waiting long for further news of Lizzie Eustace. *The Eustace Diamonds*, written between December 1869 and August 1870, had been serialized in the *Fortnightly Review* from July 1871–February 1873, and published in three volumes by Chapman & Hall in December 1872. *Phineas Redux* had already been written by this time (October 1870–April 1871) and was serialized in the *Graphic* from July 1873–January 1874, appearing in book form (two volumes) in December 1873, published by Chapman & Hall.

PHINEAS REDUX

In the *Autobiography* Trollope confesses that, since he had ended *Phineas Finn* with every intention of bringing its hero back in some future story, he had been wrong to marry him off to a simple Irish girl 'who could only be an encumbrance on such a return'. When he came to write *Phineas Redux* he was painfully compelled to dispose of that encumbrance by informing the reader that she had died due to a complication of pregnancy during the two years which have elapsed since the former part of Phineas Finn's story.

Now, in London, the Liberal Party are looking for good candidates to fight an imminent General Election, and Phineas is invited to stand for the borough of Tankerville, which he wins.

He receives an invitation from Laura Kennedy, still living in

Dresden with her father, the Earl of Brentford, to spend Christmas with them, and accepts. Word of this reaches Robert Kennedy, the husband whom Laura had gone to Dresden to escape, and he makes it plain to Phineas that he is suspicious that something mischievous is afoot between him and Laura. Phineas refuses to cancel his visit. Not long after his return he is summoned to the presence of Quintus Slide, editor of a scandal-mongering newspaper the *People's Banner*, who shows him a libellous letter from Kennedy about his wife's desertion. Phineas visits Kennedy, hoping to get him to withdraw the letter, and finds that Kennedy is clearly mad: so much so that he tries to shoot Phineas, babbling that it is he who is responsible for Laura's refusal to return to him. Phineas does not make the incident public, and Kennedy is taken quietly away by relatives to his Scottish estate, where he lapses into complete insanity and dies.

Although this affair has been successfully hushed up, Phineas is subsequently precipitated into one which becomes a public sensation. A fellow politician named Bonteen and he quarrel at their club, overheard by some other members. Shortly afterwards Bonteen is found murdered. The most obvious suspect is Lizzie Eustace's husband, Joseph Emilius, for it is known that Bonteen had been trying to find evidence to support the wide belief that Emilius had married Lizzie bigamously. However, Emilius is able to prove an alibi and is released from custody. Starting from the basis of the quarrel at the club, a strong case is now built up against Phineas Finn, and he is brought to trial. However, Marie Goesler has been busy making inquiries of her own on the Continent and turns up enough evidence to switch suspicion back to Emilius. Nothing can be proved beyond the fact that he is a bigamist, for which he goes to prison, while Phineas is acquitted of the murder charge. He resigns his seat in Parliament, but is overwhelmingly re-elected. He is offered the post of Colonial Under-secretary, but hesitates about accepting it, deciding at last to decline it and retire from politics. Laura Kennedy, whose husband is now dead, has been hoping desperately that Phineas's former love for her will be re-kindled now; but instead of proposing to her he does so to Marie Goesler, who accepts him.

During the course of the story the old Duke of Omnium has died and Plantagenet Palliser has succeeded to the title. Jewellery and money left to Marie Goesler in the old Duke's will are declined and pass instead to her friend, Adelaide Palliser, a distant relative of Plantagenet, enabling her at last to marry her impecunious suitor, Gerard Maule.

THE PRIME MINISTER

In *The Prime Minister*, the fifth of the Palliser novels, Plantagenet and Glencora are back at the very centre of events. Mr Gresham's government falls, and when he and his rival Mr Daubeny both find it impossible to form a new one, a coalition is proposed, with the Duke of Omnium (Plantagenet Palliser) as Prime Minister. He is reluctant to accept the appointment, for which he feels himself temperamentally unsuited, but accedes. He proves too sensitive and inactive – qualities, curiously enough, regarded as desirable in a statesman by Trollope, who mistrusted thrusting, ambitious men in politics – as well as too aloof and uncommunicative to make a natural Prime Minister, but his exuberant duchess, Glencora, sets out to use all the means she can to mould him into at least the semblance of one. He mixes too little with his colleagues, but she endeavours to keep his well-wishers happy with splendid receptions at Gatherum Castle, their seat in West Barsetshire, at Matching Priory, their Yorkshire home, and in London, the blatancy of her motives causing her husband a good deal of embarrassment.

She goes too far when she begins dabbling in political place-making. It is on behalf of a well-born adventurer, Ferdinand Lopez, who has married Emily Wharton, the daughter of a wealthy London lawyer, against her father's wishes, and promptly tried to make her obtain money from her father to repair his finances and further the speculations in which he is involved in partnership with a money-lender, Sextus ('Sexty') Parker. Lopez gains an invitation to one of the duchess's splendid receptions at Gatherum and impresses her with his glib talk and energetic manner as a prospective candidate for a Parliament in need of freshness and youth. She hints that she will help him gain the Palliser pocket-borough of Silverbridge, but when she tries to influence the duke he sharply rebuffs her. Believing, in spite of this, that she will be doing her husband a good turn by getting Lopez elected, she makes it known that he is the duke's favoured candidate. His rival happens to be Arthur Fletcher, who has loved Emily Wharton most of her life and had shared her father's distress at her wishing to marry Lopez. When Arthur learns that Lopez is standing against him, with the Duchess of Omnium's support, he tries to withdraw from the election, but his supporters will not let him. He wins handsomely.

Lopez furiously accuses the duke and duchess of betraying his hopes and demands financial recompense, threatening to reveal all if he is not paid £500. Learning for the first time of his wife's indiscretion in the matter, the duke gives in to this blackmail. Quintus Slide, editor of the *People's Banner*, learns of this and attacks the Prime Minister in print, provoking a question in the House. It is Phineas Finn who saves the day for the Omniums with a clever speech of exculpation.

After three years the coalition Government falls and the duke thankfully retires from political life. Lopez, however, has not retired from his money-making activities, sponging on his father-in-law for every penny he can obtain. But he is financially and socially ruined, and knows it, and when a final bid to obtain a mining appointment in Guatemala falls through he throws himself under a train. Emily, who had remained infatuated with him for all his faults, is left devastated, but recovers in due course to become the wife, after all, of Arthur Fletcher.

Trollope began writing *The Prime Minister* in April 1874 and completed it that September. It was published in eight monthly parts from November 1875–June 1876, by Chapman & Hall, who also issued it in four volumes in May 1876. It failed to please the reading public, and in a later note appended to his references to it in the *Autobiography* its author aggrievedly reported that it had been 'worse spoken of by the press than any novel I had written'.

THE DUKE'S CHILDREN

The final novel of the Palliser series, *The Duke's Children*, opens with the information that Glencora, Duchess of Omnium, is no longer in the cast of players. Back in England after their prolonged sojourn abroad, the duke had hoped to resume his political career in some capacity while the duchess looked forward to a return to the role of society hostess; but, visiting Matching Priory for a few days, she had been unable to shake off a cold, sore throat and general debility, and within a week was dead.

There are three children of the marriage, all of whom are by now grown up and showing their grief-stricken father varying degrees of concern. The eldest, Lord Silverbridge, intelligent but erratic, has been sent down from Oxford for indiscipline and is applying his mind to the form of racehorses. His younger brother, Gerald, Lord Palliser, is at Cambridge, where he is performing indifferently; during the story he will be sent down, in retribution for taking absence to watch his brother's horse run in the St Leger. The only daughter, Lady Mary Palliser, who is being cared for by Mrs Phineas Finn, is distressingly determined to marry a former fellow student of Lord Silverbridge, Frank Tregear, of whom Mary's late mother had approved but her father does not. Frank, who has neither money nor prospects, applies formally for Lady Mary's hand and is indignantly refused by the duke, who had not been aware that the duchess had sanctioned an engagement, which Mary determines to honour.

Lord Silverbridge has by now graduated from punter to owner, in partnership with a Major Tifto, and their horse 'Prime Minister' has been entered for the St Leger. Tifto becomes incensed by his aristocratic partner's manner towards him and causes their horse to go lame just before the race, its failure resulting in a loss of £70,000 to Silverbridge. The duke pays off the debt, and is able to use his magnanimous gesture to make his son give up racing and settle down to the duties of Member of Parliament for Silverbridge, the family's pocket-borough. He also believes that a good marriage will prove a steadying influence on the boy. But Silverbridge, for all his gratitude to his father for rescuing him from his creditors, is not of a character to permit a wife to be imposed on him. He has one of his own choosing in view – Isabel Boncassen, the daughter of an American scholar visiting London. The fact that Isabel is a beauty, is being received in all the best houses, and has inherited her father's intellect, for which the duke has a keen respect, are not enough to overcome his prejudice, common to almost all Victorian aristocrats, against the marriage of his heir to the daughter of a mere man of letters, the next worst thing to a tradesman. However, Silverbridge too has an inheritance – his late mother's ability to achieve desired results in the face of, or, perhaps, round the back of, the duke's disapproval. He sticks to his guns and the duke allows the marriage to go forward.

Frank Tregear secures a seat in Parliament, and the duke, perhaps mellowed by his own return to political office as President of the Council, decides that what he had formerly regarded as sheer presumption on Frank's part for seeking a wife so far above his own station had, in fact, been admirable courage. For the second time he allows a once-forbidden marriage to take place; and at the ceremony the stiff, cold, proud old man astonishes those present:

> Perhaps the matter most remarkable in the wedding was the hilarity of the Duke. One who did not know him well might have said that he was a man with very few cares, and who now took special joy in the happiness of his children – who was thoroughly contented to see them marry after their own hearts. And yet, as he stood there on the altar steps giving his daughter to that new son and looking first at his girl and then at his married son, he was reminding himself of all he had suffered.

The Duke's Children was written between May and October

1876. It was serialized in *All the Year Round* from October 1879–July 1880, when it was published by Chapman & Hall in three volumes.

MISS MACKENZIE

In the three years, less a few months, between finishing *Can You Forgive Her?* and starting *Phineas Finn* Anthony Trollope was at his most prolific. He wrote six novels, three series of sketches for the newly-founded *Pall Mall Gazette*, some of the short stories which were later to be collected into *Lotta Schmidt: and Other Stories* (published by Alexander Strahan, 1867) and reviews for the *Pall Mall Gazette* and the *Fortnightly Review*, which, in accordance with his conscientious scruples, involved thorough reading and careful thought of every work he undertook to notice. The three series of sketches were also reprinted in volume form during this period as *Hunting Sketches*, 1865, *Travelling Sketches*, 1866, and *Clergymen of the Church of England*, 1866, all published by Chapman & Hall. The first of the six novels was *Miss Mackenzie*, written between May and August 1864 and published by Chapman & Hall in two volumes in March 1865.

In dilating upon the craft and ethics of the novelist in his *Autobiography* Trollope declares that a novel can hardly be made interesting or successful without love, and admits that, having set out deliberately to prove otherwise with *Miss Mackenzie*, whom he made a 'very unattractive old maid', he had found himself compelled to surrender and let her fall in love before the end. His 'old maid' (she is thirty-five when the story begins) is Margaret Mackenzie, who has spent her best years nursing her father and her sickly brother Walter, which responsibility has prevented her marrying her one suitor, Harry Handcock. When her brother dies he leaves her comfortably off, but the years have wearied her too much for her to care about matrimony. She moves to Littlebath (Bath) and tentatively samples the pleasures of society which life has hitherto denied her. Her money inevitably attracts a succession of suitors: the Revd Jeremiah Maguire, an Evangelist in need of funds to establish himself in an independent church; Samuel Rubb junior, the son of her other brother, Tom's business partner, who swindles her out of some of her money but fails to marry her for the rest; and her cousin, John Ball, a widower with nine children, who is pushed into a proposal by his mother, who resents Miss Mackenzie's possessing money which should, she feels, have been left to her own husband, Sir John Ball.

Margaret refuses John, but he has fallen genuinely in love with her. It is then discovered that the original bequeather of the family fortune to Margaret's brothers had no legal right to do so, and that it really does belong to John Ball. To the latter's mother's dismay, he now persists in the suit she herself had initiated and persuades Margaret to marry him.

THE CLAVERINGS

THE novel following *Miss Mackenzie* was *The Claverings*, written between August–December 1864. This was the last one Trollope wrote for the *Cornhill*, which published it from February 1866– May 1867: it appeared in two volumes (Smith, Elder) in April 1867.

In *The Claverings* I did not follow the habit which had now become very common to me, of introducing personages whose names are already known to the readers of novels, and whose characters were familiar to myself. If I remember rightly, no one appears here who had appeared before or who has been allowed to appear since. I consider the story as a whole to be good, though I am not aware that the public has ever corroborated that verdict ... From beginning to end the story is well told. But I doubt now whether any one reads *The Claverings*. When I remember how many novels I have written, I have no right to expect that above a few of them shall endure even to the second year beyond publication.

Lord Ongar has about £60,000 a year; Harry Clavering, a schoolmaster, has about £300 a year: now that she has grown to womanhood Julia Brabazon has no hesitation in passing over Harry, her sweetheart since childhood, for the Ongar title and the fortune.

Harry apprentices himself to the civil engineering firm of Beilby and Burton and lodges in London with the Burton family. He soon falls in love with the daughter of the household, Florence, but his lack of income or fortune debars them from marriage. News is received from Italy that Lord Ongar, who has treated Julia brutally, has drunk himself to death with their marriage not a year old. She returns to London, where Harry engages rooms for her; before long she makes it clear that she is awaiting his proposal of marriage. When none is forthcoming she writes him one. He refuses, but has a harsh struggle with his conscience, for although he has promised himself to Florence Burton, who is irritatingly insisting on a long period of waiting before they marry, he knows he is as much in love with Julia as ever.

Count Pateroff and his sister Sophie Gordeloup, who had been familiar with the Ongars in Italy, set themselves up in London, and Pateroff tries to persuade Julia that her dying husband had expressed a wish that she should marry again, to Pateroff. He does not succeed. Harry's cousins, Sir Hugh and Archibald Clavering, are both drowned at sea, with the result that Harry inherits the family estates and Florence Burton sees no reason for further delaying their marriage.

THE BELTON ESTATE

THE next novel was *The Belton Estate*, written from January–September 1865 to help launch the *Fortnightly Review*, of which Trollope was a founder and George Eliot's partner, G. H. Lewes, was editor. Its first instalment appeared in the journal's first issue on 15 May 1865 and serialization continued until that December, when the book, in three volumes, was published by Chapman & Hall.

Belton Castle and estate, in Somersetshire, are entailed to Charles Amedroz, the son of the life-tenant there, Bernard Amedroz. Charles, who had been expelled from Harrow and sent down from Cambridge, is a compulsive gambler and has frittered away not only his own money but that of his sister Clara. His debts become insurmountable, and he commits suicide. This results in the entail passing to a distant relative, Will Belton, a handsome but uncultivated farmer in Norfolk. He visits the castle and meets Clara, with whom he quickly falls in love. However, she is intended for Captain Frederic Aylmer, M.P., whose mother's sister, Mrs Winterfield, it is supposed, has made Clara her heiress. When Mrs Winterfield dies, however, it is found that she has left her money to Captain Aylmer, with the proviso that he marry Clara. Aylmer is less than enthusiastic, and his domineering mother, Lady Aylmer, is positively hostile to the arrangement, for she has plans to marry Frederick to the very rich Lady Emily Tagmaggert.

Frederick takes Clara to visit the family seat, Aylmer Park, in Yorkshire, which gives Lady Aylmer a perfect opportunity to snub her. Frederic makes no protest at his mother's discourtesy, so Clara breaks off their engagement. Will Belton, who is now managing the Belton estate, proposes again to Clara, and is accepted.

A sub-plot concerns the tribulations of Colonel Askerton and his wife Mary, friends of Clara who live on the estate in Belton Cottage and to whom scandal is attached, for Mary had run off with the Colonel to escape her drunken husband, Jack Berdmore.

NINA BALATKA

IN the *Autobiography* Trollope tells us that he decided to publish his next novel, *Nina Balatka*, anonymously in order to test out his theory of the injustice of novel-readers giving preference to the work of authors with established names, such as himself, over unknowns. Dare one suggest that this was not such a single-minded gesture as he would have us believe, but that he knew his name was being over-exposed and wondered whether he could find a good enough sale for some of his books anonymously to enable him to reserve his name for what he considered major works? At any rate, he was soon exposed by a critic who recognized his style – and even this brought the book little success. It was written from September–December 1865, serialized in *Blackwood's Magazine* from July 1866–January 1867, and published in two volumes (Blackwood) in February 1867.

The title is the name of a 'maiden of Prague, born of Christian parents, and herself a Christian', who loves Anton Trendellsohn, the Jewish son of her father's former partner. Religious and social sentiments prevailing between the Jews and Gentiles in the old Bohemian capital inevitably cause opposition to the proposed marriage from both sides. When the young couple appear determined to go ahead defiantly, Anton's relatives bribe a servant in the Balatka house to conceal some documents in a desk drawer and arrange that Nina shall be accused of having hidden them there. Not knowing of their existence, she denies having the papers and invites Anton to search the desk, where he finds them. Horrified to see that he now mistrusts her, Nina attempts suicide but is saved. The servant confesses, Nina's father relents, and the couple marry despite the Trendellsohn family's objections.

THE LAST CHRONICLE OF BARSET

THERE is nothing in the *Autobiography* or in Trollope's correspondence to tell us why, more than four years after the publication of *Framley Parsonage*, he decided to write a further Barsetshire novel, and, with it, to bring that irregular series to an end. James Pope Hennessy suggests that it may have been a sort of gesture of liberation from his past life and work, at a time when he was turning his literary concentration towards London political circles, and, as regards his personal affairs, was contemplating the considerable step of resigning from the Post Office which he had served so long and so devotedly. The theory has a convincing ring to it; though one might wonder, additionally, whether his work at that time on the series of clerical sketches for the *Pall Mall Gazette* might not have prompted a return to the setting of Barchester Cathedral close, and to that memorable circle of ecclesiastical infighters who inhabited it and the parishes of the diocese.

Michael Sadleir advances the view that there might have been further Barchester tales but for the well-known passage between Trollope and two clergymen at the Athenaeum Club. He overheard them complaining to one another about his habit of using the same characters so often in his tales. In his impulsive, peppery way he could not help but introduce himself to the two astonished clerics, one of whom had referred disparagingly to his cherished Mrs Proudie: '"As to Mrs Proudie," I said, "I will go home and kill her before the week is over." And so I did.'

Barchester close could scarcely be Barchester close without Mrs Proudie, and perhaps her demise was, indeed, the *coup de grâce* to the series. The word *Last* in the title *The Last Chronicle of Barset* certainly distressed Trollope's readers and he received many requests to relent. But there is a pervading air of finality about *The Last Chronicle* which gives the impression that it had all along been intended as such and supports Mr Pope Hennessy's belief that, in his fifty-third year, Trollope was almost consciously discarding his old life for a new, forward-looking one.

The novel was written between January and September 1866 and issued in parts by Smith, Elder, who brought out the completed book in two volumes in 1867, when serialization ended.

The story contains many drawings-together of earlier Barchester situations, but at its core lies the case of the embittered, dejected Revd Josiah Crawley, perpetual curate of the poor parish of Hogglestock, fighting God's good fight with all his might against the odds of his poverty and near-manic despondency, sustained by his faith and by the strength and courage of his wife Mary. Compelled to accept financial assistance from Dean Arabin, he is given an envelope containing bank-notes and a cheque. The cheque, which he endorses and cashes, is one signed by Lord Lufton and mislaid by his man of business, Mr Soames, and in due course it is traced to Crawley, who gives a confused and manifestly untrue account of how he had come into possession of it. The result is that he is accused of stealing it from Mr Soames's pocket-book, which had been mislaid. Crawley is taken before the magistrates and is bailed to appear at Barchester Assizes.

As soon as the news reaches the ears of Bishop Proudie's tyrannical wife she demands Crawley's suspension from his duties: 'The man must not be allowed to desecrate the church of Hogglestock by performing the services.' The bishop feebly protests that the man has not yet been found guilty, but, as ever, bows to his wife's demands and summons Crawley to an interview, conducted more by Mrs Proudie than by the bishop. Crawley stands up to her hectoring and refuses to give up ministering to his needy flock until such time as he may be declared guilty of the theft.

Temporarily repulsed, Mrs Proudie tries to influence the Revd Dr Tempest, who is to chair an ecclesiastical commission inquiring into the Crawley affair. He rebukes her firmly, and even her husband, shocked by her blatant attempt to usurp his authority, turns sullen and silent towards her. All her efforts to win him round again fail, and, alone in her bedroom, Mrs Proudie succumbs to the heart complaint of which no one but her maid had known, and dies, characteristically remaining on her feet.

Crawley is found innocent and appointed to the better living of St Ewold's, and the great sequence of stories comes to an end. In the *Autobiography* Trollope remarks: 'I have sometimes wished to see during my lifetime a combined republication of those tales which are occupied with the fictitious county of Barsetshire. These would be *The Warden, Barchester Towers, Doctor Thorne,*

Framley Parsonage, and *The Last Chronicle of Barset*. But I have hitherto failed. The copyrights are in the hands of four different persons . . .' A footnote tells us that arrangements had since been concluded, and the first complete issue of *The Chronicles of Barsetshire* was made by Chapman & Hall in 1879, in eight volumes, adding, despite some reluctance on the author's part, *The Small House at Allington* to the five he considered represented the true Barsetshire saga.

Some time after the publication of the *Last Chronicle* Trollope was approached by a theatre manager with the proposal that he turn it into a play. He agreed, but the resulting *Did He Steal It?* was found unsatisfactory for staging. It was privately printed in 1869. In it Mr Crawley becomes a schoolmaster, Bishop and Mrs Proudie are Mr and Mrs Goshawk, a magistrate and his wife, and Caleb Thumble is Caleb Thrumble, a schoolmaster hoping to gain Crawley's place.

LINDA TRESSEL

HAVING begun writing *Phineas Finn* in November 1866, Trollope laid it aside briefly the following January to knock off a parliamentary work of a very different kind, a brief study of the life and career of Lord Palmerston. It was not published until 1882, as one in a series, 'English Political Leaders', issued by a London firm, Isbister & Co., with little success.

This done, and *Phineas Finn* completed by mid-May, he resumed his experiment in anonymous authorship with *Linda Tressel*, written in June and July and serialized in *Blackwood's Magazine* from October 1867–May 1868, reappearing in two volumes as the serialization ended.

Linda Tressel is an orphan, living in the Nuremberg home of her fanatically pious aunt Madame Charlotte Staubach. Linda is in love with a young political agitator, Ludovic Valcarm, well known to the police for his activities. Madame Staubach, fearing for the girl's moral welfare and disturbed by her lack of religious sensibilities, tries to marry her off to an old clerk in the magistrate's office, Peter Steinmarc. Rather than give in to this, Linda runs away with Ludovic, but when they arrive at Augsburg he is arrested at the station. Linda is taken back to Nuremberg and old Steinmarc, who, however, will have nothing to do with a girl of such tendencies.

THE GOLDEN LION OF GRANPÈRE

THE inferiority of *Linda Tressel*, and the failure of the experiment to prove any point or butter any commercial parsnips, caused William Blackwood to decline to publish a third work anonymously, and it was left on Trollope's hands for several years, finally appearing, under his name, in another journal, *Good Words*, in 1872: it was republished that same year, as a single volume, by Tinsley Brothers. This was *The Golden Lion of Granpère*, written in September and October 1867 and described by its author in the *Autobiography* as being on the model of *Nina Balatka* and *Linda Tressel*, but 'very inferior to either of them'. Nevertheless, some later commentators have found much more to praise in it than in either of the others.

Again, the setting is a foreign one, this time Granpère, a small town in the French province of Lorraine, where the one hotel, the Lion d'Or, is owned by the self-opinionated Michel Voss, with whom are living his second wife, Josephine, and the son of his first marriage, George. Another resident is the present Mme Voss's pretty niece, Marie Bromar. George and she are in love and wish to marry, but Michel, who 'was apt to think that his superior years enabled him to know what younger people wanted better than they would know themselves', disapproves. Unable to make him relent, George leaves home to become a landlord of an inn at Colmar. For a whole year he does not write home. Believing she has lost him for ever, Marie accepts her uncle's

F

choice of suitor, one Adrian Urmand, a Swiss linen-buyer who uses the Lion d'Or on his visits to Granpère. News of this reaches George and brings him hastening back home, where his father's joy at their reunion is so great that he permits his son and his niece to marry.

HE KNEW HE WAS RIGHT

BETWEEN finishing *Linda Tressel* and starting *The Golden Lion of Granpère*, Trollope had added to his books in print with *Lotta Schmidt: and Other Stories*, a single-volume collection of nine tales written at various times in the preceding few years. Its publication, by Alexander Strahan, was in August 1867. This was by no means to prove one of his major works; but the time of its appearance was, for quite another reason, a momentous one in his life: he was about to leave the Post Office which he had served for more than thirty years. He was fifty-two years old and needed only another eight years to become entitled to pensioned retirement. But he and his wife had agreed long before that when he had amassed savings equivalent to that pension he would shed his Civil Service harness and devote himself to writing.

As it happened, he had another secure occupation to turn to at once. The printer James Virtue had determined upon publishing a monthly journal, the *St Paul's Magazine*, and had overcome Trollope's reluctance to take on the editorship. Trollope had finally agreed, stipulating £1,000 a year, guaranteed for two years. In addition, *Phineas Finn* was bought for the handsome figure of £3,500 to be the magazine's first serial, commencing with the first issue on 1 October 1867. Trollope remained as editor of the *St Paul's* for two and a half years, working with his usual conscientiousness and enjoying the use of liberal editorial funds, despite which the magazine never became a wide success and survived only a few years after his resignation from it in 1870.

This new undertaking would have preoccupied most people sufficiently for at least a few months to keep them from their own writing; but not Anthony Trollope. On 13 November he sat down to begin a long and sombre tale, *He Knew He Was Right*, which he later termed 'nearly altogether bad', but which has been admired by Trollopians and the relatively few others who have read it for its convincing portrayal of a man driven progressively mad by his jealousy of his wife's association with an old friend. This man is Louis Trevelyan, a rich and at first mild young English landowner visiting a fictitious little British possession, the Mandarin Islands, whose governor is the Blimpish old Sir Marmaduke Rowley. Sir Marmaduke has eight daughters, with the eldest of whom, Emily, Trevelyan promptly falls in love. A marriage is sanctioned and takes place, and in due course a son, Louey, is born. But a frequent caller on Emily in England is a friend of her father's, Colonel Frederic Osborne, M.P., whose interest in other men's wives is well known. Louis requests Emily to discourage the colonel, and when she does nothing about it he makes the request an order. This proves equally in vain, for Emily's stubbornness has brought her to a position where, as she sees it, to forbid the colonel's visits would suggest to all who know her that there had been some substance to Louis's suspicions of their behaviour.

His mind increasingly troubled by his self-created fantasy, Louis becomes more and more violent in his condemnations, until Emily leaves him, taking little Louey with her. This throws him into deeper brooding, the culmination of which is his abduction of the child, whom he takes to Italy. Even this does not dispel his nightmare, though, and by the time Emily finds him he is monomaniacally disturbed. She persuades him to return to England for treatment, but his disintegration is too far advanced and he dies. An interwoven plot concerns Emily's sister Nora, who had accompanied her to England as companion after the marriage, and a friend of Louis, Hugh Stanbury. Hugh has disappointed his Aunt Jemima, his benefactress, by insisting on becoming a journalist instead of something more socially

acceptable. Nora is courted by Charles Glascock, the wealthy heir
to Lord Peterborough, but, despite the prospects of riches and a
title, true love prevails and she marries Hugh.

Trollope finished it in June 1868 and the work was issued in
weekly numbers by Strahan from October 1868–May 1869. It
was then immediately published in two volumes. Much of the
latter part of it had been written in America. Trollope was paying
his second visit there at the request of his old employers, the
General Post Office, who had flatteringly invited him to negotiate
a postal treaty on their behalf. At the same time he undertook a
commission from the Foreign Office to try to get an agreement
on international copyright, about which he felt as strongly as
most English authors and composers of the time who could only
watch more or less helplessly while American publishers un-
inhibitedly pirated their works and paid nothing for doing so.
He achieved his aim where the postal arrangements were
concerned, but got nowhere with the publishers.

THE VICAR OF BULLHAMPTON

IT was entirely characteristic of Trollope that, although so far
removed from his study at Waltham Cross and so much occupied
with official negotiations, he began a new novel only three days
after finishing this last. This was *The Vicar of Bullhampton*, completed back in England that November, 1868. Originally intended for magazine publication, it was issued instead by
Bradbury & Evans in eight monthly parts, from July 1869–May
1870, and as a single volume in April 1870.

'Not very bad, not very good', was his own later comment
on it. His preoccupation had been 'chiefly with the idea of
exciting not only pity but sympathy for a fallen woman, and of
raising a feeling of forgiveness for such in the minds of other
women'. The girl is Carry Brattle, daughter of the Bullhampton
miller, who has been seduced and abandoned in London. As if

this were not scandal enough in the eyes of Bullhampton's principal landowner, the autocratic Marquis of Trowbridge, a local farmer, Trumbull, is murdered, and Carry's brother Sam is the chief suspect. The marquis demands of Harry Gilmore, the Brattle family's landlord, that they be evicted as undesirables. Harry refuses, with the determined backing of the vicar of Bullhampton, the Revd Frank Fenwick, and his wife, who argue that the boorish Jacob Brattle, his saintly wife and the rest of their family should not be made to suffer for the transgressions of two of their children.

The marquis seeks revenge by giving some land opposite the vicarage gates to the Primitive Methodists, whose rapid rise in popularity at this time was being viewed with resentment and alarm by Anglicans everywhere. The Methodists begin to build an ugly chapel on the spot, but it is found that the site had not been the marquis's to bestow, and it has to be pulled down.

The triumphant vicar is also instrumental in the tracking down of the actual murderers, Burrows and Acorn, and the rehabilitation not only of Sam Brattle, but of Carry, whom her father at length agrees to take back. A subsidiary story concerns an attempt by the vicar and his wife to get Harry Gilmore to marry Mary Lowther, who had been going to marry her cousin, Walter Marrable, until Walter's own father embezzled his money and the son had been compelled to break off the engagement and leave for service with the army in India. Mary and Harry agree to the arrangement, but before they can be married Walter chances to come into his uncle Gregory's fortune and Harry gracefully hands Mary back to him.

SIR HARRY HOTSPUR OF HUMBLETHWAITE

FOLLOWING an unsuccessful stand as Liberal candidate for Beverley in November 1868, Trollope began a new novel which, he said later, 'had for its object the telling of some pathetic incident in life rather than the portraiture of a number of human beings'. There are, indeed, few principal characters in *Sir Harry Hotspur of Humblethwaite*. Sir Harry himself is the owner of Humblethwaite Hall, Cumberland, which, in consequence of the death of his son, seems bound to pass to the next male in line, a dissolute nephew named George Hotspur. Sir Harry wishes his daughter Emily to inherit instead, and makes a new will to that effect; but George, who is in severe financial straits, proceeds to woo her in the hope of marrying her newly acquired wealth.

Emily has no illusions about George Hotspur's weaknesses, though she will recognize no proof of his graver defects. She sees herself as his potential saviour, besides which she is infatuated by his charm and plausible manner. Sir Harry stands firm against the match, however. George marries his actress mistress, who has been his sole support, and not long afterwards dies, his death breaking the heart of the still-infatuated Emily, causing her death, too.

Sir Harry Hotspur of Humblethwaite was finished at the end of January 1869 and serialized in *Macmillan's Magazine* from May–December 1870. It appeared in one volume (Hurst & Blackett) in November 1870.

RALPH THE HEIR

THE next few weeks saw Trollope at work on his play *Did He Steal It?* (see *The Last Chronicle of Barset*). He returned to prose again in April 1869 with *Ralph the Heir*, finished in August: it ran in the *St Paul's Magazine* from January 1870–July 1871, and was published in three volumes by Hurst & Blackett in April 1871. Its author's later comment on it was: 'I have always thought it to be one of the worst novels I have written, and almost to have justified that dictum that a novelist after fifty should not write love-stories.' It also owed a good deal to his experiences in the election at Beverley. The contrived plot concerns the efforts of Gregory Newton, owner of an estate named Newton Priory, to make his natural son, Ralph, his heir, in place of his legitimate son of the same name. Just as things seem to be working out satisfactorily towards this end he is killed hunting and Ralph the heir retains his inheritance, though he gives a good portion of it to the other Ralph, who marries Mary Bonner, who had already refused Ralph the heir. The other 'romantic' element is the association between the legitimate Ralph and Polly Neefit, a breeches-maker's daughter to whom he proposes marriage in order to get his debts to her father cancelled. She resolutely refuses to contemplate becoming a 'lady', and sticks to the man of her choice, Ontario Moggs, a boot-maker's son with political and poetical inclinations.

AN EYE FOR AN EYE

IN December 1869 Trollope began *The Eustace Diamonds* (see *The Palliser Novels*). The writing of a long novel by no means precluded him from doing anything else. A few weeks before beginning it he had undertaken to contribute a volume to a series called 'Ancient Classics for English Readers', being published by Blackwood. His subject was *The Commentaries of Julius Caesar*. Painstaking as ever, he read through the Commentaries twice, in the Latin and 'without assistance either by translation or English notes', then studied everything else he could find on the subject of Caesar, in Latin and English and even, to some degree, in French, before writing his book. It was published in June 1870, but, for all the effort he had put into it, was ignored, or, at best, faintly praised.

While writing this work he had resigned from the editorship of the *St Paul's* in March. In May he was able to capitalize further on his journalistic experiences by publishing, through Strahan, a volume of stories, *An Editor's Tales*, reflecting an editor's dealings with his contributors.

The Eustace Diamonds was finished at last in August, and the following month he began a new story of the darker side of human behaviour, *An Eye for an Eye*. As its title implies, this is a tale of revenge. Its setting is Ireland, where an English cavalry lieutenant, Fred Neville, heir to the Earl of Scroope, is stationed. Visiting the spectacular coast of County Clare, Fred meets a bewitching girl, Kate O'Hara. She lives in poor circumstances with her mother, whose alcoholic husband has deserted them to live in France, in order to avoid prosecution for a variety of crimes. Fred falls in love with Kate, and her mother is only too pleased to encourage them. Kate is just as eager: too eager, for she allows Fred to seduce her.

Fred inherits the earldom and begins to see his escapade as somewhat sordid, especially when he learns that Kate is pregnant. Although he resolutely refuses his mother's demand that he marry a wealthy English girl of long lineage, Sophia Mellerby, he has no intention either of binding himself to Kate, though lacking the courage to say so outright. Mrs O'Hara divines the truth, lures him to the cliffs and pushes him over to his death. She is incarcerated in an asylum and Kate goes to France to join her father, who is able to exact a permanent allowance for their maintenance from Fred's brother Jack, who has married Sophia Mellerby and is the new Earl of Scroope.

An Eye for an Eye was completed in October 1870 but not published (the reason why is not known) for eight years: it was serialized in the *Whitehall Review* from August 1878–February 1879 and brought out in two volumes, by Chapman & Hall, in January 1879.

LADY ANNA

Phineas Redux was written next (see *The Palliser Novels*). After finishing it Trollope gave up the house at Waltham Cross and embarked with Rose on a visit to Australia to see their sheep-farmer son Fred, in New South Wales. Naturally, he had arranged a commission from Chapman & Hall to write a book arising from these travels – it appeared early in 1873 as *Australia and New Zealand* – but the day after they set sail from Liverpool in May 1871 he was already writing the first pages of another novel. *Lady Anna*: by the time they reached Melbourne two months later it was finished.

As in several of his stories, bigamy, or alleged bigamy, plays an important part in this one. A disreputable peer, Earl Lovel, had married a poor but beautiful girl of good family, Josephine Murray, only to inform her, after the birth of their daughter Anna, that he already had a wife living in Italy. The countess's life is devoted from this point to trying to prove Anna's legitimacy. The earl has returned to live in Italy and the countess and Anna, left almost penniless, have been befriended by a tailor at Keswick, Cumberland, named Thomas Thwaite. Convinced of the justice of their case, he has not only given them a home but devotes his whole means towards their upkeep and legal costs.

After twenty years Earl Lovel returns to England with an Italian mistress, to whom, at his death soon afterwards, his entire estate is left. His real heir, Frederick, a nephew, takes the case to law, but the existence or non-existence of the old earl's purported wife in Italy prevents a conclusive settlement. Marriage between Frederick, now the earl, and Lady Anna seems a logical step towards joining family ranks against the interloping ex-mistress, and when Frederick meets Anna he falls genuinely in love. But Anna has grown up alongside Thomas Thwaite's son Daniel, also a tailor, to whom she has promised herself, and will not go back on her word. Her incensed mother cajoles and threatens, even trying to murder Daniel, but Anna is not to be deterred. The law case is settled at last, with the fortune being awarded to Anna. Generously passing on a large share of it to Frederick, she emigrates with Daniel, now her husband, to Australia.

Lady Anna was serialized in the *Fortnightly Review* from April 1873–April 1874 and published in two volumes by Chapman &

Hall in May 1874. The public did not take kindly to a heroine who spurned an earl for a tailor. 'What would they have said,' demanded the author in the *Autobiography*, 'if I had allowed her to jilt the tailor and marry the good-looking young lord? How much louder, then, would have been the censure!'

THE WAY WE LIVE NOW

Lady Anna was the only novel Trollope produced during his absence from England of nearly two years, though the 250,000-word *Australia and New Zealand* involved him in much investigation and writing. He and Rose returned to London in December 1872 and soon moved into their new home, 39 Montagu Square. Here, when he began working again in May, he changed his method from writing in longhand at his regulation pace of 250 words every fifteen minutes, timed by the watch before him on his desk, to dictating to Florence Bland, his wife's niece, who acted as his secretary and librarian. As James Pope Hennessy observes, this may well account for the enormous length of some of the later novels, composed without the valuable physical limitation of longhand writing. The first of these, written at Montagu Square from May to December 1873, was *The Way We Live Now*.

This was an ill-received attack on the materialism and lack of principle Trollope saw manifested in the world of finance. He maintained of it in the *Autobiography*: 'The accusations are exaggerated. The vices are coloured, so as to make effect rather than represent truth.' But too many unpleasant characters could sour a reader then as now, and there may have been resentment in some at an over-productive (and therefore, it followed, super-ficial) writer's presuming to sit in judgment on the City of London and the Palace of Westminster. Perhaps his theme was too near the truth to be entertaining – *The Times*, at least, praised the veracity of his portraiture – but most reviews were condemnatory, and his popularity and success were never again what they had been.

The story illustrates the age-old ability of the man of suitable personality and audacity to become a public success largely through bluff. Augustus Melmotte's origins and background are obscure, but when he sets up house in Grosvenor Square, London, with his European–Jewish wife and his natural daughter, Marie, and lets it be known that he is a financier of powerful influence, he is soon being fawned upon by society and invited to participate in grandiose schemes. Titled people are only too willing to add 'glamour' to a lavish ball Melmotte gives for Marie, who, it is hinted, will some day come into a great inheritance. She soon has several hopeful noblemen in train, but unwittingly settles for the least scrupulous she could have selected, Sir Felix Carbury.

The Carburys, of Suffolk, are a mixture of the deplorable and the rectitudinous. The evil Sir Felix is in utter contrast to his second cousin Roger, a good, kind man who can recognize the corruption of commercialism. Roger wishes to marry Felix's sister, Henrietta, and has the support of the girl's literary dilettante of a mother, Lady Carbury; but Henrietta prefers Roger's friend, Paul Montague, whom she eventually does marry.

Melmotte and his wife are determined that Marie shall marry Lord Nidderdale, so she and Felix Carbury decide to elope. She steals a large sum of money from her father to pay their way, but makes the mistake of entrusting it to Felix. He loses the lot gambling and fails to keep his rendezvous with Marie. His mother's friends send him into Continental exile, escorted by a clergyman.

Marie finishes up married to Hamilton K. Fisker, an American railway promoter associated with Augustus Melmotte; and Lady Carbury takes a new husband in Nicholas Broune, an editor with no illusions about her. Melmotte, whose grand projects, free spending of other people's money and sheer panache have gained him a place in Parliament, has been suspected of having used a forged document in a land deal, and has forged another in an attempt to lay hands on Marie's inheritance. Spurned by his toadies, and disgraced by being drunk in Parliament, he kills himself. His widow eventually marries his confidential clerk, Croll, who takes her off to America in the wake of Marie and Hamilton K. Fisker.

The Way We Live Now was issued in monthly parts from February 1874–September 1875 by Chapman & Hall, who also published it in two volumes in July 1875.

HARRY HEATHCOTE OF GANGOIL

There had been an interruption to the writing of this last novel in 1873 when Trollope hesitantly accepted a commission to do a Christmas story for the *Graphic*. He disapproved of Christmas stories as such – or said he did, no doubt envying Charles Dickens the facility which had given the latter an almost proprietorial interest in Christmas – but agreed to write this one rather than miss a fee of £450. The work, taking him only four weeks to complete, was *Harry Heathcote of Gangoil: a Tale of Australian Bush Life*, which the *Graphic* published as its Christmas number that year and Sampson Low brought out as a single volume in October 1874.

There is nothing of the Dickensian Christmas about the story, which is set in Australia and is replete with antagonism and drama. Trollope's autobiographical comment is: 'I was not loath to describe the troubles to which my son had been subjected, by the mingled accidents of heat and bad neighbours, on his station in the bush.' Harry Heathcote is an English sheep-farmer in Queensland, where he lives with his wife and sons and his wife's sister, Kate Daly. The latter is in love with another Englishman, Giles Medlicot, who has a sugar mill on land adjoining Harry's Gangoil. Unfortunately, Giles's purchase of land has deprived Harry of valuable river frontage, and the two men are in dispute.

Harry, whose temper is harsh and nature obstinate, has made

enemies of other neighbours, the Brownby family, a lawless father and six sons, most of whom have been in prison and now live largely by cattle-stealing. These, together with two of Giles's hands whom Harry had earlier sacked in his impetuous way, plan to drive the Heathcotes off their property by setting fire to the tinder-dry bush in the hot month of December. They start the fire, but Giles Medlicot rallies to Harry's support, the Brownbys are vanquished and the fire extinguished, the two Englishmen are reconciled, and Giles can marry Kate Daly at last.

IS HE POPENJOY?

HAVING polished off this Christmas task Trollope went on to finish *The Way We Live Now*, and then (see *The Palliser Novels*) wrote *The Prime Minister* during the greater part of the following year, 1874. By the autumn he was free to tackle yet another permutation of the theme of disputed inheritance and suspected illegitimacy, *Is He Popenjoy?*

Lord Popenjoy is the style of the son of the Marquis of Brotherton, and the question posed in the title of the story is whether the infant brought back to England by the marquis and the 'wife' he has acquired in Italy, where he has lived for many years, is genuinely entitled to be called Popenjoy. His estate, Manor Cross, has been managed in his absence by his younger brother Lord George Germain, who has married Mary Lovelace, daughter of the dean of Brotherton, and has a son. When Lord George and his mother and sisters are ordered out of Manor Cross to make way for the returning marquis and his dubious new family, Lord George, urged by the dean, sets afoot an investigation into the legitimacy of the so-called Lord Popenjoy. Nothing definite can be discovered, but the question ceases to matter when both the child and the marquis die within a short interval of each other, so that Lord George becomes marquis and his son is the undeniable Popenjoy.

Woven throughout the story is another familiar Trollopian theme, that of the wife of a worthy man who cannot sever herself from the attentions of a handsome scapegrace. The wife is Mary Germain, and her ardent follower is a dashing Guards officer, Captain Jack de Baron, who, however, has his own pursuer in the form of Augusta Mildmay, a determined beauty who at length nails him as her prize. A sub-theme concerns the earnest but repellent members of a kind of Women's Liberation movement and the rivalry for control of their London institute, named 'Disabilities'.

Is He Popenjoy? was started in October 1874. Much of it was written during a journey Trollope made to Ceylon in the spring of the following year, and it was finished at sea, between Ceylon and Australia, in May. It was serialized in *All the Year Round* from October 1877–July 1878, and published in three volumes by Chapman & Hall in April 1878.

THE AMERICAN SENATOR

It was actually on the way back from Ceylon that *Is He Popenjoy?* was finished, for the visit there had been a brief side expedition from the real purpose of Trollope's latest travels, a further stay – the last of his life, as it transpired – with his son Fred in New South Wales. Arriving back in Australia early in June, Trollope settled down at his son's isolated sheep-station, Mortray, to write yet another novel, *The American Senator*. Sitting in these primitive surroundings, and enduring, rather than enjoying, the strange, crude way of life that characterized early Australia, he projected his thoughts more than ten thousand miles back to his own country and penned those opening pages which, Michael Sadleir has said, set before the reader the whole geographical and social pattern of an English county. Deftly though he achieved this, however, the most compelling element of the story is its 'leading lady', Arabella Trefoil, one of those utterly convincing female

portrayals which Trollope could achieve with a realism Dickens
could never have hoped – would never have tried – to approach.

Arabella is a fine, handsome specimen of a marriageable
Englishwoman, and has been close to matrimony several times;
yet, at the age of thirty, she is still single, and is determined not
to remain so much longer. Visiting Washington with her mother,
Lady Augustus Trefoil, she has become engaged to the secretary
of the British Legation there, John Morton, who has inherited
his family seat, Bragton Hall. The Trefoils return to England
with John, who also brings with him an American Senator, Elias
Gotobed, who is intent upon studying the English and their way
of life. They visit Bragton and Lady Augustus is appalled by its
dilapidated state, which, together with her discovery that John
Morton has no more than £7,000 a year, confirms her belief
that he is no fit candidate for her daughter. Arabella is more
realistic. She has been looking for a husband and a home for too
long: anyone and anywhere will do.

However, she has resources enough for one further effort, as
she discovers when she meets the sporting, handsome and very
wealthy Lord Rufford, and, disregarding John, goes all out to
get him to propose to her. When he seems to be thoroughly on
the hook Arabella makes it public that they are to marry. Rufford
firmly denies it, and Lady Augustus, whose assistance in her
campaign Arabella has continually rebuffed, threatens breach-of-
promise action for £8,000. Arabella, still confident of conquering
her objective by subtler means, refuses to be party to this; but
her tactics fail.

Despite her treachery to him, which has incurred the odium
of her relatives and friends, John Morton is a forgiving man and
when he becomes seriously ill and dies he leaves Arabella a small
fortune. Marriage comes to her at last through Mounser Green, a
Foreign Office official, and when he is appointed Ambassador to
Patagonia she leaves England with him with few remaining
regrets for the lost pleasures of life, whose pursuit has cost her so
much energy and pain.

Senator Gotobed, who has remained a background figure in a

story which is essentially Arabella Trefoil's, concludes his study
of the English and sums up his findings in a lecture at St James's
Hall which proves so unpopular that the police have to rescue
him from violence. The romantic sub-plot concerns John Morton's cousin Reginald, who inherits Bragton Hall at John's death,
and Mary Masters, a local attorney's daughter, whom he marries
despite the rival bid of a gentleman farmer, Lawrence Twentyman.

The American Senator was finished during the voyage back to
England in September 1875. It was serialized in *Temple Bar* from
May 1876–July 1877 and published in three volumes by Chap-
man & Hall in July 1877.

One further work remained to be written before Trollope
turned his mind to the last of his political stories, *The Duke's
Children* (see *The Palliser Novels*). That was *An Autobiography*,
that vivid, disjointed, at times frank and often self-delusive,
reflection of himself and his trade which he began in October
1875, on his return to England, and finished in April the following
year. He had more than six years still to live, but if he was ever
tempted to bring the *Autobiography* up to date, or to revise it, he
must have resisted it, for, apart from a note here and there, it
remains as he set it aside in 1876, having told no one of its existence save his son Harry, to whom he left the decision whether
to publish or suppress. Happily for us, Harry took the positive
course and this highly readable and informative record was
published, with an introduction by him, in two volumes by
Blackwood in 1883.

JOHN CALDIGATE

IT is not possible to record that immediately upon finishing
The Duke's Children in October 1876 Anthony Trollope drew
up fresh paper, dipped his pen again and launched straight into a
fresh novel as usual. The next one was not begun until the

following February, and just how he was occupied in the interim is not precisely stated. No doubt a good deal of the time was spent in the vast amount of reading and note-making preparatory to his writing *The Life of Cicero*, which he also began that February: it is not recorded when he finished it, but it did not appear until 1880, published in two volumes by Chapman & Hall.

After finishing the first part of *Cicero* he devoted nearly a month to a visit to South Africa, gathering material which ultimately appeared in two volumes as *South Africa* (Chapman & Hall, 1878). However, during this tedious and taxing exploration of a country he found uncongenial, he was also at work on the new novel, begun shortly before his *Cicero* and completed in July, during the voyage home. It was *John Caldigate*, serialized in *Blackwood's Magazine* from April 1878–June 1879 and published in three volumes by Chapman & Hall in the month serialization ended.

Daniel Caldigate is the squire of Folking, near Cambridge, where his son John attends university and makes friends with a fellow-student, Dick Shand, who, when John is disinherited by his father for his fondness for gambling, travels with him to Australia, to try their luck as gold-miners. Although before leaving he had fallen in love with Hester Bolton, the daughter of a banker friend of his father's, John is quickly bewitched on the voyage out by a Mrs Euphemia Smith, an actor's young widow who is going to Australia to seek work on the stage. Despite the cautionary words of the ship's captain and some of the passengers, and even from Euphemia herself, John promises himself to her.

John and Dick strike it rich in the goldfields, but Dick succumbs to the gold-digger's curse, the bottle, and disappears after a particularly heavy drinking bout. John locates Euphemia Smith, who is appearing as a dancer, and they live together until John sells out his share in his mine to a man named Tim Crinkett and sails for England without her. As a man who has made good he is welcomed by his father and marries Hester Bolton.

A son is born to them, but before he can be christened a letter

reaches John signed 'Euphemia Caldigate', and not long afterwards Euphemia arrives, with Crinkett and two other acquaintances, all ready to swear that John and she are married, and that
he had known the mine he sold to Crinkett to be already worked
out. John gives back some of the money Crinkett had paid him,
but when Euphemia's claim to be his lawful wife becomes
known he is tried for bigamy and convicted, very much on the
strength of having handed over the money as if to buy silence.
He is sentenced to two years' imprisonment. At this moment,
though, Dick Shand reappears, a shadow of the fine young man
he had once been, but able to produce evidence that clears John
of the charge and gains him a pardon. A notable feature of this
evidence, incidentally, ingeniously involves a forged postmark
on a letter purported to have been written by John to Euphemia
as 'Mrs Caldigate', a detail for which Trollope could thank his
knowledge of postal technicalities.

AYALA'S ANGEL

THE following novel, *Ayala's Angel*, was written between April–
September 1878 and published in book form only (three volumes)
by Chapman & Hall in June 1881. Hugh Walpole went so far as
to term this 'possibly the most unjustly neglected of all Trollope's
novels ... it has a gaiety and happiness and playfulness that
Trollope, gay and happy though he often was, never exceeded'.
Ayala and Lucy Dormer are respectively the younger and elder
orphaned daughters of an impecunious artist. Ayala has been
given a home by their aunt, Lady Tringle, and her wealthy
husband, while Lucy lives with a much less affluent uncle,
Reginald Dosett, an Admiralty clerk.

Ayala is one of those unworldly beings who see life only in
the most unrealistically optimistic terms, and her 'angel' of the
story's title is the 'angel of light' whom she confidently expects
to meet and find to be the perfect husband. Almost inevitably,

the men who offer themselves for consideration prove to be anything but perfect. The first is her aunt's son, Tom Tringle, a rough diamond whose insistent pursuit of her throughout the story involves him in many mishaps, from which his father has to rescue him. The second suitor is Captain Benjamin Batsby, half-brother of the Master of Foxhounds of the Rufford and Ufford United Pack: he finishes up married to one of Lady Tringle's unattractive daughters, Gertrude. Lastly comes another officer, the red-headed, good-humoured Colonel Jonathan Stubbs who, although anything but an angel of light in appearance or surface-character, has the strong backing of Ayala's friends Lady Albury and her charming sister, the Marchesa d'Baldoni, and so prevails, succeeding in bringing Ayala a love which, if not ethereal, is of a more worthwhile quality.

COUSIN HENRY

A MONTH after completing *Ayala's Angel* in 1878 Trollope began *Cousin Henry*, finished in December and serialized simultaneously in the *Manchester Weekly Times* and the *North British Weekly Mail* from March–May 1879 and published in the latter month by Chapman & Hall, in two volumes. Trollope was by now approaching the end of his career – he was sixty-three when *Cousin Henry* was written, under the shadow of approaching illness and his constitution sapped by his decades of toil and restless activity – but many readers who would find some of his more celebrated works meandering might appreciate this one more for its compelling study of a man obsessed by his misdeed.

The story concerns an inheritance dangled by old Indefer Jones, of Llanfeare in Wales, alternately before the eyes of his disliked, devious nephew Henry Jones, and his favourite niece, Isabel Broderick. A series of wills are drawn up, but when Isabel finally proves adamant that she will not marry Henry, thus enabling the estate to remain in the name of a Jones, as old

Indefer wishes, he makes what he intends will be his final will, leaving everything to Henry. However, Henry pays him a month's visit, in which he so convinces his uncle of his unworthiness that yet another will is made, leaving the estate to Isabel.

Indefer dies, but there is no trace of this last will, only of its predecessor, leaving the estate to Henry. Henry's agony of conscience begins when he chances to find the true last will hidden in a book of sermons. He cannot bring himself to destroy it, but replaces it in the book, finding as a result that he cannot bear to leave the library by night or day, but must sit staring at the shelf where is concealed the document that can deprive him of his inheritance.

Indefer Jones's lawyer, Mr Apjohn, is relentless in his search for the will, which he knows had been made. Suspecting Henry, he tries to force his hand by getting the local newspaper to print aspersive articles which must cause Henry to sue for libel, and so bring him into court, where he can be questioned. At last, though, the lawyer realizes the reason for Henry's brooding in the library and finds the will. Isabel is granted possession of the estate, pensions Henry off, and when she marries, persuades her husband to take the name Indefer Jones, thus fulfilling both her late uncle's wishes.

MARION FAY

WITH only two days to go to Christmas 1878 Trollope began work on yet another novel, *Marion Fay*. Perhaps the Spirit of Christmas took some measure of revenge upon him for this contempt of that season of festivity and slippered ease, for the book turned out to be one of his poorest. It was not completed until the following November, though this was partly due to its writing having had to be suspended for three months while two other works were begun and finished. It was serialized in the

Graphic from December 1881–June 1882, and published by Chapman & Hall in three volumes in May 1882.

Clara, Marchioness of Kingsbury, is the second wife of the marquis, and has had three sons by him. Constantly rankling in her mind is the knowledge that the inheritance of his title and estate is destined for none of them, but will go to Lord Hampstead, the son of his first marriage. Not content with hoping that Lord Hampstead might die prematurely, she endeavours to bring about his death, aided by her sycophantic chaplain, the unscrupulous Revd Thomas Greenwood; but in vain.

While the marchioness's attempts to divert the inheritance provide the book's main story line, there are two other themes, the principal of which concerns the girl of its title, Marion Fay. She is the daughter of an old Quaker clerk, and Lord Hampstead, whose radical views move him to seek the intimacy of common folk, has fallen in love with her, giving his rank-conscious stepmother additional cause for hating him. Marion refuses to marry him, for she knows that her health is declining, and their romance ends with her early death.

Lord Hampstead's other closest friend of lowly standing is a Post Office clerk, George Roden. He has fallen in love with Hampstead's sister, Lady Frances Trafford, and she with him, but the association, needless to say, is altogether disapproved of by her family. She will not give him up, though, and he suddenly becomes acceptable when it is learned that the Italian title of Duca di Crinola is his. He refuses it, but is given a responsible post in the Foreign Office, so the marriage can go forward.

DR WORTLE'S SCHOOL

THE two other works for which the writing of *Marion Fay* had to be laid aside were, respectively, a short study, *Thackeray*, for John Morley's series 'English Men of Letters' (published in one volume by Macmillan in 1879), and the novel *Dr Wortle's School*, a favourite with many Trollope enthusiasts. Once more the theme of unwitting bigamy is at the story's heart. The Revd Dr Jeffrey Wortle is the owner and headmaster of an exclusive preparatory school for Eton, named Bowick (Lowick, Northamptonshire, was where the novel was written during an April visit). He needs a classics master who is also a clergyman and can bring with him a wife capable of acting as matron to the well-bred pupils. After some difficulty, Dr Wortle finds exactly what he is looking for in the Revd Henry Peacocke, an Oxonian with several years' experience as vice-president of a classical college in America, and his American wife, Ella. The new master and matron are instant successes, professionally and with the boys, and all seems set fair for Dr Wortle's school until the intervention of the Hon Mrs Juliana Stantiloup. This relentless lady is smarting at her husband's having lost a lawsuit against Dr Wortle, arising from her demand that her son, a pupil, be accorded preferential rates. Hearing a rumour that the Peacockes' private life might not be as respectable as it appears, she precipitates an investigation, which Dr Wortle cannot refuse.

Henry Peacocke makes a clean breast of it. He had met his wife, then Ella Lefroy, after her desertion by her husband, Ferdinand Lefroy, who, with his brother Robert, had gone to join the lawless elements on the Texas–Mexican border. Peacocke had heard a report of Ferdinand Lefroy's death, had it verified by his brother, and so had married Ella. Not long after this, Ferdinand had reappeared, but had subsequently vanished again. The Peacockes had decided to maintain their 'married' state and had come to England, and to Dr Wortle's school.

The kindly, sensible Dr Wortle and his wife sympathize with the couple's position, though this now presents the headmaster with the dilemma of whether to dismiss them and safeguard his establishment's good name, or keep them on and risk the worst that Mrs Stantiloup can achieve. However, within hours of Henry Peacocke's confession a visitor arrives: it is Robert Lefroy, intent on blackmail; but as the story is already out and he is too ate, he relents and admits that his brother is truly dead. Needing absolute proof this time, Peacocke leaves for America with Lefroy, to look for Ferdinand's grave. In his absence the well-meaning Dr Wortle compromises himself and his school's reputation by innocently visiting Ella Peacocke alone in the evenings. Several valuable pupils are withdrawn when this scandal leaks out; but all ends well, with Henry returning with proof of Lefroy's death and the Peacockes, having gone through another ceremony of marriage, securely restored to the school, which is rapidly regaining its old prestige.

Dr Wortle's School was serialized in *Blackwood's Magazine* from May–December 1880 and published in two volumes by Chapman & Hall in January 1881. As has been noted, it was written in April 1879, while *Marion Fay* was still uncompleted; and it is interesting in the light of Trollope's affection-contempt attitude towards the clergy, to compare the toadying, self-seeking Dr Greenwood of the latter with the liberal-minded Dr Wortle of the former. Ironically, the house at Lowick at which Trollope wrote *Dr Wortle's School* was the rectory of a friend, to whom he wrote while there:

That I, who have belittled so many clergymen, should ever come to live in a parsonage! There will be a heaping of hot coals! You may be sure that I will endeavour to behave myself accordingly, so that no scandal shall fall upon the parish. If the bishop should come that way, I will treat him as e'er a parson in the diocese. Shall I be required to preach, as belonging to the Rectory? . . . Ought I to affect dark garments? Say the word, and I will supply myself with a high waistcoat. Will it be right to be quite genial with the curate, or ought I to patronise a little? If there be dissenters, shall I frown on them, or smile blandly? If tithe pig be brought, shall I eat him? If they take to address me as 'The Rural Anthony', will it be all right?

The ultimate irony, if Michael Sadleir's theory is to be accepted, is that in creating Dr Wortle Anthony Trollope was, consciously or not, reflecting himself. We have come to associate him, first and foremost, with his clerical figures: it seems possible that, writing of one of the most humane of them, and living in a rectory while doing so, he merged briefly and congenially with his creation – and then went back to London to finish off the story of his worst clergyman of all. He would never use a churchman as a principal character again.

KEPT IN THE DARK

ASTHMA, which had been troubling him increasingly, drove Anthony Trollope out of London in the summer of 1880. The house at 39 Montagu Square was given up in June and he wrote to his brother Henry: 'In one more week we start from town . . . It makes me melancholy; – though I believe I shall be happier there than I am here. I hate the dinner parties and all going out.'

'There' was South Harting, near Petersfield, Hampshire; not too far away for necessary visits to London, yet soothingly remote for a man whose health was running down and who had had to trade the lifelong excitement of the hunting field for passive watching for green things to show themselves in his garden, with their symbolic promise of renewal. There was no question of retirement, however. He wrote to Henry: 'Nothing really frightens me but the idea of enforced idleness. As long as I can write books, even though they be not published, I think that I can be happy.'

The first book to be written at South Harting was *Kept in the Dark*, begun in August 1880 and finished in December. It was serialized in *Good Words* from May–December 1882, and published that autumn in two volumes by Chatto & Windus. This is a return to the study of morbid psychology as exemplified in the broodings of a jealous man, such as Trollope had employed so well in *He Knew He Was Right*. The gentleman who is kept in the dark is George Western, who, while visiting Rome, meets an intellectual young woman from near Exeter, Cecilia Holt. Both are 'on the rebound': George having been jilted by a girl named Mary Tremenhere, whose beauty haunts him; Cecilia having jilted the Devonshire baronet to whom she had been engaged, Sir Francis Geraldine. But when George discloses to her the details of his past, Cecilia cannot bring herself to reciprocate. They marry with her unimportant secret undisclosed, but when it eventually reaches his ears, through the trouble-making of Sir Francis and a friend, Francesca Altifiorla, George magnifies it out of all proportion, unable to see it as anything but his wife's inability to be sincere and open with him. He leaves her, and since it would be beneath her to seek forgiveness, all seems to be over for them, until George's sister, Lady Bertha Grant, moves in with some skilful reconciliatory tactics. The story ends with the Westerns united and Cecilia happily pregnant.

THE FIXED PERIOD

Two days after finishing *Kept in the Dark*, Trollope started the most uncharacteristic and most expendable novel of his whole career, *The Fixed Period*. Written from December 1880–February 1881, it was serialized in *Blackwood's Magazine* from October 1881–March 1882, when it was published by Blackwood in two volumes. It is one of those futuristic fantasies needing the piercing percipience of a Wells or a Shaw to achieve: Trollope was as unsuited to the theme as it to him.

President John Neverbend of Britannula (even the names are Shavian), an island off Australia, has evolved a scheme whereby all residents, on reaching the age of sixty-seven, are to be housed in a 'college', where they will live comfortably until, sometime before their next birthday, they are to undergo euthanasia. President Neverbend's great friend Gabriel Crasweller, who has enthusiastically supported this 'fixed period' statute, is due to be the first to 'benefit' from it; not surprisingly, his idealistic enthusiasm wanes as his time draws nigh. He is saved by the intervention of the Royal Navy, come to claim Britannula back into the British Empire, after which the community disbands, and the subsidiary story, the romance of Neverbend's son Jack and Crasweller's daughter Eva, can proceed. A feature of the story is its futuristic trappings, such as steam tricycles with electric headlights and cricket matches in which the ball is bowled by machinery.

MR SCARBOROUGH'S FAMILY

HAVING delivered himself of this piece of nonsense, Trollope reverted to nature with a new novel of an inheritance threatened by illegitimacy. He brought especial ingenuity to the theme in *Mr Scarborough's Family*, which he wrote between March and October 1881: its serialization in *All the Year Round* began in May 1882, but he did not live to see its completion in June 1883, nor its book publication, in three volumes, by Chatto & Windus, in May that year.

John Scarborough has an almost Forsyte-like obsession with his property, a large estate in Hertfordshire. With an eye to its future, he has taken the precaution of marrying his wife twice (on the Continent), once in some secrecy, the second time, after the birth of their first son, openly. The result is that he possesses two marriage certificates. His foresight in acting in this strange fashion becomes apparent when his first son, Mountjoy, grows up to be a wastrel and a gambler and gets deeply into debt on his expectations of the inheritance. His father is able to confound him and the money-lenders who hold his many promissory notes by producing the second marriage certificate, with its implication that the wedding had not taken place until after Mountjoy's birth, so that he is illegitimate and not entitled to the inheritance. Instead, it will go to his unpleasant young brother, Augustus, born after the second 'marriage'.

For all his faults, Mountjoy is loved by his father, who has acted against him more in sorrow than in anger. When Augustus shows signs of impatience to get his hands on the estate, and behaves in other ways in keeping with his odious character, Mr Scarborough strikes again, producing the certificate of the first marriage, thus restoring Mountjoy to legitimacy and ending Augustus's expectations. In the meantime he has cunningly bought back all the promissory notes for a fraction of their value, the moneylenders having preferred to cut their losses and accept ready money rather than getting no money at all. So Mr Scarborough is ultimately able to die happy in the knowledge – or rather belief – that the future of his treasured estate is secured; though what he never sees – unless from the Other World – is Mountjoy, now happily in funds, losing no time in setting off for Monte Carlo, doubtless to dispose of the lot in his customary fashion. Side themes of the story concern the romantic ramifications of the Scarborough sons and their sister Florence.

AN OLD MAN'S LOVE

A T the beginning of 1882 Trollope published his last volume of short tales, *Why Frau Frohmann Raised Her Prices: And Other Stories* (William Isbister, one volume): they had previously appeared in issues of *Good Words* during 1877. In February he began writing the last novel he was to complete, *An Old Man's Love*. He finished it in May and it was published by Blackwood, in two volumes, at the end of 1883, by which time its author had been dead for a year.

The old (he is fifty) man of the title is William Whittlestaff, a bachelor friend of the late father of Mary Lawrie. Mary has a suitor, John Gordon, a pleasant young man of good background but no means, for which failing her stepmother forbids them to associate. He leaves for South Africa to seek his fortune in the diamond mines, but makes no formal proposal to Mary before he goes. In his absence her stepmother dies and Mary is given a home by Mr Whittlestaff, who falls in love with her and offers marriage. Mary tells him frankly that she loves John Gordon, but he has by now been absent for three years, has never written to her, and, in any case, had never proposed, so she accepts her kindly guardian's offer.

The very next day John returns, wealthy and hoping to find Mary still free. Whittlestaff, who had been jilted once, long before, is not keen to relinquish her, but, with gruff resignation, he decides at last to do so and sacrifices himself to bachelordom.

THE LANDLEAGUERS

A FEW days after finishing *An Old Man's Love* Trollope revisited Ireland, with the express intention of collecting material for a new novel. He returned and began writing it at South Harting in June 1882, but had to go to Ireland once more in August for further observation of conditions there. It was his final return to the country where he had spent many of his happiest years, had begun to write, and had set his first novels. Now he had chosen it for what was to be his last, *The Landleaguers*.

For only the second time in his career he broke his principle never to allow serialization of one of his stories to begin until the whole thing was written (the other instance had been *Framley Parsonage*). The worry of not knowing in detail how it was going to resolve itself – only a few notes about the destinies of certain characters were found when he died after completing forty-nine chapters out of the intended sixty – weighed upon him, and, together with the strain of travelling, must have caused his already chronically bad health to deteriorate more rapidly. Insufficient information was left at his death to enable anyone to finish *The Landleaguers*, and what there is of it is not of the kind or quality to inspire such scholarly speculation as has been devoted to Charles Dickens's unfinished *The Mystery of Edwin Drood*.

The members of the Land League were, in actual history, Irish agricultural tenants who, from 1879–81, used various means, from boycott to violence, to protest against the hardships caused them by high rents and evictions: Charles Stewart Parnell was one of their founders, for which he was arrested. Trollope's story, in effect a factual 'documentary' through which fictional characters move, concerns the devastation by Landleaguers of estates owned by Philip Jones, whose youngest son, Florian, aged ten, is murdered for testifying against the rioters. Another casualty is Captain Yorke Clayton, leader of the forces of law and order against them: he is shot, but not killed, and is cared for by Philip Jones's daughters, Ada and Edith, the latter of whom he marries. The other romance which relieves this grim tale of wretchedness and violence is between Philip Jones's elder son, Frank, and an Irish-American opera singer, Rachel O'Mahony, whose father, Gerald O'Mahony, is an agitator supporting the Landleaguers' cause.

The novel was published in its serial form in a weekly magazine, *Life*, from the autumn of 1882 and in two volumes, ending just where Trollope left it part-way through chapter forty-nine, in October 1883 by Chatto & Windus.

The Characters

ACORN, LAWRENCE: Murderer, with John Burrows, of Farmer Trumbull. (*The Vicar of Bullhampton*)

ALBURY, LADY ROSALINE: Wife of Sir Harry and sister of the Marchesa d'Baldoni, with whom she helps their cousin, Colonel Stubbs, win Ayala Dormer's hand. (*Ayala's Angel*)

ALF, FERDINAND: Augustus Melmotte's defeated opponent in the Parliamentary election. (*The Way We Live Now*)

AMEDROZ, CHARLES: Clara's wastrel brother, whose suicide causes the estate to pass to Will Belton. (*The Belton Estate*)

AMEDROZ, CLARA: Daughter of Bernard Amedroz and sister of Charles, she is courted by Capt. Frederic Aylmer, whom her aunt, Mrs Winterfield, intends her to marry. But Aylmer's mother disapproves and she marries her father's cousin and heir, Will Belton. *A handsome young woman, tall, well-made, active, and full of health. She carried herself as though she thought her limbs were made for use, and not simply for ease upon a sofa . . . Clara Amedroz, who was now nearly twenty-six years of age, was not a young-looking young woman. To the eyes of many men that would have been her fault; but in the eyes of Belton it was no fault. He had not made himself fastidious as to women by much consort with them, and he was disposed to think that she who was to become his wife had better be something more than a girl not long since taken out of the nursery.* (*The Belton Estate*)

ANNESLEY, HARRY: Son of the Revd and Mrs Annesley, of Buston Rectory, and brother of Fanny, Kate and Mary. The heir to his mother's brother, Peter Prosper. Despite all efforts to part him from her, he marries Florence Mountjoy. *Harry was light-haired, with long silken beard, and bright eyes, but there was usually present to his face a look of infinite joy, which was comfortable to all beholders. If not strong ... it was happy and eloquent of good temper.* (*Mr Scarborough's Family*)

ANTICANT, DR PESSIMIST: Scottish pamphleteer; a caricature of Thomas Carlyle. (*The Warden*)

APJOHN, NICHOLAS: Indefer Jones's lawyer, who persists in the quest for his late client's last will. (*Cousin Henry*)

ARABIN, 'ELLIE' and 'POSY': Daughters of Francis and Eleanor Arabin (*née* Harding), and granddaughters of Septimus Harding. (*The Last Chronicle of Barset*)

ARABIN, VERY REVD FRANCIS: Fellow of Lazarus College, later vicar of St Ewold's and ultimately dean of Barchester. He marries the former Eleanor Harding and has two daughters, Eleanor and Susan, by her. *An eloquent clergyman, a droll, odd, humorous, energetic, conscientious man ... There was a continual play of lambent fire about his eyes, which gave promise of either pathos or humour whenever he essayed to speak, and that promise was rarely broken. There was a gentle play about his mouth which declared that his wit never descended to sarcasm, and that there was no ill-nature in his repartee.* He appears in all the Barchester novels except *The Warden* and *The Small House at Allington*. (*Barchester Towers*)

ASKERTON, COLONEL and MRS MARY: Objects of scandalized talk in the Belton Estate neighbourhood because they had lived together before the death of Mary's former husband, the drunkard Jack Berdmore. She and Clara Amedroz are intimate friends. (*The Belton Estate*)

AYLMER, LADY: Frederic's domineering mother who snubs Clara Amedroz, causing her to break off their engagement and leave him free for Lady Emily Tagmaggert. Her brow-beaten husband, Sir Anthony Aylmer, is Clara's only sympathizer in the family. *She had been a beauty on a large scale, and was still aware that she had much in her personal appearance which justified pride. She carried herself uprightly, with a commanding nose and broad forehead; and though the graces of her own hair had given way to a front, there was something even in the front which added to her dignity, if it did not make her a handsome woman.* (*The Belton Estate*)

AYLMER, CAPTAIN FREDERIC, M.P.: Son of Sir Anthony and nephew and heir of Mrs Winterfield. On his aunt's insistence he half-heartedly courts Clara Amedroz, but his mother detaches him, intending him for the wealthy Lady Emily Tagmaggert. [Clara's] *heart belonged to Captain Aylmer. But she knew that she had received nothing in exchange for her heart. He had been kind to her . . . so kind, so soft in his manners, approaching so nearly to the little tenderness of incipient love-making, that the idea of regarding him as her lover, had of necessity forced itself upon her. But in nothing had he gone beyond those tendernesses, which need not imperatively be made to mean anything, though they do often mean so much.* (*The Belton Estate*)

BAGWAX, SAMUEL: Post Office clerk whose evidence, based on technical detail, proves John Caldigate's innocence. He marries Jemima Curlydown, daughter of a fellow-clerk.(*John Caldigate*)

BAKER, MARY: Niece of George Bertram, snr, she brings up his granddaughter Caroline Waddington at her home in Littlebath. Sir Lionel Bertram proposes to her, in vain. *She had had no youthful adorers, this poor, good Miss Baker; never, at least, since she had been merry as other children are, "when her little lovers came". She had advanced to her present nearly mature age without perhaps feeling the want of them. But, nevertheless, even in her bosom was living the usual feminine passion for admiration. She was no "losus naturae", but a woman with a heart, and blood in her veins; and not as yet a very old woman either.* (*The Bertrams.*) She also appears in *Miss Mackenzie.*

BALATKA, NINA: A Prague Christian, daughter of Josef Balatka, a bankrupt invalid. Her love for the Jewish Anton Trendellsohn, opposed from both sides, is the theme of the novel. (*Nina Balatka*)

BALDONI, BEATRICE, MARCHESA D': Sister of Rosaline Albury and cousin of Colonel Stubbs. The sisters help him win Ayala Dormer's hand. (*Ayala's Angel*)

BALL, JOHN (LATER SIR JOHN): Margaret Mackenzie's widower

cousin with nine children, whom she marries. *A bald-headed, stout man, somewhat past forty, who was by no means without cleverness, having done great things as a young man at Oxford; but in life he had failed. He was a director of certain companies in London, at which he used to attend, receiving his guinea for doing so, and he had some small capital . . . His zeal deserved a better success. He was always thinking of his money, excusing himself to himself and to others by the fact of his nine children.* (*Miss Mackenzie*)

BALLINDINE, LORD (Francis John Mountmorris O'Kelly – 'Frank'): His betrothal to Fanny Wyndham is broken off at the insistence of her guardian, the Earl of Cashel, but they eventually marry. (*The Kellys and the O'Kellys*)

BANMANN, BARONESS: Bavarian campaigner for women's liberation, disputing control of the movement's London institute, 'Disabilities', with her American colleague Dr Olivia Q. Fleabody. *A very stout woman, about fifty, with a double chin, a considerable moustache, a low broad forehead, and bright, round, black eyes, very far apart . . . She had a stout roll of paper in her hand, and was dressed in a black stuff gown, with a cloth jacket buttoned up to the neck, which hardly gave to her copious bust that appearance of manly firmness which the occasion almost required. But the virile collars, budding out over it, perhaps supplied what was wanting.* (*Is he Popenjoy?*)

BATSBY, CAPTAIN BENJAMIN: One of Ayala Dormer's unsuccessful suitors, he marries Gertrude Tringle. His half-brother, Sir Harry Albury, Master of the Rufford and Ufford United Foxhounds, entertains Ayala at his home, and his wife, Lady Rosaline helps Colonel Stubbs win her hand. (*Ayala's Angel*)

BEESWAX, SIR TIMOTHY, M.P.: Prominent in the Gresham and Drummond governments, and a determined opponent of the Duke of Omnium. *There were drawbacks to the utility and beauty of Sir Timothy's character as a statesman. He had no idea as to the necessity or non-necessity of any measure whatever in reference to the well-being of the country.* (*The Duke's Children*.) He also appears in *The Prime Minister*.

BELLFIELD, CAPTAIN GUSTAVUS: Successful suitor of Mrs Greenow. *He was a well-made man, nearly six feet high, with dark hair, dark whiskers, and dark moustache, nearly black, but of that suspicious hue which to the observant beholder seems always to tell a tale of the hairdresser's shop. He was handsome, too, with well-arranged features, – but carrying, perhaps, in his nose some first symptoms of the effects of midnight amusements. (Can You Forgive Her?.)* He is Captain Belleroache in the play *The Noble Jilt*.

BELTON, WILL: Farmer cousin of Bernard Amedroz, living in Norfolk with his crippled sister Mary, he inherits the estate when Charles Amedroz commits suicide. He falls in love with Clara Amedroz and, remaining constant despite her initial refusal, eventually marries her. *A big man, over six feet high, broad in the shoulders, large limbed, with bright quick grey eyes, a large mouth, teeth almost too perfect and a well-formed nose, with thick short brown hair and small whiskers which came but half way down his cheeks – a decidedly handsome man with a florid face, but still, perhaps, with something of the promised roughness of the farmer. But a more good-humoured looking countenance Clara felt at once that she had never beheld. (The Belton Estate)*

BENJAMIN, MR: Junior partner of Harter and Benjamin, London jewellers of doubtful reputation. He is sentenced for having acted as fence to Smiler after the theft of the Eustace diamonds. *That there was nothing 'too hot or too heavy' for Messrs. Harter and Benjamin was quite a creed with the police of the west end of London. (The Eustace Diamonds)*

BERTRAM, GEORGE snr: Uncle and guardian of George Bertram, jnr, and grandfather of Caroline Waddington, who takes refuge at his house at Hadley, Hertfordshire, after leaving her husband, Sir Henry Harcourt. *A notable man in the city of London . . . he was a director of the Bank of England, chairman of a large insurance company, was deep in water, far gone in gas, and an illustrious potentate in railway interests. (The Bertrams)*

BERTRAM, GEORGE jnr: Son of Sir Lionel and nephew of George Bertram snr. Having had to break his engagement to Caroline

Waddington, he eventually marries her after the death of her husband, Sir Henry Harcourt. *He was not a handsome boy, nor did he become a handsome man. His face was too solid, his cheeks too square, and his forehead too heavy; but his eyes, though small, were bright, and his mouth was wonderfully marked by intelligence.* (*The Bertrams*)

BERTRAM, SIR LIONEL: Widowed father of George Bertram, jnr. Retiring to Littlebath from an administrative post in Persia, he tries in vain to persuade either Sally Todd or Mary Baker to marry him. *He was not a man of genius, or even a man of talent. He had performed no great service for his country; had neither proposed nor carried through any valuable project of diplomacy . . . But he had been useful as a great oil-jar, from whence oil for the quiescence of troubled waters might ever and anon be forthcoming.* (*The Bertrams*)

BLAKE, WALTER ('DOT'): Gambling and horse-fancying friend of Lord Ballindine. *An effeminate-looking slight-made man, about thirty or thirty-three years of age; good looking, and gentlemanlike . . . Blake could be very amusing; but he rather laughed at people than with them, and when there were more than two in company, he would usually be found making a butt of one.* (*The Kellys and the O'Kellys*)

BLUESTONE, SERJEANT: Countess Lovel's leading counsel. His wife and their daughter Alice befriend Lady Anna Lovel when her mother turns her out. (*Lady Anna*)

BOANERGES, LORD: Intellectual guest of the old Duke of Omnium at Gatherum Castle. *Spent the morning . . . in teaching Miss Dunstable to blow soap bubbles on scientific principles.* (*Framley Parsonage.*) He also appears in *The Bertrams* and *Orley Farm*.

BOFFIN, MR, M.P.: Fellow-opponent of Sir Orlando Drought against the Prime Ministership of the Duke of Omnium. (*The Prime Minister*)

BOLD, JOHN: Young Barchester surgeon, brother of Mary. He becomes Eleanor Harding's first husband and, through misplaced zeal, precipitates her father's resignation from the

Wardenship of Hiram's Hospital. He dies before his son, Johnny, is born. *His passion is the reform of all abuses . . . Bold is thoroughly sincere in his patriotic endeavours to mend mankind, and there is something to be admired in the energy with which he devotes himself to remedying evil and stopping injustice; but I fear that he is too much imbued with the idea that he has a special mission for reforming. It would be well if one so young had a little more diffidence himself, and more trust in the honest purposes of others – if he could be brought to believe that old customs need not necessarily be evil, and that changes may possibly be dangerous.* (*The Warden*)

BOLD, MARY: John Bold's elder sister, and intimate friend of his future wife, Eleanor Harding. *She was not an unattractive young woman, though by no means beautiful. Her great merit was the kindliness of her disposition. She was not very clever, nor very animated, nor had she apparently the energy of her brother; but she was guided by a high principle of right and wrong; her temper was sweet, and her faults were fewer in number than her virtues. Those who casually met Mary Bold thought little of her; but those who knew her well loved her well, and the longer they knew her the more they loved her.* (*The Warden*.) She also appears in *Barchester Towers* and *Framley Parsonage*.

BOLTON, HESTER: Daughter of Nicholas Bolton, snr. She marries John Caldigate when he returns from Australia and stands by him when he is charged with bigamy. (*John Caldigate*)

BOLTON, NICHOLAS snr: Banker father of Nicholas, jnr, Daniel, Robert and William by a first marriage, and Hester by his second, in which he is completely dominated by his wife Mary. The sons, all professional men, and their wives are much concerned in the relationship between Hester and John Caldigate. (*John Caldigate*)

BONCASSEN, ISABEL: Daughter of an American scholar, Ezekiel Boncassen, visiting London. Lord Silverbridge falls in love with her and at length overcomes his father's objections to their marriage. *Said to be the prettiest young woman either in Europe or in America at the present time . . . Perhaps what struck*

*the beholder first was the excessive brilliancy of her complexion.
No pink was ever pinker, no alabaster whiteness was ever more like
alabaster; but under and around and through it all there was a
constantly changing hue which gave a vitality to her countenance
which no fixed colours can produce. Her eyes, too, were full of life
and brilliancy, and even when she was silent her mouth would
speak. (The Duke's Children)*

BONNER, MARY: Niece of Sir Thomas Underwood, she refuses
marriage with Ralph Newton in favour of his illegitimate
half-brother. (*Ralph the Heir*)

BONTEEN, MR, M.P.: Fellow politician of Phineas Finn. Egged
on by his wife, he tries to prove that Joseph Emilius has married Lizzie Eustace bigamously. He is murdered, for which
Phineas Finn is tried but acquitted. *When a man suddenly shoots
up into power few suffer from it very acutely. The rise of a Pitt can
have caused no heart-burning. But Mr Bonteen had been a hack
among the hacks, had filled the usual half-dozen places, had been a
junior Lord, a Vice-President, Deputy Controller, a Chief Commissioner, and a Joint Secretary. His hopes had been raised or abased
among the places of £1,000, £1,200, or £1,500 a year. He had
hitherto culminated at £2,000, and had been supposed with diligence
to have worked himself up to the top of the ladder, as far as the
ladder was accessible to him. And now he was spoken of in connection
with one of the highest offices of the State! (Phineas Redux.)* He
also appears in *Phineas Finn* and *The Eustace Diamonds*.

BOTT, MR, M.P.: Self-appointed watchdog over Lady Glencora
Palliser. He marries Mrs Marsham. *A person who certainly had
had some success in life and who had won it for himself . . . They
who sat on the same side with him in the House and watched his
political manoeuvres, knew that he was striving hard to get his
finger into the public pie. (Can You Forgive Her?)*

BOZZLE, SAMUEL: Former policeman engaged by Louis Trevelyan to assist in the abduction of his young son Louey.
(*He Knew He Was Right*)

BRABAZON, JULIA: Sister of Lady Hermione Clavering. She
jilts Harry Clavering for Lord Ongar's wealth and title and

tries in vain to regain him after her husband's death. *When she had returned to Clavering the other day, the affianced bride of Lord Ongar, he* [Harry] *had hardly known whether to admire or to deplore the settled air of established womanhood which she had assumed. Her large eyes had always lacked something of rapid glancing sparkling brightness. They had been glorious eyes to him, and in those early days he had not known that they lacked aught; but he had perceived, or perhaps fancied, that now, in her present condition they were often cold, and sometimes almost cruel. Nevertheless he was ready to swear that she was perfect in her beauty.* (*The Claverings*)

BRADY, PAT: Tool of Hyacinth Keegan against Thady Macdermot, Brady's master, whose conviction for murdering Myles Ussher he ensures. *He had that kind of external respectability about him, which a tolerably decent hat, strong brogues, and worsted stockings give to a man, when those among whom he lives are without such luxuries.* (*The Macdermots of Ballycloran*)

BRATTLE, GEORGE, SAM, CARRY, FANNY and MRS JAY: Sons and daughters of Jacob and Maggie Brattle. It is Sam who is unjustly accused of Farmer Trumbull's murder, and Carry whose 'fallen' state is the story's motivation. (*The Vicar of Bullhampton*)

BRATTLE, JACOB: Bullhampton miller, husband of Maggie and father of George, Sam, Carry, Fanny and Mrs Jay. *Crossgrained, litigious, moody and tyrannical . . . He was a silent, sad, meditative man, thinking always of the evil things that had been done to him.* (*The Vicar of Bullhampton*)

BRATTLE, MAGGIE: Jacob's wife. *One of those loving, patient, self-denying, almost heavenly human beings.* (*The Vicar of Bullhampton*)

BRENTFORD, EARL OF: Father of Laura Standish and Lord Chiltern. (*Phineas Finn* and *Phineas Redux*)

BRISKET, WILLIAM: A butcher, rival of Robinson for Maryanne Brown, but equally unsuccessful. (*The Struggles of Brown, Jones, and Robinson*)

BRODERICK, ISABEL: Niece of Indefer Jones and cousin of

Henry Jones, who hides his uncle's will when he finds the
rich inheritance has been left to Isabel instead of to him.
(*Cousin Henry*)

BROMAR, MARIE: Niece of Michel Voss, who opposes her
marriage with his son George, trying to persuade her to
accept a Swiss linen-buyer, Adrian Urmand, instead, but
relenting in the end. (*The Golden Lion of Granpère*)

BROTHERTON, FREDERICK AUGUSTUS, MARQUIS OF: Returning from Italy with an Italian 'wife', Catarina, and a small son
of doubtful legitimacy, he orders his mother, the Dowager
Marchioness, his sisters and his brother, Lord Germain, and
wife out of the family seat, but dies not long afterwards. *An
idle, self-indulgent, ill-conditioned man, who found that it suited
his tastes better to live in Italy, where his means were ample, than
on his own property, where he would have been comparatively a
poor man.* (*Is He Popenjoy?*)

BROUGHTON, DOBBS: Partner with Augustus Musselboro and
Mrs Van Siever in dubious financial activities. He is eventually
bankrupted and kills himself. (*The Last Chronicle of Barset*)

BROUNE, NICHOLAS: Editor of the *Morning Breakfast Table*
newspaper who marries Lady Carbury. (*The Way We Live
Now*)

BROWN, MR: Father of Maryanne and father-in-law of Jones,
who persuades him to enter partnership with him and Robinson in a haberdashery business, resulting in the loss of his
money. (*The Struggles of Brown, Jones and Robinson*)

BROWN, MARYANNE: Brown's younger daughter, courted by
his partner Robinson and by Brisket, the butcher, neither of
whom she accepts, remaining a spinster. (*The Struggles of
Brown, Jones, and Robinson*)

BROWNBY FAMILY: A family of cattle rustlers who try by
force to drive Harry Heathcote off his territory, but are
repulsed by Harry and his neighbour, Giles Medlicot. (*Harry
Heathcote of Gangoil*)

BUFFLE, SIR RAFFLE: Head of the Income Tax Office in which
Johnny Eames works. *The turkey-cock in his own farmyard is*

master of the occasion, and the thought of him creates fear. A bishop in his lawn, a judge on the bench, a chairman in the big room at the end of a long table, or a policeman with his bull's-eye lamp upon his beat, can all make themselves terrible by means of those appanages of majesty which have been vouchsafed to them. But how mean is the policeman in his own home, and how few thought much of Sir Raffle Buffle as he sat asleep after dinner in his old slippers! (The Small House at Allington.) He also appears in *The Last Chronicle of Barset.*

BUNCE, JACOB: Phineas Finn's London landlord and staunch defender when he is tried for murder. *He was a thoroughly hard-working man, doing pretty well in the world, for he had a good house over his head, and always could find raiment and bread for his wife and eight children; but, nevertheless, he was an unhappy man because he suffered from political grievances. (Phineas Finn.)* He also appears in *Phineas Redux.*

BUNCE, JOHN: Senior of the twelve bedesmen – or pensioners – of Hiram's Hospital. He appears in *The Warden* and *Barchester Towers.*

BURROWS, JOHN ('JACK THE GRINDER'): Murderer with Lawrence Acorn, of Farmer Trumbull. (*The Vicar of Bullhampton*)

BURTON, MR and MRS: Parents of Theodore, Florence and others. Mr Burton is junior partner of the civil engineering firm to which Harry Clavering is apprenticed. *In the purchase of great properties Mr Burton's opinion was supposed to be, or to have been, as good as any in the kingdom, and therefore there was very much to be learned in the office at Stratton. But Mr Burton was not a rich man like his partner, Mr Beilby, nor an ambitious man. He had never soared Parliamentwards, had never speculated, had never invented, and never been great. (The Claverings)*

BURTON, MRS CECILIA: Theodore's wife and staunch friend to Harry Clavering. Mother of Cissy, Sophie and Theodore jnr. (*The Claverings*)

BURTON, FLORENCE: Mr Burton's only remaining unmarried daughter, loved by, and at length married to, Harry Clavering.

Poor Florence Burton was short of stature, was brown, meagre, and poor-looking. So said Harry Clavering to himself. Her small hand, though soft, lacked that wondrous charm of touch which Julia's possessed. Her face was short, and her forehead, though it was broad and open, had none of that feminine command which Julia's look conveyed . . . He could not, as he said to himself on his return home, avoid the comparison, as she was the first girl he had seen since he had parted from Julia Brabazon. (*The Claverings*)

BURTON, THEODORE: Eldest son of Mr Burton and due to succeed him as partner in Beilby & Burton. *Harry Clavering could not bring himself to take a liking to him, because he wore cotton gloves and had an odious habit of dusting his shoes with his pocket-handkerchief. Twice Harry saw him do this on the first day of their acquaintance, and he regretted it exceedingly. The cotton gloves too were offensive, as were also the thick shoes which had been dusted; but the dusting was the great sin.* (*The Claverings*)

CALDIGATE, DANIEL: Squire of Folking, near Cambridge, and father of John, whom he disinherits but restores to favour after John makes his fortune. (*John Caldigate*)

CALDIGATE, JOHN: Only son of Daniel, he makes a fortune in Australia in partnership with Dick Shand, but has a liaison with Euphemia Smith which results in his being blackmailed after his return to England and marriage to Hester Bolton. Sentenced to prison for bigamy, he is saved by the return of Shand with proof of his innocence. (*John Caldigate*)

CAMPERDOWN, SAMUEL: The Eustace family lawyer who persists in trying to make Lizzie Eustace give up the diamonds. He is in partnership with his son John. *A better attorney, for the purposes to which his life was devoted, did not exist in London than Mr Camperdown. To say that he was honest, is nothing. To describe him simply as zealous, would be to fall very short of his merits. The interests of his clients were his own interests, and the legal rights of the properties of which he had the legal charge, were as dear to him as his own blood. But it could not be said of him that he was a learned lawyer.* (*The Eustace Diamonds*)

CANTRIP, LORD and LADY: Close friends of the Duke and

Duchess of Omnium. Lady Cantrip acts as duenna to Lady Mary Palliser after the duchess's death. They appear in several of the Palliser novels.

CARBUNCLE, MRS JANE: Aunt of Lucinda Roanoke whom she traps into marriage with Sir Griffin Tewett. Confidante of Lizzie Eustace. (*The Eustace Diamonds*)

CARBURY, SIR FELIX: Son of Lady Carbury and brother of Henrietta, both of whom he ruins financially, together with Marie Melmotte. *His heart was a stone, but he was beautiful to look at, ready-witted, and intelligent.* (*The Way We Live Now*)

CARBURY, HENRIETTA: Daughter of Lady Carbury and sister of Sir Felix. She is loved by Roger Carbury, but marries Paul Montague. *She had in her countenance a full measure of that sweetness of expression which seems to imply that consideration of self is subordinated to consideration for others.* (*The Way We Live Now*)

CARBURY, LADY MATILDA: Mother of Sir Felix and Henrietta, aspiring to literary notice. *She could write after a glib, commonplace, sprightly fashion, and had already acquired the knack of spreading all she knew very thin, so that it might cover a vast surface. She had no ambition to write a good book, but was painfully anxious to write a book that the critics would say was good.* (*The Way We Live Now*)

CARBURY, ROGER: Second cousin of Sir Felix and Henrietta, and head of the Carbury family. He loves Henrietta, but she marries his friend, Paul Montagu. *At present he was not much short of forty years of age . . . He was about five feet nine in height, having the appearance of great strength and perfect health. A more manly man to the eye was never seen.* (*The Way We Live Now*)

CARROLL, PAT: Leader of the Landleaguers in their devastation of the estates of his landlord, Philip Jones. (*The Landleaguers*)

CARRUTHERS, LORD GEORGE DE BRUCE: A friend of Lizzie Eustace, suspected by some of being behind the theft of her diamonds. She marries him after her marriage to Joseph Emilius is proved to have been bigamous. *He sometimes went into the City, and was supposed to know something about shares.*

Perhaps he played a little, and made a few bets. He generally lived with men of means; – or perhaps with one man of means at a time; but they, who knew him well, declared that he never borrowed a shilling from a friend, and never owed a guinea to a tradesman. He always had horses, but never had a home. When in London he lodged in a single room, and dined at his club. He was a Colonel of Volunteers, having got up the regiment known as the Long Shore Riflemen, – the roughest regiment of Volunteers in all England. (*The Eustace Diamonds*)

CARSTAIRS, LORD: Eldest son of Earl Bracy. A special student at Bowick School, having been expelled from Eton, he falls in love with Mary Wortle and marries her. *As far as the Doctor could see, nothing could be nicer than his young pupil's manners. He was not at all above playing with the other boys. He took very kindly to his old studies and his old haunts, and of an evening, after dinner, went away from the drawing-room to the study in pursuit of his Latin and Greek, without any precocious attempt at making conversation with Miss Wortle.* (*Dr Wortle's School*)

CASHEL, COUNTESS OF: Wife of the Earl. *A very good-natured old woman, who slept the greatest portion of her time, and knitted through the rest of her existence.* (*The Kellys and the O'Kellys*)

CASHEL, EARL OF: Father of Lady Selina Grey and of Lord Kilcullen, whom he wishes to marry off to his niece and ward, Fanny Wyndman. *About sixty-three, with considerable external dignity of appearance ... he had not done many glaringly foolish things, and, therefore, had a character for wisdom and judgment. He had run away with no man's wife, and, since his marriage, had seduced no man's daughter; he was, therefore, considered a moraι man.* (*The Kellys and the O'Kellys*)

CHADWICK, JOHN: The Bishop of Barchester's steward, responsible for the accounts of Hiram's Hospital. *The tenants on the butts and patches, as well as those on the wide episcopal domains of the see, were well pleased to have to do with so worthy and liberal a steward.* (*The Warden.*) He also appears in *Barchester Towers*, *Framley Parsonage* and *The Last Chronicle of Barset*.

CHAFFANBRASS, MR: Barrister specializing in the defence of

criminals, he appears for Alaric Tudor (*The Three Clerks*), Lady Mason (*Orley Farm*), and Phineas Finn (*Phineas Redux*). *Give him a case in which he has all the world against him: Justice with her sword raised high to strike; Truth with open mouth and speaking eyes to tell the bloody tale; outraged humanity shrieking for punishment; a case from which Mercy herself, with averted eyes, has loathing turned and bade her sterner sister to do her work; give him such a case as this, and you will see Mr. Chaffanbrass in his glory ... In person, however, Mr. Chaffanbrass is a little man, and a very dirty little man. He has all manner of nasty tricks about him, which make him a disagreeable neighbour to barristers sitting near to him. He is profuse with snuff, and very generous with his handkerchief. He is always at work upon his teeth, which do not do much credit to his industry. His wig is never at ease upon his head, but is poked about by him, sometimes over one ear, sometimes over the other, now on the back of his head, and then on his nose; and it is impossible to say in which guise he looks most cruel, most sharp, and most intolerable.* (*The Three Clerks*)

CHEESACRE, SAMUEL: Unsuccessful suitor of Mrs Greenow; she persuades him to marry Charlotte Fairstairs instead. *A stout, florid man, of about forty-five, a bachelor, apparently much attached to ladies' society, bearing no sign of age except that he was rather bald, and that grey hairs had mixed themselves with his whiskers, very fond of his farming, and yet somewhat ashamed of it when he found himself in what he considered to be polite circles. And he was, moreover, a little inclined to seek the honour which comes from a well-filled and liberally opened purse. He liked to give a man a dinner and then to boast of the dinner he had given.* (*Can You Forgive Her?*) He appears as Herr von Hoppen in *The Noble Jilt*.

CHILTERN, OSWALD STANDISH, LORD: Lady Laura Standish's violent and hard-living brother. Having spent his sister's money he courts Violet Effingham, fights a duel with Phineas Finn over her, and finally marries her. *Lord Chiltern was a red man, and that peculiarity of his personal appearance was certainly the first to strike a stranger. It imparted a certain look of ferocity to* him, *which was apt to make men afraid of him at first sight. Women are not actuated in the same way, and are accustomed to look deeper into men at the first sight than other men will trouble themselves to do.* (*Phineas Finn.*) He also appears in most of the other Palliser novels.

CLAVERING, ARCHIBALD: Brother of Sir Hugh and cousin of Harry. He tries unsuccessfully to achieve marriage with Lady Ongar after her husband's death. He is drowned with his brother, Sir Hugh. *He knew the fathers and mothers, – sires and dams I ought perhaps to say, – and grandfathers and grandmothers, and so back for some generations, of all the horses of note living in his day. He knew also the circumstances of all races, – what horses would run at them, and at what ages, what were the stakes, the periods of running, and the special interests of each affair. But . . . Captain Archibald Clavering had not yet reached the profitable stage in the career of a betting man, though perhaps he was beginning to qualify himself for it.* (*The Claverings*)

CLAVERING, FANNY: The Revd Henry's younger daughter; she marries his curate, Samuel Saul. *She was a pretty, gay-spirited girl, with bright eyes and dark brown hair, which fell into two curls behind her ears.* (*The Claverings*)

CLAVERING, HARRY: The Revd Henry's son. Jilted by Julia Brabazon, but offered marriage by her after her husband's death, he inherits the Clavering Estates and marries Florence Burton. *It will, perhaps, be complained of him that he is fickle, vain, easily led, and almost as easily led to evil as to good . . . That he had such faults and was subject to such weaknesses may be believed of him; but there may be a question whether as much evil would not be known of most men, let them be heroes or not be heroes, if their characters were, so to say, turned inside out before our eyes. Harry Clavering, fellow of his college, six feet high, with handsome face and person, and with plenty to say for himself on all subjects, was esteemed highly and regarded much by those who knew him, in spite of those little foibles which marred his character.* (*The Claverings*)

CLAVERING, REVD HENRY: Rector of Clavering and father of

Harry, Mary and Fanny. *The world had been too comfortable for him, and also too narrow; so that he had sunk into idleness. The world had given him much to eat and drink, but it had given him little to do, and thus he had gradually fallen away from his early purposes, till his energy hardly sufficed for the doing of that little.* (*The Claverings*)

CLAVERING, MRS: Wife of the Revd Henry. *His wife had given him up. She had given him up, not with disdainful rejection, nor with contempt in her eye, or censure in her voice, not with diminution of love or of outward respect. She had given him up as a man abandons his attempts to make his favourite dog take the water . . . But his dog dreads the water. As, however, he has learned to love the beast, he puts up with this mischance, and never dreams of banishing poor Ponto from his hearth because of this failure. And so it was with Mrs Clavering and her husband at the rectory.* (*The Claverings*)

CLAVERING, HERMIONE (*née* BRABAZON): Sister of Julia Brabazon and married to Sir Hugh Clavering. *Hermione had married simply a baronet, and not the richest or the most amiable among baronets; but she had married a man suitable in age and wealth, with whom any girl might have been in love. She had not sold herself to be the nurse, or not to be the nurse, as it might turn out, of a worn-out debauché. She would have hinted nothing of this, perhaps have thought nothing of this, had not Julia and Lord Ongar walked together through the Clavering groves as though they were two young people.* (*The Claverings*)

CLAVERING, SIR HUGH: Eleventh baronet, married to the former Hermione Brabazon. He is drowned with his brother Archibald in a storm at sea. *Every inch an English gentleman in appearance, and therefore popular with men and women of his own class who were not near enough to him to know him well, given to but few words, proud of his name, and rank, and place, well versed in the business of the world, a match for most men in money matters, not ignorant, though he rarely opened a book, selfish, and utterly regardless of the feelings of all those with whom he came into contact.* (*The Claverings*)

CLAVERING, MARY: The Revd Henry's elder daughter. She marries the Revd Edward Fielding. *A tall girl, less pretty than her sister, apparently less careful of her prettiness, very quiet, or, as some said, demure, but known to be good as gold by all who knew her well.* (*The Claverings*)

CLAYTON, CAPTAIN YORKE: The Landleaguers' principal opponent, shot by them and subsequently cared for by Ada and Edith Jones. He marries the latter. (*The Landleaguers*)

COMFORT, REVD CHARLES: Vicar of Cawston, counsellor of Mrs Ray, and brother-in-law to Butler Cornbury. *He that told her from the pulpit on Sundays how frightfully vain were all attempts at worldly happiness . . . would joke with her, and tell her comfortably of his grown sons and daughters, who were prospering in worldly matters, and express the fondest solicitude as to their worldly advancement. Twice or thrice a year Mrs. Ray would go to the parsonage, and such evenings would be by no means hours of wailing. Tea and buttered toast on such occasions would be very manifestly in the ascendant. Mrs Ray never questioned the propriety of her clergyman's life, nor taught herself to see a discrepancy between his doctrine and his conduct.* (*Rachel Ray*)

CORNBURY, BUTLER: Heir to the squire of Cornbury Grange and successful parliamentary candidate for Baslehurst. *Mr Butler Cornbury was the eldest son of the most puissant squire within five miles of Baslehurst, and was indeed almost as good as Squire himself, his father being a very old man.* (*Rachel Ray*)

CORNBURY, MRS PATTY: Butler Cornbury's wife; daughter of the Revd Comfort. Her influence helps to overcome Mrs Ray's and Mrs Prime's objection to Luke Rowan. *Mrs Butler Cornbury was a very pretty woman. She possessed that peculiar prettiness which is so often seen in England, and which is rarely seen anywhere else . . . I have seen in Italy and in America women perhaps as beautiful as any that I have seen in England, but in neither country does it seem that such beauty is intended for domestic use. In Italy the beauty is soft, and of the flesh. In America it is hard, and of the mind. Here it is of the heart, I think, and as such is the happiest of the three.* (*Rachel Ray*)

CRABSTICK, PATIENCE: Lizzie Eustace's personal maid. She is an accomplice in the theft of the diamonds but later turns Queen's Evidence on marrying one of the detectives investigating the case, Mr Bunfit. (*The Eustace Diamonds*)

CRABWITZ, MR: Thomas Furnival's clerk. *A gentleman who had now been with Mr Furnival for the last fifteen years, and who considered that no inconsiderable portion of the barrister's success had been attributable to his own energy and genius ... As he was unmarried, fond of ladies' society, and presumed to be a warm man in money matters, he had his social successes, and looked down from a considerable altitude on some men who from their professional rank might have been considered as his superiors.* (*Orley Farm*)

CRADELL, JOSEPH: Johnny Eames's fellow-clerk and fellow-boarder at Mrs Roper's. He marries Amelia Roper after Johnny has jilted her. (*The Small House at Allington.*) He also appears in *The Last Chronicle of Barset*.

CRASWELLER, GABRIEL: Designated to become the first 'victim' of the Fixed Period law of euthanasia in the community of Britannula. His daughter Eva loves Jack Neverbend, son of the President. (*The Fixed Period*)

CRAWLEY, GRACE: Josiah's eldest daughter, she marries Major Henry Grantly. *Nor had she the slightest pride in her own acquirements. That she had been taught in many things more than had been taught to other girls, had come of her poverty and of the desolation of her home. She had learned to read Greek and Italian because there had been nothing else for her to do in that sad house.* (*The Last Chronicle of Barset.*) She also appears in *Framley Parsonage* and the play *Did He Steal It?*

CRAWLEY, REVD JOSIAH and MRS MARY: Parents of Grace, Jane and Bob. Embittered by years of poverty, Crawley is made perpetual curate of Hogglestock, Barsetshire, and eventually vicar of St Ewold's. Suspicion of his having stolen a cheque is the central theme of *The Last Chronicle of Barset* and the play *Did He Steal It? Sometimes he was prostrate – prostrate in soul and spirit. Then he would complain with bitter voice, crying out that the world was too hard for him, that his back was broken*

I

with his burden, that his God had deserted him. For days and days, in such moods, he would stay within his cottage, never darkening the door or seeing other faces than those of his own inmates. Those days were terrible both to him and her. He would sit there unwashed, with his unshorn face resting on his hand, with an old dressing-gown hanging loose about him, hardly tasting food, seldom speaking, striving to pray, but striving so frequently in vain. And then he would rise from his chair, and, with a burst of frenzy, call upon his Creator to remove him from this misery. In these moments she never deserted him. At one period they had four children, and though the whole weight of this young brood rested on her arms, on her muscles, on her strength of mind and body, she never ceased in her efforts to comfort him. Then at length, falling utterly upon the ground, he would pour forth piteous prayers for mercy, and after a night of sleep would once more go forth to his work. (Framley Parsonage)

CROFTS, DR JAMES: Guestwick physician who marries Bell Dale. *Dr Crofts had now been practising in Guestwick nearly seven years, having settled himself in that town when he was twenty-three years old, and being at this period about thirty. During those seven years his skill and industry had been so fully admitted that he had succeeded in obtaining the medical care of all the paupers in the union, he was paid at the rate of one hundred pounds a year. He was . . . and held two or three other similar public positions, all of which attested his respectability and general proficiency. (The Small House at Allington.)* He also appears in *The Last Chronicle of Barset*.

CROLL, MR: Augustus Melmotte's confidential clerk. After Melmotte's suicide he marries his widow and they emigrate to America. (*The Way We Live Now*)

CROSBIE, ADOLPHUS: Social-climbing Civil Servant who jilts Lily Dale for Lady Alexandrina de Courcy. *Adolphus Crosbie had done more than make minutes with discretion on the papers of the General Committee Office. He had set himself down before the gates of the city of fashion, and had taken them by storm; or, perhaps, to speak with more propriety, he had picked the locks and let himself in. In his walks of life he was somebody in London. A man at the West End who did not know who was Adolphus Crosbie knew* nothing. *I do not say that he was the intimate friend of many great men; but even great men acknowledged the acquaintance of Adolphus Crosbie, and he was to be seen in the drawing-room, or at any rate on the staircases, of Cabinet Ministers.* (*The Small House at Allington.*) He also appears in *The Last Chronicle of Barset.*

CUTTWATER, CAPTAIN BARTHOLOMEW ('UNCLE BAT'), R.N.: Uncle of Mrs Woodward, living in retirement in her home at Hampton. *A tall, heavy man, on whose iron constitution hogsheads of Hollands and water seemed to have no very powerful effect. He was much given to profane oaths; but knowing that manners required that he should refrain before ladies, and being unable to bring his tongue sufficiently under command to do so, he was in the habit of 'craving the ladies' pardon' after every slip. All that was really remarkable in Uncle Bat's appearance was included in his nose. It had always been a generous, weighty, self-confident nose, inviting to itself more observation than any of his brother features demanded. But in latter years it had spread itself out in soft, porous, red excrescences, to such an extent as to make it really deserving of considerable attention.* (*The Three Clerks*)

DALE, CAPTAIN BERNARD: Christopher Dale's nephew; unsuccessful suitor of Bell Dale. *By industry, by a small but wakeful intelligence, and by some aid from patronage, he had got on till he had almost achieved the reputation of talent. His name had become known among scientific experimentalists, not as that of one who had himself invented a cannon or an antidote to a cannon, but as of a man understanding in cannons and well fitted to look at those invented by others.* (*The Small House at Allington.*) He also appears in *The Last Chronicle of Barset.*

DALE, CHRISTOPHER: Squire of Allington. Uncle of Bernard, Bell and Lily, and brother-in-law of Mrs Mary Dale. He is guardian of Johnny and Mary Eames. *Those whom he did love he loved dearly. Those whom he hated he did not ill-use beyond the limits of justice. He was close in small matters of money, and yet in certain family arrangements he was, as we shall see, capable of much liberality. He endeavoured to do his duty in accordance with his*

*lights, and had succeeded in weaning himself from personal indul-
gences, to which during the early days of his high hopes he had
become accustomed ... Mr Christopher Dale was a gentleman ...
and at the time of our story was as near to seventy as he was to sixty.
But years had treated him very lightly, and he bore few signs of age.*
(*The Small House at Allington*.) He also appears in *The Last
Chronicle of Barset*.

DALE, ISABELLA (BELL) and LILIAN (LILY): Mary Dale's daughters. Bell marries Dr Crofts; Lily, jilted by Adolphus Crosbie
and unable to accept Johnny Eames, remains a spinster. *I wish
it could be understood without any description that they were two
pretty, fair-haired girls, of whom Bell was the tallest and the prettiest,
whereas Lily was almost as pretty as her sister, and perhaps was
more attractive ... But there was, perhaps, more in the general
impression made by these girls, and in the whole tone of their
appearance, than in the absolute loveliness of their features or the
grace of their figures. There was about them a dignity of demeanour
devoid of all stiffness or pride, and a maidenly modesty which gave
itself no airs. In them was always apparent that sense of security
which women should receive from an unconscious dependence on their
own mingled purity and weakness. These two girls were never afraid
of men, – never looked as though they were so afraid. And I may
say that they had little cause for that kind of fear to which I allude.
It might be the lot of either of them to be ill-used by a man, but it
was hardly possible that either of them should ever be insulted by one.*
(*The Small House at Allington*.) They also appear in *The Last
Chronicle of Barset*.

DALE, MRS MARY: Widow of Christopher Dale's younger
brother Philip, and mother of Bell and Lily. *She had been a
beauty; according to my taste, was still very lovely; but certainly at
this time of life, she, a widow of fifteen years' standing, with two
grown-up daughters, took no pride in her beauty. Nor had she any
conscious pride in the fact that she was a lady. That she was a lady,
inwards and outwards, from the crown of her head to the sole of her
feet, in head, in heart, and in mind, a lady by education and a lady
by nature, a lady also by birth in spite of that deficiency respecting*

her grandfather, I hereby state as a fact. (*The Small House at Allington*)

DALE, COLONEL ORLANDO and LADY FANNY: Parents of Bernard Dale. *An effete, invalid, listless couple, pretty well dead to all the world beyond the region of the Torquay card-tables. He it was who had made for himself quite a career in the Nineteenth Dragoons. This he did by eloping with the penniless daughter of that impoverished earl, the Lord de Guest. After the conclusion of that event circumstances had not afforded him the opportunity of making himself conspicuous; and he had gone on declining gradually in the world's esteem – for the world had esteemed him when he first made good his running with the Lady Fanny – till now, in his slippered years, he and his Lady Fanny were unknown except among those Torquay Bath chairs and card-tables. His elder brother was still a hearty man, walking in thick shoes, and constant in his saddle; but the colonel, with nothing beyond his wife's title to keep his body awake, had fallen asleep somewhat prematurely among his slippers. (The Small House at Allington*)

DALRYMPLE, CONWAY: Artist friend of Johnny Eames, he raises himself from obscurity to celebrity and paints and marries the wealthy Clara van Siever. (*The Last Chronicle of Barset*)

DALY, KATE: Harry Heathcote's sister-in-law, living with him and his family in Australia. She loves Giles Medlicot, with whom Harry is in dispute, and eventually marries him. (*Harry Heathcote of Gangoil*)

DAUBENY, MR: Conservative M.P. for East Barsetshire and sometime Prime Minister (said to represent Benjamin Disraeli). *The bucolic mind of East Barsetshire took warm delight in the eloquence of the eminent personage who represented them, but was wont to extract more actual enjoyment from the music of his periods than from the strength of his arguments. When he would explain to them that he had discovered a new, or rather hitherto unknown, Conservative element in the character of his countrymen, which he could best utilise by changing everything in the Constitution, he manipulated his words with such grace, was so profound, so broad, and so exalted, was so brilliant in mingling a deep philosophy with the ordinary politics of the day, that the bucolic mind could only admire.* (*Phineas Redux.*) He also appears in *Phineas Finn* and *The Prime Minister.*

DAVIS, MRS: Landlady of the 'Cat and Whistle'. She tries in vain to engineer Charley Tudor's marriage with her barmaid, Norah Geraghty. *Her customers were chiefly people who knew her and frequented her house regularly. Lawyers' clerks, who were either unmarried, or whose married homes were perhaps not so comfortable as the widow's front parlour; tradesmen, not of the best sort, glad to get away from the noise of their children* ... (*The Three Clerks*)

DE BARON, CAPTAIN JACK: Guardsman-about-town, cousin of Adelaide Houghton and persistent follower of Lady Germain (Mary Lovelace). He in turn is pursued, and finally captured, by Augusta Mildmay. *He was about the middle height, light-haired, broad-shouldered, with a pleasant smiling mouth and well-formed nose; but, above all, he had about him that pleasure-loving look, that appearance of taking things jauntily, and of enjoying life* ... *Captain De Baron was a very popular man. There was a theory abroad about him that he always behaved like a gentleman, and that his troubles were misfortunes rather than faults. Ladies always liked him, and his society was agreeable to men because he was neither selfish nor loud.* (*Is He Popenjoy?*)

DE COURCY, LADY ALEXANDRINA: Youngest daughter of the Earl, she marries Adolphus Crosbie, but they part after a few weeks and she dies not long afterwards. *Alexandrina was the beauty of the family, and was in truth the youngest. But even she was not very young, and was beginning to make her friends uneasy lest she, too, should let the precious season of hay-harvest run by without due use of her summer's sun. She had, perhaps, counted too much on her beauty, which had been beauty according to law rather than beauty according to taste, and had looked, probably, for too bounteous a harvest* ... *Her glass and her maid assured her that her sun shone still as brightly as ever; but her spirit was becoming weary with waiting, and she dreaded lest she should become a terror* to all, as was her sister Rosina, or an object of interest to none, as was Margaretta. (*The Small House at Allington.*) She also appears in *Barchester Towers* and *Doctor Thorne*.

DE COURCY, LADY AMELIA: The Earl's eldest daughter, she marries Mortimer Gazebee. *Mrs Gazebee was now the happy mother of many babies, whom she was wont to carry with her on her visits to Courcy Castle, and had become an excellent partner to her husband. He would perhaps have liked it better if she had not spoken so frequently to him of her own high position as the daughter of an earl, or so frequently to others of her low position as the wife of an attorney. But, on the whole, they did very well together.* (*The Small House at Allington.*) She also appears in *Barchester Towers* and *Doctor Thorne*.

DE COURCY, EARL: Head of the De Courcy family and brother of Lady Arabella Gresham. His wife is the Countess Rosina and they have three sons – Lord Porlock, the Hon. George and the Hon. John de Courcy – and four daughters – the Ladies Amelia, Rosina, Margaretta and Alexandrina. *A man who had been much given to royal visitings and attendances, to parties in the Highlands . . . for the Earl de Courcy had been a great courtier. But of late gout, lumbago, and perhaps also some diminution in his powers of making himself generally agreeable, had reconciled him to domestic duties, and the earl spent much of his time at home. The countess, in former days, had been heard to complain of her lord's frequent absence. But it is hard to please some women, – and now she would not always be satisfied with his presence.* (*The Small House at Allington.*) He also appears in *Doctor Thorne*.

DE COURCY, HON. GEORGE: Second son of the Earl, he had married a coal-merchant's daughter for her money. *Having been a spendthrift all his life, he had now become strictly parsimonious. Having reached the discreet age of forty, he had at last learned that beggary was objectionable; and he, therefore, devoted every energy of his mind to saving shillings and pence wherever pence and shillings might be saved. When first this turn came upon him both his father and mother were delighted to observe it; but, although it had hardly yet lasted over twelve months, some evil* results were beginning to appear. Though possessed of an income, he would take no steps towards possessing himself of a house. He hung by the paternal mansion, either in town or country; drank the paternal wines, rode the paternal horses, and had even contrived to obtain his wife's dresses from the maternal milliner. (*The Small House at Allington.*) He also appears in *Barchester Towers*, *Doctor Thorne*, and *The Last Chronicle of Barset*.

DE COURCY, HON. JOHN: Third son of the Earl. *He had as yet taken to himself no wife, and as he had not hitherto made himself conspicuously useful in any special walk of life his family were beginning to regard him as a burden. Having no income of his own to save, he had not copied his brother's virtue of parsimony; and, to tell the truth plainly, had made himself so generally troublesome to his father, that he had been on more than one occasion threatened with expulsion from the family roof. But it is not easy to expel a son.* (*The Small House at Allington.*) He also appears in *Barchester Towers* and *Doctor Thorne*.

DE COURCY, LADY MARGARETTA: The Earl's third daughter and her mother's favourite. *The world called her proud, disdainful, and even insolent; but the world was not aware that in all that she did she was acting in accordance with a principle which had called for much self-abnegation. She had considered it her duty to be a De Courcy and an earl's daughter at all times; and consequently she had sacrificed to her idea of duty all popularity, adulation, and such admiration as would have been awarded to her as a well-dressed, tall, fashionable, and by no means stupid young woman. To be at all times in something higher than they who were manifestly below her in rank, – that was the effort that she was ever making.* (*The Small House at Allington.*) She also appears in *Barchester Towers* and *Doctor Thorne*.

DE COURCY, LADY ROSINA: The Earl's second daughter. *The Lady Rosina was very religious; and I do not know that she was conspicuous in any other way, unless it might be that she somewhat resembled her father in her temper. It was of the Lady Rosina that the servants were afraid, especially with reference to that so-called day of rest which, under her dominion, had become to many of them a day of restless torment. It had not always been so with the Lady Rosina; but her eyes had been opened by the wife of a great church dignitary in the neighbourhood, and she had undergone regeneration. How great may be the misery inflicted by an energetic, unmarried, healthy woman in that condition, – a woman with no husband, no children, or duties, to distract her from her work – I pray that my readers may never know.* (*The Small House at Allington.*) She also appears in *Barchester Towers* and *The Prime Minister*.

DE GUEST, LADY JULIA: Sister of Earl de Guest, for whom she manages Guestwick Manor. *No suitor had been fortunate enough to induce the Lady Julia to run with him. Therefore she still lived, in maiden blessedness, as mistress of Guestwick Manor; and as such had no mean opinion of the high position which destiny had called upon her to fill. She was a tedious, dull, virtuous old woman, who gave herself infinite credit for having remained all her days in the home of her youth, probably forgetting, in her present advanced years, that her temptations to leave it had not been strong or numerous.* (*The Small House at Allington.*) She also appears in *The Last Chronicle of Barset*.

DE GUEST, THEODORE, EARL: Brother-in-law of Christopher Dale. Johnny Eames saves him from an attack by a bull and receives the Earl's grateful patronage. *A thorough-going old Tory, whose proxy was always in the hand of the leader of his party; and who seldom himself went near the metropolis, unless called thither by some occasion of cattle-showing. He was a short, stumpy man, with red cheeks and a round face; who was usually to be seen till dinner-time dressed in a very old shooting coat, with breeches, gaiters, and very thick shoes. He lived generally out of doors, and was almost as great in the preserving of game as in the breeding of oxen. He knew every acre of his own estate, and every tree upon it, as thoroughly as a lady knows the ornaments in her drawing-room.* (*The Small House at Allington*)

DESMOND, CLARA, DOWAGER COUNTESS OF: Mother of Clara and Patrick. She loves Clara's lover, Owen Fitzgerald, but is left bitter and alone at the story's end. *She was beautiful, proud, and clever; and if it would suit her to marry a handsome young*

*fellow with a good house and an unembarrassed income of eight
hundred a year, why should she not do so?* (*Castle Richmond*)

DESMOND, LADY CLARA: Daughter of the Dowager Countess.
  She loves Owen Fitzgerald but at length marries Herbert
  Fitzgerald. *Poor Clara! what had the great family done for her, or
  how had she been taught to maintain its honour? She knew that she
  was an earl's daughter, and that people called her Lady Clara;
  whereas other young ladies were only called Miss So-and-So. But
  she had not been taught to separate herself from the ordinary throng
  of young ladies by any other distinction.* (*Castle Richmond*)

DESMOND, PATRICK, EARL OF: Son of the Dowager Countess,
  he succeeded to the title on his father's death. Brought home
  from Eton aged sixteen, he resumes an intense friendship with
  Owen Fitzgerald and they ultimately go abroad together.
  *He had met no other friend to whom he could talk of sport and a
  man's outward pleasures when his mind was that way given, and to
  whom he could also talk of soft inward things, – the heart's feelings,
  and aspirations, and wants. Owen would be as tender with him as a
  woman, allowing the young lad's arm round his body, listening to
  words which the outer world would have called bosh – and have
  derided as girlish. So at least thought the young earl to himself. And
  all boys long to be allowed utterance occasionally for these soft tender
  things; – as also do all men, unless the devil's share in the world has
  become altogether uppermost with them.* (*Castle Richmond*)

DIE, NEVERSAYE: London barrister with whom George Bertram
  (*The Bertrams*) and Herbert Fitzgerald (*Castle Richmond*) study,
  and who is consulted over Sir Roger Scatcherd's will (*Doctor
  Thorne*).

DOCKWRATH, SAMUEL: Lawyer husband of Miriam Usbech,
  he is made to give up his tenancy of part of the Orley Farm
  estate and retaliates by re-investigating the case of Sir Joseph
  Mason's will. *A little man, with sandy hair, a pale face, and stone-
  blue eyes. In judging of him by appearance only and not by the ear,
  one would be inclined to doubt that he could be a very sharp attorney
  abroad and a very persistent tyrant at home. But when Mr Dockwrath began to talk, one's respect for him began to grow. He talked*

well and to the point, and with a tone of voice that could command where command was possible, persuade where persuasion was required, mystify when mystification was needed, and express with accuracy the tone of an obedient humble servant when servility was thought to be expedient. (*Orley Farm*)

DORMER, AYALA and LUCY: Younger and elder daughters of the late Egbert Dormer and nieces of Lady Tringle and Reginald Dosett. Ayala's search for the perfect husband, her 'Angel of Light', leads her past Tom Tringle and Capt. Benjamin Batsby to end at Col. Jonathan Stubbs. Lucy marries Isadore Hamel. *Ayala the romantic; Ayala the poetic! Her long dark black locks, which had never hitherto been tucked up, which were never curled, which were never so long as to be awkward, were already known as being the loveliest locks in London. She sang as though Nature had intended her to be a singing-bird, – requiring no education, no labour. She had been once for three months in Paris, and French had come naturally to her. Her father had taught her something of his art, and flatterers had already begun to say that she was born to be the one great female artist of the world.* (*Ayala's Angel*)

DOSETT, REGINALD and MRS MARGARET: Uncle and aunt of Ayala and Lucy Dormer whom they assist – he willingly, she less freely – after their father's death. (*Ayala's Angel*)

DROUGHT, SIR ORLANDO, M.P.: Leading Conservative opponent of the Prime Ministership of the Duke of Omnium. (*The Prime Minister.*) He also appears in *Phineas Redux* and *The Way We Live Now*.

DRUMMOND, LORD: The Duke of Omnium's successor as Prime Minister. He appears in *Phineas Redux*, *The Prime Minister*, *The Duke's Children* and *The American Senator*.

DUMBELLO, LORD GUSTAVUS: See Hartletop, Marquis of.

DUNSTABLE, MARTHA: Heiress to the manufacturer of a patent medicine, 'Ointment of Lebanon', she directs the business after his death. Lady Arabella Gresham wishes her to marry her unwilling son Frank, but she eventually marries Dr Thorne. *In age she was about thirty; but Frank, who was no great judge in such matters, and who was accustomed to have very young girls* round him, at once put her down as being ten years older. *She had a very high colour, very red cheeks, a large mouth, big white teeth, a broad nose, and bright, small, black eyes. Her hair also was black and bright, but very crisp and strong, and was combed close round her face in small crisp black ringlets.* Since she had been brought out into the fashionable world some one of her instructors in fashion had given her to understand that curls were not the thing. '*They'll always pass muster*,' Miss Dunstable had replied, '*when they are done up with bank-notes.*' (*Doctor Thorne.*) She also appears in *Framley Parsonage* and *The Last Chronicle of Barset*.

EAMES, JOHNNY: A poor clerk in London, he loves Lily Dale, but promises to marry Amelia Roper. Advanced through Lord de Guest's interest, he jilts Amelia, but his love for Lily remains unrequited. *He had declared his passion in the most moving language a hundred times; but he had declared it only to himself. He had written much poetry about Lily, but he kept his lines safe under lock and key. When he gave the reins to his imagination, he flattered himself that he might win not only her but the world at large also by his verses; but he would have perished rather than exhibit them to the human eye . . . He had no real hope, unless when he was in one of those poetic moods. He had acknowledged to himself, in some indistinct way, that he was no more than a hobbledehoy, awkward, silent, ungainly, with a face unfinished, as it were, or unripe.* (*The Small House at Allington.*) Johnny Eames is said to be Trollope's closest self-portrait from his youth. He helps to clear the Revd Crawley of the allegation of theft in *The Last Chronicle of Barset*.

EAMES, MRS: Widow of an unsuccessful farmer, and mother of Johnny and a daughter Mary. *A poor forlorn woman – forlorn even during the time of her husband's life, but very woebegone now in her widowhood. In matters of importance the squire had been kind to her; arranging for her her little money affairs, advising her about her house and income, also getting for her that appointment for her son. But he snubbed her when he met her, and poor Mrs Eames held him in great awe.* (*The Small House at Allington*)

EFFINGHAM, VIOLET: Laura Standish's closest friend, wooed by many men, including Phineas Finn and Lord Chiltern, who fight a duel over her. She marries the latter. *A woman who wanted to depreciate Violet Effingham had once called her a pug-nosed puppet; but I, as her chronicler, deny that she was pug-nosed, – and all the world who knew her soon came to understand that she was no puppet. In figure she was small, but not so small as she looked to be. Her feet and hands were delicately fine, and there was a softness about her whole person, an apparent compressibility, which seemed to indicate that she might go into very small compass. Into what compass, and how compressed, there were very many men who held very different opinions. (Phineas Finn.)* She appears in all the Palliser novels, and in *The American Senator*.

EMILIUS, REVD JOSEPH: Fashionable preacher; he bigamously marries Lizzie Eustace. *It was said that he was born a Jew in Hungary, and that his name in his own country had been Mealyus. At the present time he was among the most eloquent of London preachers, and was reputed by some to have reached such a standard of pulpit-oratory, as to have had no equal within the memory of living hearers. In regard to his reading it was acknowledged that no one since Mrs Siddons had touched him. (The Eustace Diamonds.)* He also appears in *Phineas Redux*, perhaps murdering Bonteen.

ERLE, BARRINGTON, M.P.: Private Secretary to Prime Minister Mildmay, his uncle, he introduces Phineas Finn to his cousin, Laura Standish. He appears in *Phineas Finn, The Eustace Diamonds, Phineas Redux, The Prime Minister* and *The Duke's Children*.

EUSTACE, LADY LIZZIE: Frank Greystock's cousin, widow of Sir Florian Eustace. Her machinations over the family diamonds provide the story of *The Eustace Diamonds*, at the end of which she marries Joseph Emilius. After he is proved to be a bigamist she marries Lord George Carruthers. *Her figure was lithe, and soft, and slim, and slender. If it had a fault it was this, – that it had in it too much of movement. There were some who said that she was almost snake-like in her rapid bendings and the almost too easy gestures of her body; for she was much given to action, and to the expression of her thought by the motion of her limbs. She might certainly have made her way as an actress, had fortune called upon her to earn her bread in that fashion. And her voice would have suited the stage . . . Her eyes, in which she herself thought that the lustre of her beauty lay, were blue and clear, bright as cerulean waters. They were long, large eyes, – but very dangerous. To those who knew how to read a face, there was danger plainly written in them . . . She forgot nothing, listened to everything, understood quickly, and was desirous to show not only as a beauty but as a wit. There were men at this time who declared that she was simply the cleverest and the handsomest woman in England.* (*The Eustace Diamonds.*) She also appears in *Phineas Redux* and *The Prime Minister.*

FAIRSTAIRS, CHARLOTTE, FANNY and JOE: Protégés at Yarmouth of Mrs Greenow, who makes a match between Charlotte and her own suitor, Samuel Cheesacre. *There were the two Miss Fairstairs, whom Mrs Greenow had especially patronized, and who repaid that lady for her kindness by an amount of outspoken eulogy which startled Kate by its audacity . . . There came in also a brother of the Fairstairs girls, Joe Fairstairs, a lanky, useless, idle young man, younger than them, who was supposed to earn his bread in an attorney's office at Norwich, or rather to be preparing to earn it at some future time, and who was a heavy burden upon all his friends.* (*Can You Forgive Her?*)

FAWN, FREDERICK, VISCOUNT: Undistinguished Government official, unsuccessful suitor of Violet Effingham and Marie Goesler. *A young man of about thirty-five, a Peer of Parliament and an Under-Secretary of State, – very prudent and very diligent, – of whom his mother and sisters stood in great awe . . . Lord Fawn had suffered a disappointment in love, but he had consoled himself with blue-books, and mastered his passion by incessant attendance at the India Board. The lady he had loved had been rich, and Lord Fawn was poor; but nevertheless he had mastered his passion.* (*The Eustace Diamonds.*) He also appears in *Phineas Finn, Phineas Redux,* and *The Prime Minister.*

FAWN, LADY: Mother of Lord Fawn and eight daughters; employer and friend of Lucy Morris. *Lady Fawn was known as a miracle of Virtue, Benevolence, and Persistency. Every good quality that she possessed was so marked as to be worthy of being expressed with a capital. But her virtues were of that extraordinarily high character that there was no weakness in them, – no getting over them, no perverting them with follies or even exaggerations.* (*The Eustace Diamonds*)

FAY, MARION: Only surviving daughter of an old Quaker clerk, Zachary Fay, she is loved by Lord Hampstead but will not marry him because she foresees, correctly, that she will die young. (*Marion Fay*)

FENWICK, REVD FRANK: The vicar of Bullhampton.

FENWICK, MRS JANET (*née* BALFOUR): Frank Fenwick's wife and close friend of Harry Gilmore and Mary Lowther. *As good a specimen of an English country parson's wife as you shall meet in a county, – gay, good-looking, fond of the society around her, with a little dash of fun, knowing in blankets and corduroys and coals and tea; knowing also as to beer and gin and tobacco; acquainted with every man and woman in the parish; thinking her husband to be quite as good as the squire in regard to position, and to be infinitely superior to the squire, or any other man in the world, in regard to his personal self; a handsome, pleasant, well-dressed lady, who has no nonsense about her.* (*The Vicar of Bullhampton*)

FILLGRAVE, DR: Dr Thorne's principal rival amongst the Barsetshire medical profession. *If the bulgy roundness of his person and the shortness of his legs in any way detracted from his personal importance, these trifling defects were, he was well aware, more than atoned for by the peculiar dignity of his countenance. If his legs were short, his face was not; if there was any undue preponderance below the waistcoat, all was in due symmetry above the necktie . . . His eyes were not brilliant, but were very effective, and well under command. He was rather short-sighted, and a pair of eyeglasses was always on his nose, or in his hand. His nose was long, and well pronounced, and his chin, also, was sufficiently prominent; but the great feature of his face was his mouth. The amount of secret medical knowledge of which he could give assurance by the pressure of those lips was truly wonderful.* (*Doctor Thorne.*) He also appears in *Barchester Towers* and *The Last Chronicle of Barset*.

FINN, PHINEAS: Irish Parliamentarian and protégé of Laura Standish. Romantic objective of several ladies, he marries his childhood sweetheart, Mary Jones, who dies young; and later, after his acquittal of the murder of Bonteen, he marries Marie Goesler. *Phineas himself, it may be here said, was six feet high, and very handsome, with bright blue eyes, and brown wavy hair, and light silken beard. Mrs Low had told her husband more than once that he was much too handsome to do any good. Mr Low, however, had replied that young Finn had never shown himself to be conscious of his own personal advantages. 'He'll learn it soon enough,' said Mrs Low. 'Some woman will tell him, and then he'll be spoilt.'* (*Phineas Finn*)

FISKER, HAMILTON K.: American railway promoter who marries Marie Melmotte. *A shining little man, – perhaps about forty years of age, with a well-twisted moustache . . . He was troubled by no shyness, by no scruples, and by no fears. His mind was not capacious, but such as it was it was his own, and he knew how to use it.* (*The Way We Live Now*)

FITZGERALD, BURGO: Nephew of Lady Monk. Lady Glencora Palliser's infatuation for him is a principal theme of *Can You Forgive Her?* *A terribly handsome man about town, who had spent every shilling that anybody would give him, who was very fond of brandy, who was known, but not trusted, at Newmarket, who was said to be deep in every vice, whose father would not speak to him; – and with him the Lady Glencora was never tired of dancing.* (*The Small House at Allington*)

FITZGERALD, HERBERT: Sir Thomas's son and heir. He marries Lady Clara Desmond. *Owen Fitzgerald had called him a prig; but Herbert was no prig. Nor yet was he a pedant; which word might, perhaps, more nearly have expressed his cousin's meaning. He liked little bits of learning, the easy outsides and tags of classical acquirements, which come so easily within the scope of the memory when a man has passed some ten years between a public school and a university. But though he did love to chew the cud of these morsels of Attic grass which he had cropped, certainly without any great or sustained effort,* he had no desire to be ostentatious in doing so, or to show off more than he knew. *Indeed, now that he was away from his college friends, he was rather ashamed of himself than otherwise when scraps of quotations would break from him in his own despite.* (*Castle Richmond*)

FITZGERALD, MARY: Formerly Mary Wainwright, she married Sir Thomas Fitzgerald after the supposed death of her worthless husband, Matthew Mollett, and had three children, Herbert, Emmeline and Mary, only to learn that Mollett was still alive. *She also was old for her age, and woebegone, not only in appearance, but also in the inner workings of her heart. But then it was known of her that she had undergone deep sorrows in her early youth, which had left their mark upon her brow, and their trace upon her inmost thoughts.* (*Castle Richmond*)

FITZGERALD, OWEN: A scapegrace relative of the Fitzgeralds of Castle Richmond, living at Hap House. Debarred from marrying Lady Clara Desmond, he goes abroad instead with her young brother Patrick, the new Earl, with whom he has a close relationship. *He was a very handsome man . . . He was clever, too, though perhaps not educated as carefully as might have been: his speech was usually rapid, hearty, and short, and not seldom caustic and pointed. Had he fallen among good hands, he might have done very well in the world's fight; but with such a character, and lacking such advantages, it was quite as open to him to do ill. Alas! the latter chance seemed to have fallen to him.* (*Castle Richmond*)

FITZGERALD, SIR THOMAS: Owner of Castle Richmond and father of Herbert, Emmeline and Mary. The strain of his years of being blackmailed by Mollett finally kills him. *He had, one may say, all that a kind fortune could give him; he had a wife who was devoted to him; he had a son on whom he doted, and of whom all men said all good things; he had two sweet, happy daughters; he had a pleasant house, a fine estate, position and rank in the world . . . That he did, however, in this mental privacy of his carry some heavy burden, was made plain enough to all who knew him.* (*Castle Richmond*)

K

FITZGIBBON, HON LAURENCE, M.P.: Son of Lord Claddaugh and younger brother of Aspasia Fitzgibbon. Close friend of Phineas Finn whom he persuades to enter Parliament. He appears in *Phineas Finn*, *The Eustace Diamonds*, *Phineas Redux* and *The Prime Minister*.

FLANNELLY, JOE and SALLY: See KEEGAN, HYACINTH (*The Macdermots of Ballycloran*)

FLEABODY, DR OLIVIA Q.: Baroness Banmann's rival for control of the women's liberation institute in London, 'Disabilities'. *What would have been a pretty face, had it not been marred by a pinched look of studious severity and a pair of glass spectacles, of which the glasses shone in a disagreeable manner. There are spectacles which are so much more spectacles than other spectacles, that they make the beholder feel that there is before him a pair of spectacles carrying a face, rather than a face carrying a pair of spectacles. So it was with the spectacles of Olivia Q. Fleabody.* (*Is He Popenjoy?*)

FLETCHER, ARTHUR, M.P.: Sweetheart from childhood of Emily Wharton, whom he marries after the suicide of her husband, Ferdinand Lopez, whom Fletcher had defeated in the election at Silverbridge. His brother John is the husband of Sir Alured Wharton's daughter Sarah. *The very pearl of the Fletcher tribe. Though a younger brother, he had a very pleasant little fortune of his own. Though born to comfortable circumstances, he had worked so hard in his young days as to have already made for himself a name at the bar. He was a fair-haired, handsome fellow ... He looked like one of those happy sons of the gods who are born to success.* (*The Prime Minister*)

FOTHERGILL, MR: The old Duke of Omnium's man of business, dismissed after the duke's death by Lord Chiltern for his indifference to fox-hunting. *He was not exactly his agent; that is to say, he did not receive his rents; but he 'managed' for him, saw people, went about the county, wrote letters, supported the electioneering interest, did popularity when it was too much trouble for the duke to do it himself, and was, in fact, invaluable.* (*Framley Parsonage.*) He also appears in *The Small House at Allington*, *The Last Chronicle of Barset* and *Phineas Redux*.

FURNIVAL, MRS KITTY: Thomas Furnival's wife and mother of Sophia; she believes his friendship with Lady Mason to be something deeper. *All the charms of her youth – had they not been given to him, and also all her solicitude, all her anxious fighting with the hard world? When they had been poor together, had she not patched and turned and twisted, sitting silently by his side into the long nights, because she would not ask him for the price of a new dress? And yet now, now that they were rich – ? (Orley Farm)*

FURNIVAL, SOPHIA: Thomas Furnival's daughter, briefly engaged to Lucius Mason. *A clever, attractive girl, handsome, well-read, able to hold her own with the old as well as with the young, capable of hiding her vanity if she had any, mild and gentle to girls less gifted, animated in conversation, and yet possessing an eye that could fall softly to the ground, as a woman's eye always should fall upon occasions. Nevertheless she was not altogether charming. 'I don't feel quite sure that she is real,' Mrs. Orme had said of her, when on a certain occasion Miss Furnival had spent a day and a night at The Cleeve. (Orley Farm)*

FURNIVAL, THOMAS, M.P.: Counsel and friend of Lady Mason who appears in her defence in both trials. Father of Sophia. *Not that he was becoming old, or weak, or worn; but his eye had lost its fire – except the fire peculiar to his profession; and there were wrinkles in his forehead and cheeks; and his upper lip, except when he was speaking, hung heavily over the lower; and the loose skin below his eye was forming into saucers; and his hair had become grizzled; and on his shoulders, except when in court, there was a slight stoop. As seen in his wig and gown he was a man of commanding presence . . . His eyes were very gray, and capable to an extraordinary degree both of direct severity and of concealed sarcasm. Witnesses have been heard to say that they could endure all that Mr Furnival could say to them, and continue in some sort to answer all his questions, if only he would refrain from looking at them. But he would never refrain. (Orley Farm)*

GAUNTLET, ADELA: In love with Arthur Wilkinson, but unable to marry him until late in the story because he is compelled to support, and share his vicarage with, his mother. *He was not worthy of her. That is, the amount of wealth of character which he brought into that life partnership was, when counted up, much less than her contribution. But that she was fully satisfied with her bargain – that she was so then and so continued – was a part of her worthiness. If ever she weighed herself against him, the scale in which he was placed never in her eyes showed itself to be light.* (*The Bertrams*)

GAZEBEE, MORTIMER, M.P.: Formerly junior partner of Gumption, Gazebee and Gazebee, property agents, he marries Lady Amelia de Courcy and becomes Member of Parliament for Barchester. *He never received a shilling of dowry, but that he had not expected. Nor did he want it . . . But, on the whole, Mr Gazebee did not repent his bargain; when he asked friends to dine, he could tell them that Lady Amelia would be very glad to see them; his marriage gave him some* éclat *at his club, and some additional weight in the firm to which he belonged; he gets his share of the Courcy shooting, and is asked about to Greshambury and other Barsetshire houses, not only 'to dine at table and all that', but to take his part in whatever delights country society there has to offer.* (*Doctor Thorne.*) He also appears in *The Small House at Allington* and *The Last Chronicle of Barset.*

GERAGHTY, NORAH: Barmaid at the 'Cat and Whistle'. Charley Tudor wavers perilously close to marrying her, but is reprieved by her sudden marriage to Mr Peppermint. *Charley got up and took her hand; and as he did so, he saw that her nails were dirty. He put his arms round her waist and kissed her; and as he caressed her, his olfactory nerves perceived that the pomatum in her hair was none of the best. He thought of those young lustrous eyes that would look up so wondrously into his face; he thought of the gentle touch, which would send a thrill through all his nerves; and then he felt very sick.* (*The Three Clerks*)

GERALDINE, SIR FRANCIS: Jilted by Cecilia Holt, he and a trouble-making woman friend, Francesca Altifiorla, cause a rift between Cecilia and the man she married instead, George Western. (*Kept in the Dark*)

GERMAIN, LORD GEORGE: Younger brother of the Marquis of

Brotherton and husband of Mary Lovelace. When his brother and his son die he becomes the new marquis and his son becomes Lord Popenjoy. *He was a tall, handsome, dark-browed man, silent generally, and almost gloomy, looking, as such men do, as though he were always revolving deep things in his mind, but revolving in truth things not very deep – how far the money would go, and whether it would be possible to get a new pair of carriage-horses for his mother. Birth and culture had given to him a look of intellect greater than he possessed; but I would not have it thought that he traded on this, or endeavoured to seem other than he was. He was simple, conscientious, absolutely truthful, full of prejudice, and weak-minded. (Is He Popenjoy?)*

GERMAIN, LADIES SARAH, SUSANNA and AMELIA: The Marquis of Brotherton's pious and domineering spinster sisters. The fourth sister is Lady Alice Holdenough. *But Lady Sarah could be very severe; and Lady Susanna could be very stiff; and Lady Amelia always re-echoed what her elder sisters said. (Is He Popenjoy?)*

GIBSON, REVD THOMAS: Rector of St Peter's-cum-Pumpkin and a minor canon at Exeter Cathedral, much sought after by the opposite sex. *He had a house and an income, and all Exeter had long decided that he was a man who would certainly marry . . . He was fair game, and unless he surrendered himself to be bagged before long, would subject himself to just and loud complaint. (He Knew He Was Right)*

GILMORE, HARRY: Squire of Bullhampton. He unselfishly relinquishes Mary Lowther to her former suitor, Walter Marrable. *A man with a good heart, and a pure mind, generous, desirous of being just, somewhat sparing of that which is his own, never desirous of that which is another's. (The Vicar of Bullhampton)*

GLASCOCK, HON. CHARLES (LATER LORD PETERBOROUGH): Unsuccessful rival of Hugh Stanbury for Nora Rowley, he marries Caroline Spaulding, daughter of the American Minister to Italy. *(He Knew He Was Right)*

GOESLER, MARIE: Widow of a Viennese banker, she is instrumental in clearing Phineas Finn of the charge of murdering

Bonteen, and becomes his second wife. *Probably something over thirty years of age. She had thick black hair, which she wore in curls, – unlike anybody else in the world, – in curls which hung down low beneath her face, covering, and perhaps intended to cover, a certain thinness in her cheeks which would otherwise have taken something from the charm of her countenance. Her eyes were large, of a dark blue colour, and very bright, – and she used them in a manner which is as yet hardly common with Englishwomen. She seemed to intend that you should know that she employed them to conquer you, looking as a knight may have looked in olden days who entered a chamber with his sword drawn from the scabbard and in his hand.* (*Phineas Finn.*) She also appears in most of the other Palliser novels.

GOLIGHTLY, CLEMENTINA: Daughter of Mrs Val Scott by her first marriage. She marries Victoire Jaquêtanàpe. *In the common parlance of a large portion of mankind, a 'doosed fine gal'. She stood five feet six, and stood very well, on very good legs, but with rather large feet. She was as straight as a grenadier, and had it been her fate to carry a milk-pail, she would have carried it to perfection. Instead of this, however, she was permitted to expend an equal amount of energy in every variation of waltz and polka that the dancing professors of the age had been able to produce. Waltzes and polkas suited her admirably; for she was gifted with excellent lungs and perfect powers of breathing.* (*The Three Clerks*)

GORDELOUP. SOPHIE: Sister of Count Pateroff. She becomes a parasite on Julia Brabazon after Lord Ongar's death, *A little, dry, bright woman she was, with quick eyes, and thin lips, and small nose, and mean forehead, and scanty hair drawn back quite tightly from her face and head; very dry, but still almost pretty with her quickness and her brightness. She was fifty, was Sophie Gordeloup, but she had so managed her years that she was as active on her limbs as most women are at twenty-five. And the chicken and the bread-sauce, and the sweetbread, and the champagne were there, all very good of their kind; for Sophie Gordeloup liked such things to be good, and knew how to indulge her own appetite, and to coax that of another person.* (*The Claverings*)

GORDON, JOHN: Unable to offer marriage to Mary Lawrie because he has no money, he goes to South Africa, where in some years he makes a small fortune. He returns to find Mary about to marry her father's friend, William Whittlestaff; but the older man relinquishes her to him. (*An Old Man's Love*)

GOTOBED, ELIAS: The American Senator studying English life with the assistance of John Morton. He delivers a controversial lecture in London about his findings and has to be smuggled out of the hall for safety. (*The American Senator*)

GOWRAN, ANDY: Manager of Lizzie Eustace's estate in Scotland. *An honest, domineering, hard-working, intelligent Scotchman, who had been brought up to love the Eustaces, and who hated his present mistress with all his heart. He did not leave her service, having an idea in his mind that it was now the great duty of his life to save Portray from her ravages.* (*The Eustace Diamonds.*) He also appears in *Phineas Redux*.

GRAHAM, FELIX: One of Lady Mason's defending counsel at her second trial. He attempts unsuccessfully to transform Mary Snow into a fitting wife for him, but eventually marries Madeline Staveley. *He had ideas of his own that men should pursue their labours without special conventional regulations, but should be guided in their work by the general great rules of the world, – such for instance as those given in the commandments: – Thou shalt not bear false witness; Thou shalt not steal; and others. His notions no doubt were great, and perhaps were good; but hitherto they had not led him to much pecuniary success in his profession. A sort of a name he had obtained, but it was not a name sweet in the ears of practising attorneys.* (*Orley Farm*)

GRANT, LADY BERTHA: George Western's sister, who engineers the reconciliation between him and his wife. (*Kept in the Dark*)

GRANTLY, FLORINDA: A daughter of the archdeacon of Barchester and sister of the Marchioness of Hartletop. *The two little girls Florinda and Grizzel were nice little girls enough, but they did not possess the strong sterling qualities of their brothers; their voices were not often heard at Plumstead Episcopi; they were bashful and timid by nature, slow to speak before company even*

*when asked to do so; and though they looked very nice in their clean
white muslin frocks and pink sashes, they were but little noticed by
the archdeacon's visitors.* (*The Warden.*) She also appears in
Barchester Towers and *The Small House at Allington.*

GRANTLY, GRISELDA (GRIZZELL): One of the archdeacon of
Barchester's two daughters, she begins life in the Barchester
series (Lord Lufton declines to marry her and she marries Lord
Dumbello, becoming Marchioness of Hartletop), and reappears in two Palliser novels. *She was decidedly a beauty, but
somewhat statuesque in her loveliness. Her forehead was high and
white, but perhaps too like marble to gratify the taste of those who are
fond of flesh and blood. Her eyes were large and exquisitely formed,
but they seldom showed much emotion. She, indeed, was impassive
herself, and betrayed but little of her feeling.* (*Framley Parsonage.*)
She also appears in *The Warden, Barchester Towers, The Small
House at Allington, The Last Chronicle of Barset, Can You Forgive
Her?, Phineas Finn* and *Miss Mackenzie.*

GRANTLY, MAJOR HENRY, V.C.: Second and favourite son of the
archdeacon of Barchester. He wins the Victoria Cross in India,
where his first wife dies, leaving him with a daughter, Edith.
Retiring to the Plumstead district, he eventually marries Grace
Crawley. He appears in *The Warden, Barchester Towers*, and
The Last Chronicle of Barset. His equivalent in the play *Did He
Steal It?* is Captain Oakley.

GRANTLY, REVD CHARLES JAMES: Eldest son of the archdeacon.
He becomes a fashionable London preacher, married to a Lady
Anne. As a boy *he well knew how much was expected from the
eldest son of the Archdeacon of Barchester, and was therefore mindful
not to mix too freely with other boys.* (*The Warden.*) He also
appears in *Barchester Towers* and *The Last Chronicle of Barset.*

GRANTLY, RT REVD DR: Bishop of Barchester and father of
Theophilus. *A bland and kind old man, opposed by every feeling
to authoritative demonstrations and episcopal ostentation.* (*The
Warden.*) His death is recounted at the beginning of *Barchester
Towers.*

GRANTLY, SAMUEL ('SOAPY'): Third son of the archdeacon of

Barchester. *He was soft and gentle in his manners, and attractive in his speech; the tone of his voice was melody, and every action was a grace; unlike his brothers, he was courteous to all, he was affable to the lowly, and meek even to the very scullery maid . . . To speak the truth, Samuel was a cunning boy, and those even who loved him best could not but own that for one so young, he was too adroit in choosing his words, and too skilled in modulating his voice.* (*The Warden.*) He also appears in *Barchester Towers.*

GRANTLY, VEN. DR THEOPHILUS: Son of the bishop of Barchester, archdeacon of the cathedral and rector of Plumstead Episcopi. He hopes to succeed his father as bishop, but is passed over for Dr Proudie. He is married to the former Susan Harding. *A fitting impersonation of the church militant here on earth; his shovel hat, large, new, and well-pronounced, a churchman's hat in every inch, declared the profession as plainly as does the Quaker's broad brim; his heavy eyebrow, large, open eyes, and full mouth and chin expressed the solidity of his order; the broad chest, amply covered with fine cloth, told how well to do was his estate; one hand ensconced within his pocket, evinced the practical hold which our mother church keeps on her temporal possessions; and the other, loose for action, was ready to fight if need be for her defence; and, below these, the decorous breeches and neat black gaiters showing so admirably that well-turned leg, betokened the decency, the outward beauty, and grace of our church establishment.* (*The Warden.*) He appears in all six Barchester novels.

GREEN, MOUNSER: Foreign Office official and man-about-town who marries Arabella Trefoil and is appointed Ambassador to Patagonia. (*The American Senator*)

GREENOW, MRS ARABELLA: Only daughter and youngest child of Squire Vavasor; sister of John Vavasor. She had a brief but happy marriage with a much older man. *Though she had enjoyed the name of being a beauty, she had not the usual success which comes from such repute. At thirty-four she was still unmarried. She had, moreover, acquired the character of being a flirt; and I fear that the stories which were told of her, though doubtless more than half false, had in them sufficient of truth to justify the character . . . She was married to the old man; and the marriage fortunately turned out satisfactorily, at any rate for the old man and for her family . . . Her husband was a retired merchant, very rich, not very strong in health, and devoted to his bride. Rumours soon made their way to Vavasor Hall, and to Queen Anne Street, that Mrs Greenow was quite a pattern wife, and that Mr Greenow considered himself to be the happiest old man in Lancashire.* (Can You Forgive Her?)

GREENWOOD, REVD THOMAS: The Kingsbury family chaplain and private secretary to the marquis, he abets the marchioness's attempts to divert the course of the inheritance. (*Marion Fay*)

GRESHAM, AUGUSTA: One of Frank's sisters, engaged to Gustavus Moffat until he breaks it off in his pursuit of Martha Dunstable. She falls in love with Mortimer Gazebee, but is talked out of it by her cousin Lady Amelia de Courcy, who marries him herself. *Augusta Gresham had perceived early in life that she could not obtain success either as an heiress or as a beauty, nor could she shine as a wit; she therefore fell back on such qualities as she had, and determined to win the world as a strong-minded, useful woman. That which she had of her own was blood; having that, she would in all ways do what in her lay to enhance its value.* (*Doctor Thorne.*) She also appears in *The Small House at Allington.*

GRESHAM, BEATRICE: One of Frank's sisters in whom he confides his love for Mary Thorne. She marries the Revd Caleb Oriel. *Not that Beatrice had ever wished to promote a marriage between them, or had even thought of such a thing. She was girlish, thoughtless, imprudent, inartistic, and very unlike a De Courcy. Very unlike a De Courcy she was in all that; but, nevertheless, she had the De Courcy veneration for blood.* (*Doctor Thorne*)

GRESHAM, FRANCIS NEWBOLD jnr (FRANK): Son and heir of the Greshams of Greshambury, he is discouraged from courting Mary Thorne because of her lower social status, but permitted to marry her when she is found to be an heiress. *Those who don't approve of a middle-aged bachelor country doctor as a hero, may take the heir to Greshambury in his stead, and call the book, if it so please them, 'The Loves and Adventures of Francis Newbold*

Gresham the Younger'. And Master Frank Gresham was not ill-adapted for playing the part of hero of this sort. He did not share his sisters' ill-health, and though the only boy of the family, he excelled all his sisters in personal appearance. The Greshams from time immemorial had been handsome. They were broad browed, blue eyed, fair haired, born with dimples in their chins, and that pleasant, aristocratic, dangerous curl of the upper lip which can equally express good humour or scorn. Young Frank was every inch a Gresham, and was the darling of his father's heart. (Doctor Thorne.) He also appears in *Framley Parsonage, The Last Chronicle of Barset* and *The Prime Minister.*

GRESHAM, FRANCIS NEWBOLD snr: Squire of Greshambury, and failed politician. Henpecked husband of Lady Arabella (de Courcy) and father of Frank and nine daughters. *His father had been member for Barsetshire all his life, and he looked forward to similar prosperity as though it were part of his inheritance; but he failed to take any of the steps which had secured his father's seat . . . A high Tory, with a great Whig interest to back him, is never a popular person in England. No one can trust him, though there may be those who are willing to place him, untrusted, in high position. Such was the case with Mr Gresham. (Doctor Thorne)*

GRESHAM, LADY ARABELLA: Wife of the above. Sister of Earl de Courcy. She endeavours in vain to discourage the attachment between her son Frank, and Mary Thorne. *A fashionable woman, with thorough Whig tastes and aspirations, such as became the daughter of a great Whig earl; she cared for politics, or thought that she cared for them, more than her husband did: for a month or two previous to her engagement she had been attached to the Court, and had been made to believe that much of the policy of England's rulers depended on the political intrigues of England's women. She was one who would fain be doing something if only she knew how, and the first important attempt she made was to turn her respectable young Tory husband into a second-rate Whig bantling. (Doctor Thorne)*

GRESHAM, MR: Prime Minister of England (said to represent William Ewart Gladstone). *Said to be the greatest orator in*

Europe ... *Mr Gresham is a man with no feelings for the past,
void of historical association, hardly with memories, – living altogether for the future which he is anxious to fashion anew out of
the vigour of his own brain.* (*Phineas Finn.*) He also appears in
Phineas Redux, *The Prime Minister*, and *The Eustace Diamonds*.

GREX, LADY MABEL: Daughter of Earl Grex and sister of the
gambler Lord Percival. She loves Frank Tregear, but they
agree to part since neither has money. She endeavours to win
Lord Silverbridge, but in vain. (*The Duke's Children*)

GREY, JOHN: Alice Vavasor's worthy but possessive suitor,
whom she throws over for the more wayward George Vavasor,
but eventually marries. *Mr Grey was a man of high character, of
good though moderate means; he was, too, well educated, of good
birth, a gentleman, and a man of talent. No one could deny that the
marriage would be highly respectable, and her father had been more
than satisfied ... She loved him much, and admired him even more
than she loved him. He was noble, generous, clever, good, – so good
as to be almost perfect; nay, for aught she knew he was perfect.
Would that he had some faults! Would that he had!* (*Can You
Forgive Her?*)

GREY, JOHN: John Scarborough's lawyer. (*Mr Scarborough's
Family*)

GREY, LADY SELINA: Only unmarried daughter of the Earl of
Cashel, and sister to Lord Kilcullen. *Lady Selina was not in her
première jeunesse, and, in manner, face, and disposition, was something like her father: she was not, therefore, very charming ...
She was plain, red-haired, and in no ways attractive; but she had
refused the offer of a respectable country gentleman, because he was
only a country gentleman.* (*The Kellys and the O'Kellys*)

GREYSTOCK, FRANK, M.P.: Barrister son of the Dean of Greystock, he contemplates marriage with his cousin, Lizzie Eustace,
but marries Lucy Morris, to whom he is already engaged.
*He was quick, ready-witted, self-reliant, and not over scrupulous in
the outward things of the world. He was desirous of doing his duty
to others, but he was specially desirous that others should do their
duty to him. He intended to get on in the world, and believed that*

happiness was to be achieved by success . . . There certainly was no apostasy. He had now and again attacked his father's ultra-Toryism, and rebuked his mother and sisters when they spoke of Gladstone as Apollyon, and called John Bright the Abomination of Desolation. But it was easy to him to fancy himself a Conservative, and as such he took his seat in the House without any feeling of discomfort. (The Eustace Diamonds)

GRIMES, JACOB: Landlord of the Handsome Man public house in London, George Vavasor's headquarters for his first election campaign. *Mr Grimes might have been taken as a fair sample of the English innkeeper, as described for many years past. But in his outer garments he was very unlike that description. He wore a black, swallow-tailed coat, made, however, to set very loose upon his back, a black waistcoat, and black pantaloons. He carried, moreover, in his hands a black chimney-pot hat. Not only have the top-boots and breeches vanished from the costume of innkeepers, but also the long, particoloured waistcoat, and the bird's-eye fogle round their necks. They get themselves up to look like Dissenting ministers or undertakers, except that there is still a something about their rosy gills which tells a tale of the spigot and corkscrew. (Can You Forgive Her?)*

HAMEL, ISADORE: Young sculptor who marries Lucy Dormer. *(Ayala's Angel)*

HAMPSTEAD, LORD: Eldest son and heir of the Marquis of Kingsbury and brother of Lady Frances Trafford. He loves Marion Fay. *(Marion Fay)*

HAPHAZARD, SIR ABRAHAM: Celebrated lawyer consulted by Septimus Harding in *The Warden* and about Sir Roger Scatcherd's will in *Doctor Thorne. Coruscations flew from him; glittering sparkles, as from hot steel; but no heat; no cold heart was ever cheered by warmth from him, no unhappy soul ever dropped a portion of its burden at his door. (The Warden)*

HARCOURT, SIR HENRY, M.P.: Solicitor-general and socially ambitious, he marries Caroline Waddington for her supposed fortune, but she leaves him, and, deeply in debt and out of office, he commits suicide. *Might it not be safely predicted of a man who was solicitor-general before he was thirty, that he would*

be lord-chancellor or lord chief-justice, or at any rate some very
bigwig indeed before he was fifty? ... For our friend Sir Henry
every joy was present. Youth and wealth and love were all his, and
his all together. He was but eight-and-twenty, was a member of
Parliament, solicitor-general, owner of a house in Eaton Square,
and possessor of as much well-trained beauty as was to be found at
that time within the magic circle of any circumambient crinoline
within the bills of mortality. (*The Bertrams*)

HARDING, ELEANOR: Younger daughter of Septimus Harding
and sister to Susan. She marries John Bold and bears his son
Johnny after his death, and later marries again to Francis
Arabin, by whom she has two daughters, Eleanor and Susan.
*Her loveliness was like that of many landscapes, which require to be
often seen to be fully enjoyed. There was a depth of dark clear brightness in her eyes which was lost upon a quick observer, a character
about her mouth which showed itself to those with whom she familiarly
conversed, a glorious form of head the perfect symmetry of which
required the eye of an artist for its appreciation. (Barchester Towers.)*
She appears in all the Barchester novels. Her equivalent in the
play *Did He Steal It?* is Mrs Lofty.

HARDING, REVD SEPTIMUS: Widowed father of Susan Grantly
and Eleanor. He is, successively, precentor of Barchester Cathedral and Warden of Hiram's Hospital; rector of Crabtree
Parva; rector of St Cuthbert's, Barchester; vicar of St Ewold's,
author of the book *Harding's Church Music*. *A small man,
now verging on sixty years, but bearing few signs of age; his
hair is rather grizzled, though not grey; his eye is very mild,
but clear and bright, though the double glasses which are held swing-
ing from his hand, unless when fixed on his nose, show that time
has told upon his sight; his hands are delicately white, and both
hands and feet are small; he always wears a black frock coat, black
knee-breeches, and black gaiters, and somewhat scandalises some of
his more hyper-clerical brethren by a black neck-handkerchief. (The
Warden).* He appears in all six Barchester novels.

HARDING, SUSAN. See GRANTLY, VEN. DR THEOPHILUS.

HARDLINES, SIR GREGORY, K.C.B.: Chief Commissioner of the

Civil Service Examination Board, having been promoted from chief clerkship of the Weights and Measures Office. Patron of Alaric Tudor. *In days long ago there were, as we all know, three kings at Brentford. So also were there three kings at the Civil Service Examination Board. But of these three Sir Gregory was by far the greatest king. He sat in the middle, had two thousand jewels to his crown, whereas the others had only twelve hundred each, and his name ran first in all the royal warrants. Nevertheless, Sir Gregory, could he have had it so, would, like most kings, have preferred an undivided sceptre.* (*The Three Clerks*)

HARFORD, REVD DR: Elderly Rector of Baslehurst. *He had nearly completed half a century of work in that capacity, and had certainly been neither an idle nor an inefficient clergyman. But, now in his old age, he was discontented and disgusted by the changes which had come upon him; and though some bodily strength for further service still remained to him, he had no longer any aptitude for useful work ... But perhaps hatred of Mr Prong was the strongest passion of Dr Harford's heart at the present moment.* (*Rachel Ray*)

HART, MR: London tailor who unsuccessfully opposes Butler Cornbury in the Baslehurst parliamentary election. *The Jewish hero, the tailor himself, came among them, and astonished their minds by the ease and volubility of his speeches. He did not pronounce his words with any of those soft slushy Judaic utterances by which they had been taught to believe he would disgrace himself. His nose was not hookey, with any especial hook, nor was it thicker at the bridge than was becoming. He was a dapper little man, with bright eyes, quick motion, ready tongue, and a very new hat. It seemed that he knew well how to canvass. He had a smile and a good word for all, – enemies as well as friends.* (*Rachel Ray*)

HARTLETOP, GUSTAVUS, MARQUIS OF: Formerly Lord Dumbello; son of the Dowager Marchioness of Hartletop. He marries Griselda Grantly, whose willing slave he becomes. *It satisfied his ambition to be led about as the senior lacquey in his wife's train ... and considered himself to be distinguished even among the elder sons of marquises, by the greatness reflected from the parson's daughter whom he had married.* (*The Small House at*

Allington.) He also appears in *Framley Parsonage* and *The Last Chronicle of Barset*.

HEATHCOTE, HARRY: English sheep-farmer in Australia, living at Gangoil with his wife Mary, two children and sister-in-law Kate Daly. His territorial disputes with his neighbour, Giles Medlicot, and their joint battle with the marauding Brownbys are the substance of the story. (*Harry Heathcote of Gangoil*)

HOLDENOUGH, LADY ALICE: Wife of Canon Holdenough, and only married sister of the Marquis of Brotherton and the Ladies Sarah, Susanna and Amelia. (*Is He Popenjoy?*)

HOLT, CECILIA: Marrying George Western without daring to admit that she had jilted an earlier lover, Sir Francis Geraldine, she is deserted by him when he learns of it, but they are reconciled with the help of George's sister, Lady Grant. (*Kept in the Dark*)

HOTSPUR, EMILY: Daughter of Sir Harry, wooed for her property by George Hotspur, but infatuated with him, she is heartbroken at his death and dies too. (*Sir Harry Hotspur of Humblethwaite*)

HOTSPUR, GEORGE: Cousin of Emily, whom he is prevented from marrying, for her property, by her father. He marries his actress mistress, Mrs Morton. (*Sir Harry Hotspur of Humblethwaite*)

HOTSPUR, SIR HARRY: Father of Emily, whose marriage to George Hotspur he manages to prevent. (*Sir Harry Hotspur of Humblethwaite*)

HOUGHTON, MRS ADELAIDE (*née* DE BARON): Cousin of Jack de Baron. She had married the elderly Jeffrey Houghton after rejecting Lord George Germain, whom she takes pleasure in embarrassing after his marriage to Mary Lovelace. *She consulted her glass, and told herself that, without self-praise, she must regard herself as the most beautiful woman of her own acquaintance.* (*Is He Popenjoy?*)

HURTLE, MRS WINIFRED: American widow with a past, from his engagement with whom Paul Montague extricates himself with difficulty. *She was certainly a most beautiful woman, and she* knew it. She looked as though she knew it, – but only after that fashion in which a woman ought to know it. (*The Way We Live Now*)

JAQUÊTANAPÉ, VICTOIRE: Frenchman-about-town, who marries Clementina Golightly for her fortune. *The happy Victoire was dressed up to the eyes. That, perhaps, is not saying much, for he was only a few feet high; but what he wanted in quantity he fully made up in quality. He was a well-made, shining, jaunty little Frenchman, who seemed to be perfectly at ease with himself and all the world. He had to be perfectly at ease with himself and all the world. He had the smallest little pair of moustaches imaginable, the smallest little imperial, the smallest possible pair of boots, and the smallest possible pair of gloves. Nothing on earth could be nicer, or sweeter, or finer, than he was.* (*The Three Clerks*)

JONES, ADA and EDITH: Philip Jones's elder and younger daughters who care for Captain Clayton after he has been shot. Although Ada is the beauty, it is Edith whom he loves. (*The Landleaguers*)

JONES, FLORIAN: Philip Jones's youngest child, aged ten, whose testimony against the Landleaguers results in his being shot and killed. (*The Landleaguers*)

JONES, FRANK: Philip Jones's eldest son, in love with Rachel O'Mahony. (*The Landleaguers*)

JONES, HENRY: Purported heir to his wealthy uncle Indefer Jones, whose will he hides when he discovers the inheritance has been left to his cousin, Isabel Broderick. (*Cousin Henry*)

JONES, MARY FLOOD: Phineas Finn's Irish childhood sweetheart. She becomes his first wife, but dies young. *One of those girls, so common in Ireland, whom men, with tastes that way given, feel inclined to take up and devour on the spur of the moment; and when she liked her lion, she had a look about her which seemed to ask to be devoured.* (*Phineas Finn*)

JONES, MR: Husband of Brown's daughter Sarah Jane, whom he persuades to influence her father to invest disastrously in a haberdashery business with himself and Robinson. (*The Struggles of Brown, Jones, and Robinson*)

L

JONES, MRS MONTACUTE: Lady Mary Germain's matchmaking confidante. *A stout-built but very short old lady, with grey hair curled in precise rolls down her face, with streaky cheeks, giving her a look of extreme good health, and very bright grey eyes. She was always admirably dressed, so well dressed that her enemies accused her of spending enormous sums on her toilet. She was very old – some people said eighty, adding probably not more than ten years to her age – very enthusiastic, particularly in reference to her friends; very fond of gaiety, and very charitable. (Is He Popenjoy?)*

JONES, PHILIP: Father of Frank, Florian, Ada and Edith and owner of Irish estates which become devastated by local troublemakers led by one of his tenants, Pat Carroll. (*The Landleaguers*)

KANTWISE, MR: Commercial traveller in hardware; crony of Mr Moulder and a leading habitué of the Bull Inn, Leeds. *He looked as though a skin rather too small for the purpose had been drawn over his head and face so that his forehead and cheeks and chin were tight and shiny. His eyes were small and green, always moving about in his head, and were seldom used by Mr Kantwise in the ordinary way. At whatever he looked he looked sideways; it was not that he did not look you in the face, but he always looked at you with a sidelong glance, never choosing to have you straight in front of him. And the more eager he was in conversation – the more anxious he might be to gain his point, the more he averted his face and looked askance; so that sometimes he would prefer to have his antagonist almost behind his shoulder.* (*Orley Farm*)

KEEGAN, HYACINTH: Attorney married to Sally, the daughter of Joe Flannelly. Flannelly holds the mortgage on Ballycloran and Keegan is his principal instrument in trying to dispossess the Macdermots. (*The Macdermots of Ballycloran*)

KELLY, JOHN: Martin's elder brother: an attorney's clerk. (*The Kellys and the O'Kellys*)

KELLY, MARTIN: Mary Kelly's farmer son, brother of John, Meg and Jane and distantly related to his landlord, Lord Ballindine.

He schemes to marry Anty Lynch for her money, but eventually does so for love as well. *He was a good-looking young fellow, about twenty-five years of age, with that mixture of cunning and frankness in his bright eye, which is so common among those of his class in Ireland.* (*The Kellys and the O'Kellys*)

KELLY, MRS MARY: Widowed mother of Martin, John, Meg and Jane. She keeps an inn and grocery shop, and takes in Anty Lynch when she flies from her brother's murderous attempt. *Her husband had left her for a better world some ten years since, with six children; and the widow, instead of making continual use, as her chief support, of that common wail of being a poor, lone woman, had put her shoulders to the wheel.* (*The Kellys and the O'Kellys*)

KENNEBY, JOHN: Brother of Mrs Moulder. Professed witness to Sir Joseph Mason's will. Formerly in love with Miriam Usbech, he is persuaded by his sister to marry Mrs Smiley. *John Kenneby, after one or two attempts in other spheres of life, had at last got into the house of Hubbles and Grease, and had risen to be their book-keeper. He had once been tried by them as a traveller, but in that line he had failed. He did not possess that rough, ready, self-confident tone of mind which is almost necessary for a man who is destined to move about quickly from one circle of persons to another.* (*Orley Farm*)

KENNEDY, ROBERT, M.P.: Member of Parliament for several Scottish boroughs, he marries Lady Laura Standish and tries to kill Phineas Finn when he suspects he has influenced her to leave him. He dies insane. *He was possessed of over a million and a half of money, which he was mistaken enough to suppose he had made himself; whereas it may be doubted whether he had ever earned a penny. His father and uncle had created a business in Glasgow, and that business now belonged to him ... He never spoke much to anyone, although he was constantly in society. He rarely did anything, although he had the means of doing everything. He had very seldom been on his legs in the House of Commons, though he sat there for ten years. He was seen about everywhere, sometimes with one acquaintance and sometimes with another; – but it may be doubted whether he had any friend.* (*Phineas Finn.*) He also appears in *Phineas Redux*.

KILCULLEN, ADOLPHUS, LORD: Son of the Earl of Cashel and brother to Lady Selina Grey. Much in debt from gambling, he is unsuccessful in trying to marry his father's ward, the heiress Fanny Wyndhan. *Lord Kilcullen, when about to marry, would be obliged to cashier his opera-dancers and their expensive crews; and, though he might not leave the turf altogether, when married he would gradually be drawn out of turf society, and would doubtless become a good steady family nobleman, like his father.* (*The Kellys and the O'Kellys*)

KINGSBURY, MARQUIS OF, and CLARA, MARCHIONESS OF: The Marquis has two children, Lady Frances Trafford and Lord Hampstead, by an earlier marriage, and three sons by this one. The Marchioness's attempts to get the inheritance away from Lord Hampstead to her own sons is the main theme of the story. (*Marion Fay*)

LAROCHEJAQUELIN, AGATHA: Sister (invented by Trollope) of the real-life Henri Larochejaquelin, commander-in-chief of the Vendéan forces in the counter-Revolutionary uprising of 1793. She rejects the hand of Henri's friend and fellow-Royalist Adolph Denot (real character), who exacts revenge by leading Republican forces against his comrades. She is also loved by the real-life Vendéan leader Jacques Cathelineau, and tends him as he is dying of battle wounds. (*La Vendée.*) (N.B. The many other characters in this work, mostly drawn from real life, are excluded from this section.)

LAWRIE, MARY: In love with John Gordon, who had never declared himself before leaving to seek his fortune in South Africa, she eventually accepts her father's friend, William Whittlestaff. When John returns, rich, the older man relinquishes his claim. (*An Old Man's Love*)

LEFROY, ELLA (*née* BEAUFORT): American 'widow' of Ferdinand Lefroy, who unwittingly makes a bigamous marriage with Henry Peacocke. She becomes house-mother at Dr Wortle's school in England, and the marriage is legitimized when

Lefroy is learned to be dead at last. *She was a woman something over thirty years of age when she first came to Bowick, in the very pride and bloom of woman's beauty ... Her features were regular, but with a great show of strength. She was tall for a woman, but without any of that look of length under which female altitude sometimes suffers. She was strong and well-made, and apparently equal to any labour to which her position might subject her.* (*Dr Wortle's School*)

LEFROY, FERDINAND and ROBERT: American brothers, the first of whom marries Ella Beaufort, then disappears, believed killed. The latter tries to blackmail Ella and her new husband, Henry Peacocke, as bigamists. *They were both handsome, and, in spite of the sufferings of their State, an attempt had been made to educate them like gentlemen. But no career of honour had been left open to them, and they had fallen by degrees into dishonour, dishonesty, and brigandage.* (*Dr Wortle's School*)

LINLITHGOW, LADY PENELOPE: Lizzie Eustace's aunt. *She was one of those old women who are undoubtedly old women – who in the remembrance of younger people seem always to have been old women, – but on whom old age appears to have no debilitating effects. If the hand of Lady Linlithgow ever trembled, it trembled from anger; – if her foot ever faltered, it faltered for effect. In her way Lady Linlithgow was a very powerful human being. She knew nothing of fear, nothing of charity, nothing of mercy, and nothing of the softness of love. She had no imagination. She was worldly, covetous, and not unfrequently cruel. But she meant to be true and honest, though she often failed in her meaning.* (*The Eustace Diamonds*)

LONGESTAFFE, ADOLPHUS and FAMILY: A Suffolk squire, he becomes financially involved with Augustus Melmotte, and his scheming wife, Lady Pomona, tries to persuade their ineffectual son, Adolphus jnr ('Dolly'), to court Marie Melmotte for her money. Dolly has two dull sisters, Sophia and Georgiana. (*The Way We Live Now.*) Dolly also appears in *The Duke's Children*.

LOPEZ, FERDINAND: Adventurer in partnership with Sexty

Parker. He marries Emily Wharton for her father's money, fails to gain election to Parliament, blackmails the Duchess of Omnium, and, finally discredited, kills himself. *He had been at a good English private school ... Thence at the age of seventeen he had been sent to a German University, and at the age of twenty-one had appeared in London, in a stockbroker's office, where he was soon known as an accomplished linguist, and as a very clever fellow, – precocious, not given to many pleasures, apt for work, but hardly trustworthy by employers, not as being dishonest, but as having a taste for being a master rather than a servant ... He was certainly a handsome man, – his beauty being of a sort which men are apt to deny and women to admit lavishly. He was nearly six feet tall, very dark, and very thin, with regular, well-cut features indicating little to the physiognomist unless it be the great gift of self-possession.* (*The Prime Minister*)

LOVEL, LADY ANNA: Daughter of the Earl and Countess: the latter's fight to prove her daughter's legitimacy is the story's main theme. Anna is offered marriage by the 'young Earl', Frederick, but prefers a tailor, Daniel Thwaite. (*Lady Anna*)

LOVEL, COUNTESS: Formerly Josephine Murray, she had married the old Earl Lovel, but is subsequently informed by him that he is married already and that their daughter, Lady Anna, is therefore illegitimate. (*Lady Anna*)

LOVEL, FREDERICK: The 'young Earl', nephew and heir of the old Earl. He offers marriage to Lady Anna, but she prefers a tailor, Daniel Thwaite. (*Lady Anna*)

LOVELACE, REVD HENRY: Widowed Dean of Brotherton and father of Mary, on whose and her husband's behalf he challenges the legitimacy of Lord Popenjoy, the Marquis of Brotherton's small son and heir. *When a poor curate, a man of very humble origin, with none of what we commonly call Church interest, with nothing to recommend him but a handsome person, moderate education, and a quick intellect, he had married a lady with a considerable fortune, whose family had bought for him a living. Here he preached himself into fame.* (*Is He Popenjoy?*)

LOVELACE, MARY: The Dean of Brotherton's daughter, married

to Lord George Germain. *She was a sweet, innocent, ladylike, high-spirited, joyous creature ... She was so nice that middle-aged men wished themselves younger that they might make love to her, or older that they might be privileged to kiss her. Though keenly anxious for amusement, though over head and ears in love with sport and frolic, no unholy thought had ever polluted her mind. That men were men, and that she was a woman, had of course been considered by her.* (*Is He Popenjoy?*)

LOWTHER, MARY: Object of the vicar's and his wife's matchmaking attempt for Harry Gilmore, who relinquishes her to Walter Marrable. *If you judged her face by any rules of beauty, you would say that it was too thin, but feeling its influence with sympathy, you could never wish it to be changed.* (*The Vicar of Bullhampton*)

LUFTON, LADY, of Framley Court: Widowed mother of Lord Lufton. She appoints Mark Robarts to the living of Framley and finds him a wife, but considers his sister Lucy unworthy of her son, though she eventually relents. *She liked cheerful, quiet, well-to-do people, who loved their Church, their country, and their Queen, and who were not too anxious to make a noise in the world. She desired that all the farmers round her should be able to pay their rents without trouble, that all the old women should have warm flannel petticoats, that the working men should be saved from rheumatism by healthy food and dry houses, that they should all be obedient to their pastors and masters – temporal as well as spiritual. That was her idea of loving her country.* (*Framley Parsonage*)

LUFTON, LUDOVIC, LORD: School and university friend of Mark Robarts, whose sister Lucy he marries after his mother withdraws her stubborn opposition. *Lord Lufton himself was a fine, bright-looking young man; not so tall as Mark Robarts, and with perhaps less intelligence marked on his face; but his features were finer, and there was in his countenance a thorough appearance of good humour and sweet temper. It was, indeed, a pleasant face to look upon, and dearly Lady Lufton loved to gaze at it.* (*Framley Parsonage*)

LUPEX, ORSON and MRS MARIA: A scene-painter and his flirtatious wife lodging at Mrs Roper's boarding-house. (*The Small House at Allington*)

LYNCH, BARRY: Anty's Old Etonian brother and would-be murderer for her share of their late father, Simeon's, estate. *If, at this moment, there was a soul in all Ireland over whom Satan had full dominion – if there was a breast unoccupied by one good thought – if there was a heart wishing, a brain conceiving, and organs ready to execute all that was evil, from the worst motives, they were to be found in that miserable creature, as he stood there urging himself on to hate those whom he should have loved – cursing those who were nearest to him – fearing her, whom he had ill-treated all his life.* (*The Kellys and the O'Kellys*)

MACDERMOT, EUPHEMIA ('FEEMY'): Daughter of Larry and sister of Thady. Her seduction by Myles Ussher brings tragedy to them all. *A tall, dark girl, with that bold, upright, well-poised figure, which is so peculiarly Irish. She walked as if all the blood of the old Irish princes was in her veins.* (*The Macdermots of Ballycloran*)

MACDERMOT, LAWRENCE ('LARRY'): Father of Thady and Feemy and owner of the run-down estate of Ballycloran. (*The Macdermots of Ballycloran*)

MACDERMOT, THADY: Son of Larry and brother of Feemy, whose seducer, Myles Ussher, he kills. (*The Macdermots of Ballycloran*)

MCGRATH, REVD JOHN: Priest whose parish includes Ballycloran and who acts as moderator of his flock's passions. (*The Macdermots of Ballycloran*)

MACKENZIE, MARGARET: The spinster whose story this is, prevented from accepting her suitor Harry Handcock by having to nurse her sick father and brother. She is released by their deaths and acquires a fortune and several suitors, finally marrying her cousin John Ball. *During those fifteen years, her life had been very weary. A moated grange in the country is bad enough for the life of any Mariana, but a moated grange in town is much worse. Her life in London had been altogether of the moated grange kind, and long before her brother's death it had been very wearisome to her.* (*Miss Mackenzie*)

MACKENZIE, MRS SARAH: Margaret Mackenzie's sister-in-law, incensed that the family inheritance had not gone to her late husband, Thomas. (*Miss Mackenzie*)

MACLEOD, LADY: Widow of Sir Archibald Macleod, K.C.B., and cousin of Alice Vavasor, whom she brings up. *She was a Calvinistic Sabbatarian in religion, and in worldly matters she was a devout believer in the high rank of her noble relatives. She could almost worship a youthful marquis, though he lived a life that would disgrace a heathen among heathens; and she could and did, in her own mind, condemn crowds of commonplace men and women to all eternal torments which her imagination could conceive, because they listened to profane music in a park on Sunday. Yet she was a good woman. Out of her small means she gave much away. She owed no man anything. She strove to love her neighbours. She bore much pain with calm, unspeaking endurance, and she lived in trust of a better world.* (*Can You Forgive Her?*)

MCKEON, TONY: Ballycloran farmer who works to gain Thady Macdermot's acquittal. His wife befriends Feemy. (*The Macdermots of Ballycloran*)

M'RUEN, JABESH: Moneylender into whose toils Charley Tudor falls. *Mr Jabesh M'Ruen was in the habit of relieving the distresses of such impoverished young gentlemen as Charley Tudor; and though he did this with every assurance of philanthropic regard, though in doing so he made only one stipulation, 'Pray be punctual, Mr Tudor, now pray do be punctual, sir, and you may always count on me,' nevertheless, in spite of all his goodness, Mr M'Ruen's young friends seldom continued to hold their heads well up over the world's water.* (*The Three Clerks*)

MAGUIRE, REVD JEREMIAH: One of Margaret Mackenzie's suitors, wanting her money to build an Independent church. He marries a Miss Colza, who had acted as his spy on Margaret's circumstances. *The possessor of a good figure, of a fine head of jet black hair, of a perfect set of white teeth, of whiskers which were also black and very fine, but streaked here and there with a grey hair, – and of the most terrible squint in his right eye which ever disfigured a face that in all other aspects was fitted for an Apollo. (Miss Mackenzie)*

MARRABLE, COLONEL: Father of Walter, whom he swindles. *Good-tempered, sprightly in conversation, and had not a scruple in the world. (The Vicar of Bullhampton)*

MARRABLE, SIR GREGORY: Father of Gregory, brother of John and Colonel Marrable, and uncle of Walter. *He rose late, took but little exercise, and got through his day with the assistance of his steward, his novel, and occasionally of his doctor. He slept a good deal, and was never tired of talking to himself. (The Vicar of Bullhampton)*

MARRABLE, GREGORY: Sickly son of Sir Gregory. His early death leaves Walter Marrable Sir Gregory's heir. *(The Vicar of Bullhampton)*

MARRABLE, REVD JOHN: Sir Gregory's brother and Walter's uncle. *(The Vicar of Bullhampton)*

MARRABLE, SARAH: The aunt with whom Mary Lowther lives in London. *(The Vicar of Bullhampton)*

MARRABLE, CAPTAIN WALTER: Son of Colonel Marrable and nephew of Sir Gregory, whose estate he inherits, enabling him to marry his cousin Mary Lowther. *(The Vicar of Bullhampton)*

MARSHAM, MRS: A girlhood friend of Plantagenet Palliser's mother. She marries Mr Bott with whom she had been watchdog over Palliser's wife, Lady Glencora. *One of those women who are ambitious of power, and not very scrupulous as to the manner in which they obtain it. She was hardhearted, and capable of pursuing an object without much regard to the injury she might do. She would not flatter wealth or fawn before a title, but she was not above any artifice by which she might ingratiate herself with those whom it suited her purpose to conciliate. She thought evil rather than good. She was herself untrue in action, if not absolutely in word. I do not say that she would coin lies, but she would willingly leave false impressions. (Can You Forgive Her?)*

MARTY, FATHER: Parish priest of Kilmacrenny, only friend of Kate O'Hara and her mother. *(An Eye for an Eye)*

MASON, JOSEPH: Sir Joseph's heir and half-brother to Lucius. His wife's name is Diana, and they have two sons, Joseph and John, and three daughters, Diana, Creusa and Penelope. *A big, broad, heavy-browed man, in whose composition there was nothing of tenderness, nothing of poetry, and nothing of taste; but I cannot say that he was on the whole a bad man. He was just in his dealings, or at any rate endeavoured to be so. He strove hard to do his duty as a county magistrate against very adverse circumstances. He endeavoured to enable his tenants and labourers to live. He was severe to his children, and was not loved by them; but nevertheless they were dear to him, and he endeavoured to do his duty by them. The wife of his bosom was not a pleasant woman, but nevertheless he did his duty by her; that is, he neither deserted her, nor beat her, nor locked her up ... But yet he was a bad man in that he could never forget and never forgive.* (*Orley Farm*)

MASON, SIR JOSEPH: Owner of Groby Park, Yorkshire, and Orley Farm, near London. Elderly husband of Lady Mason. Father of Joseph and three daughters by his first marriage, and Lucius by his second. (*Orley Farm*)

MASON, LUCIUS: Lady Mason's only son. She forges the codicil to her husband's will to give Lucius possession of Orley Farm. He is unsuccessful in wooing Sophia Furnival, and finally emigrates to Australia. *A handsome, well-mannered lad, tall and comely to the eye, with soft brown whiskers sprouting on his cheek, well grounded in Greek, Latin, and Euclid, grounded also in French and Italian, and possessing many more acquirements than he would have learned at Harrow. But added to these, or rather consequent of them, was a conceit which public-school education would not have created.* (*Orley Farm*)

MASON, LADY MARY (formerly Johnson): Sir Joseph's second wife and mother of Lucius, for whose benefit she forges the codicil to her husband's will. *She was now forty-seven years of age, and had a son who had reached man's estate; and yet perhaps she had more of woman's beauty at this present time than when she stood at the altar with Sir Joseph Mason. The quietness and repose of her manner suited her years and her position; age had given fulness to her tall form; and the habitual sadness of her countenance was in fair accordance with her condition and character. And yet she was not really sad, – at least so said those who knew her. The melancholy was in her face rather than in her character. (Orley Farm)*

MASTERS, MARY: Daughter of a Dillsborough attorney, Gregory Masters, she had been largely brought up at Bragton Hall and marries Reginald Morton when he inherits it. (*The American Senator*)

MAULE, GERARD: Son of Maurice Maule. Suitor of Adelaide Palliser, but too poor to marry until Mme Goesler refuses the Duke of Omnium's bequest and it passes to Adelaide. '*When he's out he rides hard; but at other times there's a ha-ha, lack a-daisical air about him which I hate ... A man can't suppose that he'll gain anything by pretending that he never reads, and never thinks, and never does anything, and never speaks, and doesn't care what he has for dinner, and, upon the whole, would just as soon lie in bed all day as get up. It isn't that he is really idle. He rides and eats, and does get up, and I daresay talks and thinks. It's simply a poor affectation.*' – Finn (*Phineas Redux.*) He also appears in *The Duke's Children*. His father unsuccessfully courts Mme Goesler.

MEDLICOT, GILES: Harry Heathcote's closest neighbour, a fellow-Englishman, in love with Harry's sister-in-law, Kate Daly, but in dispute with Harry over territory. He and Harry are reconciled when Giles sides with Harry in battle with the marauding Brownbys. (*Harry Heathcote of Gangoil*)

MELLERBY, SOPHIA: A duke's granddaughter whom Fred Neville refuses to marry. She marries his brother Jack and becomes Countess of Scroope. (*An Eye for an Eye*)

MELMOTTE, AUGUSTUS: Bogus financier whose success carries him into Parliament but at length to ruin and suicide. Natural father of Marie. *A large man with bushy whiskers and rough thick hair, with heavy eyebrows, and a wonderful look of power about his mouth and chin.* (*The Way We Live Now*)

MELMOTTE, MADAME: Augustus Melmotte's Bohemian-Jewish wife and conniver at his social manoeuvres. *There was certainly very little ... to recommend her, unless it was a readiness to spend* money on any object that might be suggested to her by her new acquaintances. It sometimes seemed that she had a commission from her husband to give away presents to any who would accept them. (*The Way We Live Now*)

MELMOTTE, MARIE: Augustus Melmotte's natural daughter. She marries Hamilton Fisker. *She was not beautiful, she was not clever, and she was not a saint.* (*The Way We Live Now*)

MIDLOTHIAN, MARGARET, COUNTESS OF: Imposing relative of Alive Vavasor and meddler in her romantic affairs. Mother of Lady Jane and Lady Mary. *She made no pretension either to youth or beauty, – as some ladies above sixty will still do, – but sat confessedly an old woman in all her external relations ... Very small she was, but she carried in her grey eyes and sharp-cut features a certain look of importance which saved her from being considered as small in importance. Alice, as soon as she saw her, knew that she was a lady over whom no easy victory could be obtained.* (*Can You Forgive Her?*)

MILBOROUGH, DOWAGER COUNTESS OF: Old family friend who warns Louis Trevelyan of Colonel Osborne's interest in his wife. She befriends Nora Rowley. (*He Knew He Was Right*)

MILDMAY, AUGUSTA ('GUSS'): A determined beauty in pursuit of Jack de Baron, whom she at length gets to the altar. *She was certainly handsome, but she carried with her that wearied air of being nearly worn out by the toil of searching for a husband which comes upon some young women after the fourth or fifth year of their labours ... Guss Mildmay had no money to speak of, but she had beauty enough to win either a working barrister or a rich old sinner. She was quite able to fall in love with the one and flirt with the other at the same time; but when the moment for decision came, she could not bring herself to put up with either. At present she was in real truth in love with Jack de Baron, and had brought herself to think that if Jack would ask her, she would risk everything.* (*Is He Popenjoy?*)

MILDMAY, JULIA ('AUNT JU'): A leader of the women's liberation movement responsible for inviting Baroness Banmann to lecture at the 'Disabilities' institute. (*Is He Popenjoy?*)

MILDMAY, WILLIAM: Prime Minister, uncle of Barrington Erle, related to Laura Standish. He appears in *Phineas Finn, Phineas Redux,* and *The Prime Minister.*

MOFFAT, GUSTAVUS, M.P.: Intended by her mother for Augusta Gresham's husband, he breaks the engagement to pursue Martha Dunstable, though without success. *Mr Moffat was a young man of very large fortune, in parliament, inclined to business, and in every way recommendable. He was not a man of birth, to be sure; that was to be lamented; – in confessing that Mr Moffat was not a man of birth, Augusta did not go so far as to admit that he was the son of a tailor; such, however, was the rigid truth in the matter.* (*Doctor Thorne*)

MOGGS, ONTARIO: Ambitious bootmaker's son who marries Polly Neefit whom he impresses by his attempt (unsuccessful) to enter Parliament. *It was the glory of Ontario Moggs to be a politician; – it was his ambition to be a poet; – it was his nature to be a lover; – it was his disgrace to be a bootmaker.* (*Ralph the Heir*)

MOLLETT, ABRAHAM ('ABY'): Matthew Mollett's rascally son and associate in his blackmailing activities. *Free living had told more upon him, young as he was, than upon his father . . . his hand on a morning was unsteady; and his passion for brandy was stronger than that for beef-steaks.* (*Castle Richmond*)

MOLLETT, MATTHEW: Bigamous husband of Mary Wainwright, whose marriage with Sir Thomas Fitzgerald after Mollett's presumed death enables him to blackmail Sir Thomas. His own wife, through whom he is traced by the lawyer Prendergast, is also named Mary, as is their daughter, who had adopted the surname Swan. *He was a hale hearty man, of perhaps sixty years of age, who had certainly been handsome, and was even now not the reverse. Or rather, one may say, that he would have been so were it not that there was a low, restless, cunning legibile in his mouth and eyes, which robbed his countenance of all manliness.*

MONK, JOSHUA, M.P.: Radical Member for Pottery Hamlets, who, after two decades of obscurity, attains Cabinet rank and eventually becomes Prime Minister. He is a staunch friend of

Phineas Finn. *A thin, tall, gaunt man, who had devoted his whole life to politics, hitherto without any personal reward.* (*Phineas Finn*) He also appears in *Phineas Redux* and *The Prime Minister*.

MONK, LADY: Wife of Sir Cosmo Monk, M.P., and aunt of Burgo Fitzgerald, of whom her husband disapproves. *Lady Monk was a woman now about fifty years of age, who had been a great beauty, and who was still handsome in her advanced age. Her figure was very good. She was tall and of fine proportion, though by no means verging to that state of body which our excellent American friend and critic Mr Hawthorne has described as beefy and has declared to be the general condition of English ladies of Lady Monk's age. Lady Monk was not beefy. She was a comely, handsome, upright dame, – one of whom, as regards her outward appearance, England might be proud.* (*Can You Forgive Her?*)

MONTAGUE, PAUL: Friend of Roger Carbury who marries Henrietta Carbury. (*The Way We Live Now*)

MORRIS, LUCY: Friend of Lady Fawn, in whose household she is governess. She marries Frank Greystock. *A treasure though no heroine. She was a sweetly social, genial little human being whose presence in the house was ever felt to be like sunshine. She was never forward, but never bashful. She was always open to familiar intercourse without ever putting herself forward. There was no man or woman with whom she would not so talk as to make the man or woman feel that the conversation was remarkably pleasant, – and she could do the same with any child.* (*The Eustace Diamonds*)

MORTON, JOHN: Secretary of the British Legation at Washington. Engaged to Arabella Trefoil, to whom he leaves a fortune at his death, despite her unfaithfulness to him. He is cousin to Reginald Morton. (*The American Senator*)

MORTON, REGINALD: Cousin to John, at whose death he inherits Bragton Hall and marries Mary Masters. (*The American Senator*)

MOULDER, MR: Commercial traveller in groceries and spirits; brother-in-law of John Kenneby. *Short and very fat; – so fat that he could not have seen his own knees for some considerable time past. His face rolled with fat, as also did all his limbs. His eyes were large, and bloodshot. He wore no beard, and therefore showed plainly the triple bagging of his fat chin. In spite of his overwhelming fatness, there was something in his face that was masterful and almost vicious. His body had been overcome by eating, but not as yet his spirit – one would be inclined to say . . . Mr Moulder did not get drunk. His brandy and water went into his blood, and into his eyes, and into his feet, and into his hands, – but not into his brain.* (Orley Farm)

MOULDER, MRS MARY ANNE: Wife of the above and sister of John Kenneby, whom she marries off to the widow Maria Smiley. *Mrs Moulder was no doubt a happy woman. She had quite fallen into the mode of life laid out for her. She had a little bit of hot kidney for breakfast at about ten; she dined at three, having seen herself to the accurate cooking of her roast fowl, or her bit of sweetbread, and always had her pint of Scotch ale. She turned over all her clothes almost every day. In the evening she read Reynolds's Miscellany, had her tea and buttered muffins, took a thimbleful of brandy and water at nine, and then went to bed. The work of her life consisted in sewing buttons to Moulder's shirts, and seeing that his things were properly got up when he was at home.* (Orley Farm)

MOUNTJOY, FLORENCE: Daughter of Sarah Mountjoy, who intends her to marry her cousin, Mountjoy Scarborough; but Florence loves Harry Annesley, and despite all efforts to part them she marries him. *'She's not such a wonderful beauty, after all,' once said of her a gentleman, to whom it may be presumed that she had not taken the trouble to be peculiarly attractive. 'No,' said another; 'no. But, by George! I shouldn't like to have the altering of her.' It was thus that men generally felt in regard to Florence Mountjoy. When they came to reckon her up they did not see how any change was to be made for the better.* (Mr Scarborough's Family)

MOUNTJOY, LADY: Sir Magnus's wife. *There were those who declared that Lady Mountjoy was of all women the most over-bearing and impertinent. But they were generally English residents at Brussels, who had come to live there as a place at which education for their children would be cheaper than at home. Of these Lady Mountjoy had been heard to declare that she saw no reason why*

*because she was the minister's wife she should be expected to enter-
tain all the second-class world of London ... It cannot therefore be
said that Lady Mountjoy was popular; but she was large in figure,
and painted well, and wore her diamonds with an air which her
peculiar favourites declared to be majestic.* (*Mr Scarborough's
Family*)

MOUNTJOY, SIR MAGNUS: British Minister at Brussels who
entertains his niece Florence at his Legation for a period as
part of the scheme to detach her from Harry Annesley. *A stout,
tall, portly old gentleman, sixty years of age, but looking somewhat
older, whom it was a difficulty to place on horseback, but who,
when there, looked remarkably well. He rarely rose to a trot during
his two hours of exercise, which to the two attachés who were told
off for the duty of accompanying him, was the hardest part of their
allotted work. But other gentlemen would lay themselves out to meet
Sir Magnus and to ride with him, and in this way he achieved that
character for popularity which had been a better aid to him in life
than all the diplomatic skill which he possessed.* (*Mr Scarborough's
Family*)

MOUNTJOY, MRS SARAH: Florence's mother, sister of John and
Martha Scarborough. (*Mr Scarborough's Family*)

MUSSELBORO, AUGUSTUS: Partner with Dobbs Broughton
and Mrs van Siever in dubious financial activities, he marries
Mrs Broughton after her husband's suicide. (*The Last Chronicle
of Barset*)

NEEFIT, POLLY: Daughter of Thomas Neefit, a breeches-maker,
to whom Ralph (the heir) Newton is in debt. She refuses her
father's attempt to make her a lady through marriage with
Ralph, and chooses instead Ontario Moggs, a bootmaker's son
with ambitions towards poetry and politics. (*Ralph the Heir*)

NERONI, SIGNORA MADELINE: Younger daughter of Dr Stanhope. Crippled and deserted by her Italian husband, she returns
with her daughter Julia to her family and accompanies them
to Barchester, where her allurements prove to be Obadiah
Slope's downfall. *The beauty of her face was uninjured, and that
beauty was of a peculiar kind ... Her eyes were long and large,*

M

and marvellously bright; might I venture to say, bright as Lucifer's, I should perhaps best express the depth of their brilliancy. They were dreadful eyes to look at, such as would absolutely deter any man of quiet mind and easy spirit from attempting a passage of arms with such foes. There was talent in them, and the fire of passion and the play of wit, but there was no love. Cruelty was there instead, and courage, a desire of masterhood, cunning, and a wish for mischief. And yet, as eyes, they were very beautiful. (Barchester Towers)

NEVERBEND, JOHN: President of Britannula and narrator of the story. His wife is named Sarah, and his son is Jack, in love with Eva Crasweller. (*The Fixed Period*)

NEVILLE, FRED: Nephew and heir of the Earl of Scroope and brother of Jack Neville. Refusing to marry the high-born Sophia Mellerby, he seduces Kate O'Hara, a beautiful but poor girl living in Ireland where he is a cavalry lieutenant: she becomes pregnant. He succeeds to the title but will not marry her, and is murdered by her mother. (*An Eye for an Eye*)

NEVILLE, JACK: Fred's younger brother. He inherits the earldom at Fred's death and marries Sophia Mellerby. (*An Eye for an Eye*)

NEWTON, GREGORY: Owner of Newton Priory. He tries to buy out his heir, Ralph, from his inheritance in favour of his natural son, also named Ralph. (*Ralph the Heir*)

NEWTON, RALPH: Gregory Newton's heir, about to marry Polly Neefit when he is saved by his father's death and the consequent inheritance. (*Ralph the Heir*)

NEWTON, RALPH: Gregory Newton's natural son. He marries Mary Bonner, who has refused the legitimate Ralph Newton for love of the illegitimate one. (*Ralph the Heir*)

NIDDERDALE, LORD: Eldest son of the Marquis of Auld Reekie and cousin to the Duke of Omnium. He is a suitor for Marie Melmotte, but eventually marries the daughter of Lord Cantrip, another of the Duke's friends. *He had a commonplace, rough face, with a turn-up nose, high cheek bones, no especial complexion, sandy-coloured whiskers, and bright laughing eyes.* (*The Way We Live Now.*) He also appears in *The Duke's Children.*

NORMAN, HENRY (HARRY): Fellow clerk of Alaric Tudor in the Weights and Measures. He marries his cousin, Linda Woodward, and leaves the Civil Service on inheriting his family's estate. *He was, as a boy, somewhat shy and reserved in his manners, and as he became older he did not shake off the fault. He showed it, however, rather among men than with women, and, indeed, in spite of his love of exercise, he preferred the society of ladies to any of the bachelor gaieties of his unmarried acquaintance. He was, nevertheless, frank and confident in those he trusted, and true in his friendships, though, considering his age, too slow in making a friend.* (*The Three Clerks*)

O'HARA, KATE: An Irish girl seduced and left pregnant by Fred Neville. Her mother kills Fred and is condemned to an asylum, and Kate, who loses the child, goes to live in France with her father, who successfully blackmails Fred's family into making them a permanent allowance. (*An Eye for an Eye*)

O'KELLY FAMILY: Lord Ballindine (Frank) is its head; his mother is the Hon. Mrs O'Kelly; his sisters are Augusta and Sophia ('Guss' and 'Sophy'). (*The Kellys and the O'Kellys*)

O'MAHONY, RACHEL: Irish-American opera singer in love with Frank Jones. He will not marry her because of his poverty and she becomes engaged to her patron, Lord Castlewell, but when she loses her voice and career she returns to Frank. Her father, Gerald O'Mahony, is an advocate of the Landleaguers' cause. (*The Landleaguers*)

OMNIUM, DUKE OF (THE 'OLD DUKE'): Senior member of the Whig party and leading resident of Barsetshire. Uncle of Plantagenet Palliser. *He rarely went near the presence of majesty, and when he did so, he did it merely as a disagreeable duty incident to his position. He was very willing that the Queen should be queen so long as he was allowed to be Duke of Omnium . . . Their revenues were about the same, with the exception, that the duke's were his own, and he could do what he liked with them. This remembrance did not unfrequently present itself to the duke's mind. In person, he was a plain, thin man, tall, but undistinguished in appearance, except that there was a gleam of pride in his eye which seemed every moment to be saying, 'I am the Duke of Omnium.' He was unmarried, and, if report said true, a great debauchee; but if so he had always kept his debaucheries decently away from the eyes of the world.* (Doctor Thorne.) He also appears in *Framley Parsonage, The Small House at Allington, Can You Forgive Her?, Phineas Finn, The Eustace Diamonds* and *Phineas Redux*.

OMNIUM, DUKE and DUCHESS OF: See Palliser, Plantagenet and Glencora.

ONGAR, LORD: Julia Brabazon's elderly, debauched husband, who dies within a year of their marriage. *The Peerage said that he was thirty-six, and that, no doubt, was in truth his age, but anyone would have declared him to be ten years older ... He was, moreover, weak, thin, and physically poor, and had, no doubt, increased this weakness and poorness by hard living. Though others thought him old, time had gone swiftly with him, and he still thought himself a young man. He hunted, though he could not ride. He shot, though he could not walk. And, unfortunately, he drank, though he had no capacity for drinking! His friends at last had taught him to believe that his only chance of saving himself lay in marriage, and therefore he had engaged himself to Julia Brabazon, purchasing her at the price of a brilliant settlement.* (The Claverings)

ORIEL, REVD CALEB: Rector of Greshambury, where he lives with his sister Patience. He is loved by all the local girls, and, though 'not a marrying man', succumbs to Beatrice Gresham. *Mr Oriel was a man of family and fortune, who, having gone to Oxford with the usual views of such men, had become inoculated there with very high-church principles, and had gone into orders influenced by a feeling of enthusiastic love for the priesthood. He was by no means an ascetic – such men, indeed, seldom are – nor was he a devotee. He was a man well able, and certainly willing, to do the work of a parish clergyman; and when he became one, he was efficacious in his profession. But it may perhaps be said of him, without speaking slanderously, that his original calling, as a young man, was rather to the outward and visible signs of religion than to its inward and spiritual graces.* (*Doctor Thorne.*) He also appears in *The Last Chronicle of Barset.*

ORME, MRS EDITH: Widow of Sir Peregrine Orme's only son, Peregrine, and mother of Peregrine the younger. *She had been a great beauty, very small in size and delicate of limb, fair haired with soft blue wondering eyes, and a dimpled cheek. Such she had been when young Peregrine Orme brought her home to The Cleeve, and the bride at once became the darling of her father-in-law. One year she had owned of married joy, and then all the happiness of the family had been utterly destroyed ... All this happened now twenty years since, but the widow still wears the colours of mourning. Of her also the world of course said that she would soon console herself with a second love; but she too has given the world the lie.* (*Orley Farm*)

ORME, PEREGRINE: Son of Edith and grandson and heir of Sir Peregrine; sent down from Oxford for practical-joking. He is an unsuccessful suitor of Madeline Staveley. *The chief fault in the character of young Peregrine Orme was that he was so young. There are men who are old at one-and-twenty, – are quite fit for Parliament, the magistrate's bench, the care of a wife, and even for that much sterner duty, the care of a balance at the bankers; but there are others who at that age are still boys, – whose inner persons and characters have not begun to clothe themselves with the 'toga virilis'. . . . Mrs Orme, his mother, no doubt thought that he was perfect. Looking at the reflex of her own eyes in his, and seeing in his face so sweet a portraiture of the nose and mouth and forehead of him whom she had loved so dearly and lost so soon, she could not but think him perfect.* (*Orley Farm*)

ORME, SIR PEREGRINE: Aged owner of The Cleeve and lord of the manor of Hamworth, which embraces Orley Farm. Grandfather of Peregrine the younger. Loyal friend to Lady Mason despite her rejection of marriage and confession of her crime. *He was a fine, handsome English gentleman with white hair, keen gray eyes, a nose slightly aquiline, and lips now too closely pressed together in consequence of the havoc which time had made among his teeth. He was tall, but had lost something of his height from stooping, – was slight in his form, but well made, and vain of the smallness of his feet and the whiteness of his hands. He was generous, quick-tempered, and opinionated; generally very mild to those who would agree with him and submit to him, but intolerant of contradiction, and conceited as to his experience of the world and the wisdom which he had thence derived.* (Orley Farm)

OSBORNE, COLONEL FREDERIC, M.P.: An old friend of the Rowleys whose attentions towards Emily trigger off the manic jealousy of her young husband, Louis Trevelyan. *We all know the appearance of that old gentleman, how pleasant and dear a fellow he is, how welcome is his face within the gate, how free he makes with our wine, generally abusing it, how he tells our eldest daughter to light his candle for him, how he gave silver cups when the girls were born, and now bestows tea-services as they get married, – a most useful, safe, and charming fellow, not a year younger-looking or more nimble than ourselves, without whom life would be very blank. We all know that man; but such a man was not Colonel Osborne in the house of Mr Trevelyan's young bride.* (He Knew He Was Right)

PALLISER, ADELAIDE: Related to Plantagenet Palliser, she wishes to marry Gerard Maule, and is enabled to do so when the Duke of Omnium's bequest to Mme Goesler is passed on to her. *A tall, fair girl, exquisitely made, with every feminine grace of motion, highly born, and carrying always the warranty of her birth in her appearance; but with no special loveliness of face . . . She had resolved long since that the gift of personal loveliness had not been bestowed upon her. And yet after a fashion she was proud of her own appearance. She knew that she looked like a lady, and she knew also that she had all that command of herself which health and strength can give to a woman when she is without feminine affectation.* (Phineas Redux.) She also appears in *The Duke's Children*.

PALLISER, EUPHEMIA and IPHIGENIA THEODATA: Elderly cousins of Plantagenet Palliser. (*Can You Forgive Her?*)

PALLISER, LADY GLENCORA (*née* MacCluskie): Daughter of the Lord of the Isles and Plantagenet Palliser's heiress bride, she

becomes Duchess of Omnium when he succeeds to the duke-
dom. She is mother of Lord Silverbridge, Lord Gerald and
Lady Mary Palliser. *To love and fondle some one, – to be loved
and fondled, were absolutely necessary to her happiness. She wanted
the little daily assurance of her supremacy in the man's feelings, the
constant touch of love, half accidental half contrived, the passing
glance of the eye telling perhaps of some little joke understood only
between them two rather than of love, the softness of an occasional
kiss given here and there when chance might bring them together,
some half-pretended interest in her little doings, a nod, a wink, a
shake of the head, or even a pout. It should have been given to her
to feed upon such food as this daily, and then she would have forgotten
Burgo Fitzgerald. But Mr. Palliser understood none of these things;
and therefore the image of Burgo Fitzgerald in all his beauty was
ever before her eyes. (Can You Forgive Her?.)* She is a principal
figure throughout the Palliser series, and also appears in *The
Small House at Allington, The Last Chronicle of Barset, The
American Senator* and *Miss Mackenzie.*

PALLISER, PLANTAGENET: The character from whom the
Palliser series derives its name. He is heir to the Duke of
Omnium, whom he succeeds. He marries Lady Glencora
MacCluskie, and they have three children, Lord Silverbridge,
Lord Gerald and Lady Mary Palliser. A dedicated politician,
Palliser becomes Chancellor of the Exchequer, and, as Duke
of Omnium, Prime Minister of the coalition Government.
*He had wealth, position, power, and the certainty of attaining the
highest rank among, perhaps, the most brilliant nobility of the world.
He was courted by all who could get near enough to court him. It is
hardly too much to say that he might have selected a bride from all
that was most beautiful and best among English women. If he would
have bought race-horses, and have expended thousands on the turf,
he would have gratified his uncle by doing so. He might have been
the master of hounds, or the slaughterer of hecatombs of birds. But
to none of these things would he devote himself. He had chosen to
be a politician, and in that pursuit he laboured with a zeal and
perseverance which would have made his fortune at any profession*

*or in any trade. He was constant in committee-rooms up to the very
middle of August. He was rarely absent from any debate of importance, and never from any important division. Though he seldom
spoke, he was always ready to speak if his purpose required it. No
man gave him credit for any great genius – few even considered that
he could become either an orator or a mighty statesman. But the
world said that he was a rising man ... He was a thin-minded,
plodding, respectable man, willing to devote all his youth to work,
in order that in old age he might be allowed to sit among the Coun-
cillors of the State.* (*The Small House at Allington.*) He appears
throughout the Palliser series.

PARKER, SEXTUS ('SEXTY'): Ferdinand Lopez's partner in his
financial schemes. (*The Prime Minister*)

PATEROFF, COUNT EDOUARD: Brother of Sophie Gordeloup,
with whom he joins in sponging off Julia Brabazon after her
husband's death. *He was a fair man, with a broad, fair face, and
very light blue eyes; his forehead was low, but broad; he wore no
whiskers, but bore on his lip a heavy moustache, which was not
grey, but perfectly white – white it was with years, of course, but
yet it gave no sign of age to his face. He was well made, active, and
somewhat broad in the shoulders, though rather below the middle
height. But for a certain ease of manner which he possessed, accompanied by something of restlessness in his eye, anyone would have
taken him for an Englishman. And his speech hardly betrayed that
he was not English.* (*The Claverings*)

PEACOCKE, REVD HENRY: English president of an American
college, he marries the supposedly widowed Ella Lefroy, only
to discover soon after that her husband is still alive. Back in
England, working at Dr Wortle's school, Peacocke is approached by Lefroy's brother with an attempt at blackmail,
but Lefroy is learned to be dead at last. *A small, wiry man,
anything but robust in appearance, but still capable of great bodily
exertion. He was a great walker. Labour in the school never seemed
to fatigue him. The addition of a sermon to preach every week
seemed to make no difference to his energies in the school.* (*Dr
Wortle's School*)

PIE, SIR OMICRON: Fashionable London physician who attends leading characters in several of the works: e.g. *Barchester Towers, Doctor Thorne, The Prime Minister* and *The Bertrams.*

POPENJOY, LORD: Style of the son of the Marquis of Brotherton. (*Is He Popenjoy?*)

POPPLECOURT, LORD: The Duke of Omnium's unsuccessful choice as husband for his daughter Lady Mary Palliser. (*The Duke's Children*)

PORLOCK, LORD: Eldest son of Earl de Courcy. *All the sons and daughters were there, – excepting Lord Porlock, the eldest, who never met his father. The earl and Lord Porlock were not on terms, and indeed hated each other as only such fathers and such sons can hate.* (*The Small House at Allington.*) He also appears in *Doctor Thorne.*

PRENDERGAST, MR: Sir Thomas Fitzgerald's elderly lawyer whose energetic measures defeat the blackmailer, Mollett. *No one would have dreamed of calling Mr Prendergast an old man. He was short of stature, well made, and in good proportion; he was wiry, strong, and almost robust. He walked as though in putting his foot to the earth he always wished to proclaim that he was afraid of no man and no thing. His hair was grizzled, and his whiskers were grey, and round about his mouth his face was wrinkled; but with him even these things hardly seemed to be signs of old age. He was said by many who knew him to be a stern man, and there was that in his face which seemed to warrant such a character. But he had also the reputation of being a very just man; and those who knew him best could tell tales of him which proved that his sternness was at any rate compatible with a wide benevolence.* (*Castle Richmond*)

PRIME, MRS DOROTHEA: Widowed sister of Rachel Ray, with whom and their mother she lives. *She had ever been brown and homely, but her features had been well-formed, and her eyes had been bright. Now, as she approached to thirty years of age, she might have been as well-looking as at any earlier period of her life if it had been her wish to possess good looks. But she had had no such wish. On the contrary, her desire had been to be ugly, forbidding, unattractive, almost repulsive; so that, in very truth, she might be known to be a widow indeed. (Rachel Ray)*

PRONG, REVD SAMUEL: Evangelical clergyman at Baslehurst, interested in Dorothea Prime. *An energetic, severe, hardworking, and, I fear, intolerant young man, who bestowed very much laudable care upon his sermons. The care and industry were laudable, but not so the pride with which he thought of them and their results. He spoke much of preaching the Gospel, and was sincere beyond all doubt in his desire to do so; but he allowed himself to be led away into a belief that his brethren in the ministry around him did not preach the Gospel, – that they were careless shepherds, or shepherds' dogs indifferent to the wolf, and in this way he had made himself unpopular among the clergy and gentry of the neighbourhood. (Rachel Ray)*

PROSPER, PETER: Squire of Buston and uncle of Harry Annesley, his heir. He courts Matilda Thoroughbung until deterred by the domestic stipulations she makes for marriage. *He would have been young-looking for his age, but for an air of ancient dandyism which had grown upon him. He was somewhat dry, too, and skinny, with high cheek-bones and large dull eyes. But he was clean, and grave, and orderly, – a man promising well to a lady on the look-out for a husband. (Mr Scarborough's Family)*

PROUDIE, MRS: The bishop's wife who dominates him and the cathedral close until her death from apoplexy during the Crawley affair (*Last Chronicle*). *It was not only that she was a tyrant, a bully, a would-be priestess, a very vulgar woman, and one who would send headlong to the nethermost pit all who disagreed with her; but that at the same time she was conscientious, by no means a hypocrite, really believing in the brimstone which she threatened, and anxious to save the souls around her from its horrors. And as her tyranny increased so did the bitterness of the moments of her repentance increase, in that she knew herself to be a tyrant – till that bitterness killed her. Since her time others have grown up equally dear to me, – Lady Glencora and her husband, for instance; but I have never dissevered myself from Mrs Proudie, and still live much in company with her ghost. (Autobiography.)* She first appears in

Barchester Towers, then in the four succeeding works of the six. Her equivalent in the play *Did He Steal It?* is Mrs Goshawk.

PROUDIE, RT REVD DR THOMAS: Appointed bishop of Barchester in succession to Dr Grantly. He and his wife have a large family, among them Olivia, Augusta and Netta. *In person Dr Proudie is a good looking man, spruce and dapper, and very tidy. He is somewhat below middle height, being about five feet four, but he makes up for the inches which he wants by the dignity with which he carries those which he has. It is no fault of his own if he has not a commanding eye, for he studies hard to assume it. His features are well formed, though perhaps the sharpness of his nose may give to his face . . . an air of insignificance. If so, it is greatly redeemed by his mouth and chin, of which he is justly proud. (Barchester Towers.)* He also appears in the succeeding four novels, and in *The Claverings*. His equivalent in the play *Did He Steal It?* is the magistrate, Goshawk.

PUCKER, MISS: Gossip-spreading friend of Mrs Ray. *Rachel greatly disliked Miss Pucker. She disliked that lady's squint, she disliked the tone of her voice, she disliked her subservience to Mrs Prime, and she especially disliked the vehemence of her objection to – young men. (Rachel Ray)*

PUDDICOMBE, REVD: Neighbour and uncompromising adviser of Dr Wortle. (*Dr Wortle's School*)

QUIVERFUL, MRS LETITIA: The Revd Quiverful's wife, who becomes Matron of Hiram's Hospital when he is made Warden. *To her the outsides and insides of her husband and fourteen children were everything. In her bosom every other ambition had been swallowed up in that maternal ambition of seeing them and him and herself duly clad and properly fed. It had come to that with her that life had now no other purpose. (Barchester Towers.)* She also appears in *Framley Parsonage*.

QUIVERFUL, REVD: Vicar of Puddingdale and father of fourteen children. He is appointed Warden of Hiram's Hospital in succession to Septimus Harding. *Mr Quiverful was an honest, painstaking, drudging man; anxious, indeed, for bread and meat, anxious for means to quiet his butcher and cover with returning*

*smiles the now sour countenance of his baker's wife, but anxious
also to be right with his own conscience. He was not careful, as
another might be who sat on an easier worldly seat, to stand well
with those around him, to shun a breath which might sully his name,
or a rumour which might affect his honour. He could not afford such
niceties of conduct, such moral luxuries. It must suffice for him to be
ordinarily honest according to the ordinary honesty of the world's
ways, and to let men's tongues wag as they would.* (Barchester
Towers.) He also appears in *The Warden* and *The Last Chronicle
of Barset*.

RAY, MRS: Mother of Rachel and Dorothea (Prime). *She was a
woman all over, and had about her so much of a woman's prettiness,
that she had not altogether divested herself of it, even when her
weepers had been of the broadest. To obtain favour in men's eyes
had never been in her mind since she had first obtained favour in the
eyes of him who had been her lord; but yet she had never absolutely
divested herself of her womanly charms, of that look, half retreating,
half beseeching, which had won the heart of the ecclesiastical lawyer.
Gradually her weeds and her deep heavy crapes had fallen away
from her, and then, without much thought on the matter, she dressed
herself much as did other women of forty or forty-five.* (Rachel Ray)

RAY, RACHEL: Sister of Dorothea Prime; in love with Luke
Rowan, whom she eventually marries. *A fair-haired, well-
grown, comely girl, – very like her mother in all but this, that
whereas about the mother's eyes there was always a look of weakness,
there was a shadowing of coming strength of character round those of
the daughter. On her brow there was written a capacity for sustained
purpose which was wanting to Mrs Ray ... A little wickedness
now and then, to the extent, perhaps, of a vain walk into Baslehurst
on a summer evening, a little obstinacy in refusing to explain whither
she had been and whom she had seen, a yawn in church, or a word
of complaint as to the length of the second Sunday sermon, – these
were her sins; and when rebuked for them by her sister, she would
of late toss her head, and look slyly across to her mother, with an
eye that was not penitent.* (Rachel Ray)

REYNOLDS, JOE: Leader of the illegal potheen distillers and

plotter to kill Myles Ussher, who had arrested his brother Tim. (*The Macdermots of Ballycloran*)

RICHARDS, MRS: The three clerks' landlady, who is instrumental in getting help for Charley Tudor when he is arrested for debt. *To Mrs Richards herself Charley was not in debt, and she had therefore nothing to embitter her own feelings against him. Indeed, she had all that fondness for him which a lodging-house keeper generally has for a handsome, dissipated, easy-tempered young man.* (*The Three Clerks*)

ROANOKE, LUCINDA: American niece of Jane Carbuncle who traps her into marriage with Sir Griffin Tewett. She goes mad on her wedding day. (*The Eustace Diamonds*)

ROBARTS, BLANCHE: Eldest sister of Mark. She marries Squire Crowdy, of Creamclotted Hall, Devonshire, where her sister Jane lives with them. *Blanche had a bright complexion, and a fine neck, and a noble bust,* et vera incessu patuit Dea – *a true goddess, that is, as far as the eye went. She had a grand idea, moreover, of an apple-pie, and had not reigned eighteen months at Creamclotted Hall before she knew all the mysteries of pigs and milk, and most of those appertaining to cider and green geese.* (*Framley Parsonage*)

ROBARTS, FANNY (*née* MONSELL): Mark's wife. *If high principles without asperity, female gentleness without weakness, a love of laughter without malice, and a true loving heart, can qualify a woman to be a parson's wife, then was Fanny Monsell qualified to fill that tradition. In person she was somewhat larger than common. Her face would have been beautiful but that her mouth was large. Her hair, which was copious, was of a bright brown; her eyes also were brown, and, being so, were the distinctive feature of her face, for brown eyes are not common. They were liquid, large, and full either of tenderness or of mirth. Mark Robarts still had his accustomed luck, when such a girl as this was brought to Framley for his wooing.* (*Framley Parsonage*)

ROBARTS, JOHN (JACK): Mark's youngest brother. A Government clerk, promoted to private secretary to the Lord Petty Bag. *Jack Robarts had been a well-built, straight-legged, lissome young fellow, pleasant to the eye because of his natural advantages, but rather given to a harum-skarum style of gait, and occasionally careless, not to say slovenly, in his dress. But now he was the very pink of perfection. His jaunty frockcoat fitted him to perfection; not a hair of his head was out of place; his waistcoat and trousers were glossy and new, and his umbrella, which stood in the umbrella-stand in the corner, was tight and neat, and small, and natty. 'Well, John, you've become quite a great man,' said his brother.* (Framley Parsonage)

ROBARTS, LUCY: Mark's youngest sister, living with him and his wife at Framley Parsonage. Regarded by Lady Lufton as too 'insignificant' to marry her son, she proves her qualities by her devoted nursing of Mrs Crawley. *What eyes she had! ... Green, probably, for most eyes are green – green or grey, if green be thought uncomely for an eyecolour. But it was not their colour, but their fire, which struck one with such surprise. Lucy Robarts was thoroughly a brunette. Sometimes the dark tint of her cheeks was exquisitely rich and lovely, and the fringes of her eyes were soft and long, and her small teeth, which one so seldom saw, were white as pearls, and her hair, though short, was beautifully soft – by no means black, but yet of so dark a shade of brown.* (Framley Parsonage)

ROBARTS, REVD MARK: Brother of Gerald, John, Blanche (Crowdy), Jane and Lucy, Vicar of Framley, through the influence of Lady Lufton, he narrowly escapes ruin through financial involvement with Nathaniel Sowerby. *Much had been done to spoil him, but in the ordinary acceptation of the word he was not spoiled. He had too much tact, too much common sense, to believe himself to be the paragon which his mother thought him. Self-conceit was not, perhaps, his greatest danger. Had he possessed more of it, he might have been a less agreeable man, but his course before him might on that account have been the safer. In person he was manly, tall, and fair-haired, with a square forehead, denoting intelligence rather than thought.* (Framley Parsonage)

ROBINSON, GEORGE: An advertising enthusiast in partnership with Brown and Jones in their haberdashery enterprise. He is

Brisket's equally unsuccessful rival for Maryanne Brown. (*The Struggles of Brown, Jones, and Robinson*)

RODEN, GEORGE: A Post Office clerk, loved by Lady Frances Trafford, but disapproved of by her family. He becomes acceptable when it is revealed that he has inherited the Italian title of Duca di Crinola. (*Marion Fay*)

ROPER, AMELIA: Daughter of the London boarding-house keeper with whom Johnny Eames lodges. Jilted by him, she marries his fellow-boarder, Joseph Cradell. *A tall, well-grown young woman, with dark hair and dark eyes; – not handsome, for her nose was thick, and the lower part of her face was heavy, but yet not without some feminine attractions. Her eyes were bright; but then, also, they were mischievous. She could talk fluently enough; but then, also, she could scold. She could assume sometimes the plumage of a dove; but then again she could occasionally ruffle her feathers like an angry kite. I am quite prepared to acknowledge that John Eames should have kept himself clear of Amelia Roper; but then young men so frequently do those things which they should not do!* (*The Small House at Allington*)

ROUND and CROOK: Joseph Mason's attorneys in the Orley Farm trials. *Mr Crook had usually done the dirty work of the firm, having been originally a managing clerk; and he still did the same – in a small way. He had been the man to exact penalties, look after costs, and attend to any criminal business, or business partly criminal in its nature, which might chance to find its way to them. But latterly in all great matters Mr Round junior, Mr Matthew Round – his father was Richard – was the member of the firm on whom the world in general placed the greatest dependence.* (*Orley Farm*)

ROWAN, LUKE: Left an interest in the brewery of Bungall and Tappitt, he refuses to be bought out but takes over the firm, improves the product, and marries Rachel Ray. *He was a young man, by no means of a bad sort, meaning to do well, with high hopes in life, one who had never wronged a woman, or been untrue to a friend, full of energy and hope and pride. But he was conceited, prone to sarcasm, sometimes cynical, and perhaps sometimes affected. It may be that he was not altogether devoid of that Byronic weakness which was so much more prevalent among young men twenty years since than it is now. His two trades had been those of an attorney and a brewer, and yet he dabbled in romance, and probably wrote poetry in his bedroom. Nevertheless, there were worse young men about Baslehurst than Luke Rowan.* (Rachel Ray)

ROWAN, MARY: Luke's sister, for whom the Tappitt family give a ball. *Very willing to be pleased, with pleasant round eager eyes, and a kindly voice.* (Rachel Ray)

ROWAN, MRS: Mother of Luke and Mary, she disapproves of his love for Rachel Ray and connives with Mrs Ray to try to end their association. *A somewhat stately lady, slow in her movements and careful in her speech, so that the girls were at first very glad that they had valiantly worked up their finery before her coming.* (Rachel Ray)

ROWLEY, EMILY: Sister of Nora and one of the eight daughters of Sir Marmaduke Rowley, Governor of the Mandarin Islands, she marries Louis Trevelyan, who becomes jealous of her friendship with Colonel Osborne and abducts their infant son Louey. *She was very strong, as are some girls who come from the tropics, and whom a tropical climate has suited. She could sit on her horse the whole day long, and would never be weary with dancing at the Government House balls.* (He Knew He Was Right)

ROWLEY, NORA: Emily's sister and companion after her marriage. After a struggle with her sensibilities, she rejects the wealthy Charles Glascock for the impecunious Hugh Stanbury. *Her education had been of that nature which teaches girls to believe that it is a crime to marry a man without an assured income. Assured morality in a husband is a great thing. Assured good temper is very excellent. Assured talent, religion, amiability, truth, honesty, are all desirable. But an assured income is indispensable.* (He Knew He Was Right)

RUBB, SAMUEL jnr: One of Margaret Mackenzie's suitors, the son of her brother Tom's partner. He swindles her out of some of her money but then falls in love with her, though in vain. *Mr Rubb carried with him an air of dignity, and had about*

his external presence a something of authority . . . as Miss Macken-
zie said to herself, there was certainly no knowing that he belonged
to the oil-cloth business from the cut of his coat or the set of his
trousers. (Miss Mackenzie)

RUFFORD, LORD: Sporting landowner in unsuccessful pursuit
of whom Arabella Trefoil jilts her fiancé John Morton. Arabella's mother charges him with breach of promise when he
will not propose, and he is relieved to escape into marriage
with Caroline Penge. (*The American Senator.*) He also appears
in *Ayala's Angel.*

ST BUNGAY, DUCHESS OF: Wife of the Duke and an aunt of
Lady Laura Standish. *No breath of slander had ever touched her*
name. I doubt if any man alive had ever had the courage even to
wink at her since the Duke had first called her his own. Nor was
she a spendthrift, or a gambler. She was not fast in her tastes, or
given to any pursuit that was objectionable. She was simply a fool,
and as a fool was ever fearing that she was the mark of ridicule.
(Can You Forgive Her?)

ST BUNGAY, DUKE OF: A senior politician, sometime President
of the Council, prominent throughout the Palliser novels.
He was a minister of very many years' standing, being as used to
cabinet sittings as other men are to their own arm-chairs; but he had
never been a hard-working man. Though a constant politician, he
had ever taken politics easy whether in office or out. The world had
said before now that the Duke might be Premier, only that he would
not take the trouble . . . He was never reckless in politics, and never
cowardly. He snubbed no man, and took snubbings from no man.
He was a Knight of the Garter, a Lord Lieutenant of his county,
and at sixty-two had his digestion unimpaired and his estate in
excellent order. He was a great buyer of pictures, which, perhaps,
he did not understand, and a great collector of books which certainly
he never read. All the world respected him, and he was a man to
whom the respect of all the world was as the breath of his nostrils.
(Can You Forgive Her?)

SAUL, REVD SAMUEL: The Revd Henry Clavering's unprepossess-
sing curate, he becomes Rector of Clavering and marries Fanny

N

Clavering. *Mr Saul was very tall and very thin, with a tall thin head, and weak eyes, and a sharp, well-cut nose, and, so to say, no lips, and very white teeth, with no beard, and a well-cut chin. His face was so thin that his cheekbones obtruded themselves unpleasantly. He wore a long rusty black coat, and a high rusty black waistcoat, and trousers that were brown with dirty roads and general ill-usage. Nevertheless, it never occurred to anyone that Mr Saul did not look like a gentleman, not even to himself, to whom no ideas whatever on that subject ever presented themselves. But that he was a gentleman I think he knew well enough, and was able to carry himself before Sir Hugh and his wife with quite as much ease as he could do in the rectory. (The Claverings)*

SCARBOROUGH, AUGUSTUS: John's younger son and brother of Mountjoy. His father's declaration of Mountjoy's illegitimacy makes Augustus heir, but he so displeases his parent that he is deprived of the inheritance again. *He had been called but two years when the story was made known of his father's singular assertion. As from that time it became unnecessary for him to practise his profession, no more was heard of him as a lawyer. But they who had known the young man in the chambers of that great luminary, Mr Rugby, declared that a very eminent advocate was now spoilt by a freak of fortune. (Mr Scarborough's Family)*

SCARBOROUGH, JOHN: Owner of Tretton Park, Hertfordshire, whose ingenious scheme for ensuring that it is inherited by whichever of his sons, Mountjoy or Augustus, is best fitted to cherish it is the theme of the story. He is brother to Martha Scarborough and Sarah Mountjoy. *He was luxurious and self-indulgent, and altogether indifferent to the opinion of those around him. But he was affectionate to his children, and anxious above all things for their welfare, or rather happiness. Some marvellous stories were told as to his income, which arose chiefly from the Tretton delf-works and from the town of Tretton, which had been built chiefly on his very park, in consequence of the nature of the clay and the quality of the water. (Mr Scarborough's Family)*

SCARBOROUGH, MARTHA: Spinster sister of John Scarborough

and Sarah Mountjoy, living with her brother at Tretton Park.
(*Mr Scarborough's Family*)

SCARBOROUGH, CAPTAIN MOUNTJOY: John's elder son and
brother of Augustus. His father announces his illegitimacy
when he seems unfit to inherit his estate, but later ensures that
he becomes sole heir. *Mountjoy was dark-visaged, with coal-
black whiskers and moustaches, with sparkling angry eyes, and
every feature of his face well cut and finely formed, But there was
absent from him all look of contentment or satisfaction.* (*Mr Scarborough's Family*)

SCATCHERD, LADY: Wife of Sir Roger and mother of Louis
Philippe, she had acted as foster-mother to Frank Gresham.
*Lady Scatcherd was no fit associate for the wives of English baronets;
– was no doubt by education and manners much better fitted to sit in
their servants' halls; but not on that account was she a bad wife or a
bad woman. She was painfully, fearfully anxious for that husband
of hers, whom she honoured and worshipped, as it behoved her to do,
above all other men.* (*Doctor Thorne.*) She also appears in *Framley
Parsonage.*

SCATCHERD, LOUIS-PHILIPPE: Sir Roger's only son and heir.
Expelled from Eton and Cambridge, he succeeds to his father's
estate and title soon after coming of age, but dies of drink
within a few months. *He was acute, crafty, knowing, and up to
every damnable dodge practised by men of the class with whom he
lived. At one-and-twenty he was that most odious of all odious
characters – a close-fisted reprobate. He was a small man, not ill-
made by Nature, but reduced to unnatural tenuity by dissipation . . .
His hair was dark red, and he wore red moustaches, and a great
deal of red beard beneath his chin, cut in a manner to make him
look like an American. His voice also had a Yankee twang, being a
cross between that of an American trader and an English groom;
and his eyes were keen and fixed, and cold and knowing.* (*Doctor
Thorne*)

SCATCHERD, MARY: Roger Scatcherd's sister, mother of Mary
Thorne, having been seduced by Henry Thorne, who is killed
for it by her brother. She marries a workman named

Tomlinson, who takes her to America, leaving the child to be brought up by Dr Thorne. (*Doctor Thorne*)

SCATCHERD, SIR ROGER: Killer of Henry Thorne, who had seduced Scatcherd's sister Mary, he becomes a millionaire after leaving prison and gains control of much of the Gresham estates. He dies of drink. *While conquering the world Roger Scatcherd had not conquered his old bad habits. Indeed, he was the same man at all points that he had been when formerly seen about the streets of Barchester with his stonemason's apron tucked up around his waist. The apron he had abandoned, but not the heavy prominent thoughtful brow, with the wildly-flashing eye beneath it. He was still the same good companion, and still also the same hardworking hero. In this only had he changed, that now he would work, and some said equally well, whether he were drunk or sober.* (*Doctor Thorne*)

SCOTT, HON. UNDECIMUS ('UNDY'), M.P.: Son of Lord Gaberlunzie, brother of Val, and M.P. for the Tillietudlum district of Scotland. He involves Alaric Tudor in his crooked financial dealings and causes his downfall. *The one strong passion of his life was the desire of a good income at the cost of the public. He had an easy way of getting intimate with young men when it suited him, and as easy a way of dropping them afterwards when that suited him. He had no idea of wasting his time or opportunities in friendships.* (*The Three Clerks*)

SCOTT, CAPTAIN THE HON. VALENTINE: Brother of 'Undy'. He marries Clementina Golightly's widowed mother for her money. *He had not Undy's sharpness, his talent for public matters, or his aptitude for the higher branches of the Civil Service; but he had wit to wear his sash and epaulets with an easy grace, and to captivate the heart, person, and some portion of the purse, of the Widow Golightly. The lady was ten years older than the gentleman; but then she had a thousand a-year.* (*The Three Clerks*)

SCOTT, HON. MRS VALENTINE: Remarried widow of Jonathan Golightly and mother of Clementina. *Mrs Val Scott as she was commonly called, was a very pushing woman ... To tell the truth, Mrs Val, who had in her day encountered, with much patience, a good deal of snubbing, and who had had to be thankful when she was patronised, now felt that her day for being a great lady had come, and that it behoved her to patronise others.* (*The Three Clerks*)

SCROOPE, LADY MARY: Second wife of the Earl of Scroope, whom she induces to get Fred Neville to promise that he will not marry Kate O'Hara. (*An Eye for an Eye*)

SCRUBY, MR: George Vavasor's unscrupulous election agent. *An attorney from Great Marlborough Street, supposed to be very knowing in the ways of metropolitan elections.* (*Can You Forgive Her?*)

SENTIMENT, MR POPULAR: A widely-read novelist; a caricature of Charles Dickens. (*The Warden*)

SHAND, DICK: John Caldigate's friend from Cambridge days who partners him in the Australian gold-mining venture, but drinks too much and disappears. He returns to England just in time to gain John's release from prison by producing vital evidence. (*John Caldigate*)

SLIDE, QUINTUS: Editor of the scandal-mongering newspaper *People's Banner. Mr Quintus Slide was certainly well adapted for his work. He could edit his paper with a clear appreciation of the kind of matter which would best conduce to its success, and he could write telling leading articles himself. He was indefatigable, unscrupulous, and devoted to his paper. Perhaps his great value was shown most clearly in his distinct appreciation of the low line of public virtue with which his readers would be satisfied. A highly-wrought moral strain would he knew well create either disgust or ridicule. 'If there is any beastliness I 'ate it is 'igh-faluting,' he has been heard to say to his underlings.* (*Phineas Redux*)

SLOPE, REVD OBADIAH: Bishop Proudie's domestic chaplain and Mrs Proudie's rival for dominance over cathedral affairs. His infatuation for Madeline Neroni is his undoing and he is dismissed, later marrying a rich widow and occupying a living in London. *His hair is lank, and of a dull pale reddish hue. It is always formed into three straight lumpy masses, each brushed with admirable precision, and cemented with much grease . . . His face is nearly the same colour as his hair, though perhaps a little redder; it is not unlike beef, – beef, however, one would say, of a bad quality. His forehead is capacious and high, but square and heavy, and unpleasantly shining. His mouth is large, though his lips are thin and bloodless; and his big, prominent, pale brown eyes inspire anything but confidence. His nose, however, is his redeeming feature: it is pronounced, straight, and well-formed; though I myself should like it better did it not possess a somewhat spongy, porous appearance, as though it had been cleverly formed out of red coloured cork. (Barchester Towers.)* He also appears in *Framley Parsonage.*

SLOW and BIDEAWHILE: Adolphus Longestaffe's family lawyers. *Piqued themselves on the decorous and orderly transaction of their business. It had grown to be a rule in the house that anything done quickly must be done badly. (The Way We Live Now.)* They also act for clients in *Framley Parsonage, Orley Farm, Miss Mackenzie,* and *He Knew He Was Right.*

SMILER, MR: Well-known thief sentenced for stealing the Eustace diamonds. *A gentleman for whom the whole police of London entertained a feeling which approached to veneration. (The Eustace Diamonds)*

SMILEY, MRS MARIA: Widowed owner of brickfields and friend of Mrs Moulder, who pushes her reluctant brother John Kenneby into marriage with the widow. *Mrs Smiley was a firm set, healthy-looking woman of about forty. She had large, dark, glassy eyes, which were bright without sparkling. Her cheeks were very red, having a fixed settled colour that never altered with circumstances. Her black wiry hair was ended in short crisp curls, which sat close to her head. It almost collected like a wig, but the hair was in truth her own. Her mouth was small, and her lips thin, and they gave to her face a look of sharpness that was not quite agreeable. Nevertheless she was not a bad-looking woman, and with such advantages as two hundred a year and the wardrobe which Mrs Moulder had described, was no doubt entitled to look for a second husband. (Orley Farm)*

SMITH, MRS EUPHEMIA: An actress ('Mademoiselle Cettini') and adventuress with whom John Caldigate lives for a time in Australia. She and Tim Crinkett, a former mining partner of

John's, blackmail him and get him convicted of bigamy, but are foiled when the trick by which they have achieved it is revealed. (*John Caldigate*)

SMITH, HAROLD, M.P.: Brother-in-law of Nathaniel Sowerby. An ambitious politician, he achieves minor Ministerial posts. *Harold, in early life, had intended himself for the cabinet; and if working hard at his trade could ensure success, he ought to obtain it sooner or later. He had already filled more than one subordinate station, had been at the Treasury, and for a month or two at the Admiralty, astonishing official mankind by his diligence ... Mr Harold Smith was not personally a popular man with any party, though some judged him to be eminently useful. He was laborious, well-informed, and, on the whole, honest; but he was conceited, long-winded, and pompous.* (*Framley Parsonage*.) He also appears in *The Last Chronicle of Barset*.

SMITH, MRS HAROLD: Nathaniel Sowerby's sister, married to the above. *She was a clever, bright woman, good-looking for her time of life – and she was now over forty – with a keen sense of the value of all worldly things, and a keen relish for all the world's pleasures. She was neither laborious, nor well-informed, nor perhaps altogether honest – what woman ever understood the necessity or recognized the advantage of political honesty? – but then she was neither dull nor pompous, and if she was conceited, she did not show it.* (*Framley Parsonage*.) She also appears in *The Last Chronicle of Barset*.

SNAPE, THOMAS: Head clerk of the Internal Navigation Office. *Poor Mr Snape had selected for his own peculiar walk in life a character for evangelical piety ... He was not by nature an ill-natured man, but he had become by education harsh to those below him, and timid and cringing with those above.* (*The Three Clerks*)

SNOW, MARY: Daughter of a drunken engraver, she is taken up by Felix Graham, who tries unsuccessfully to educate her into a suitable wife for himself. She marries Albert Fitzallen, an apothecary, whose love for her is more spontaneous. *He* [Felix Graham] *was one of those few wise men who have determined not to take a partner in life at hazard, but to mould a young mind and*

*character to those pursuits and modes of thought which may best fit a
woman for the duties she will have to perform ... He had found
her pretty, halfstarved, dirty, ignorant, and modest; and so finding
her had made himself responsible for feeding, cleaning, and teaching
her, – and ultimately for marrying her. (Orley Farm)*

SOWERBY, NATHANIEL, M.P.: Owner of Chaldicotes, which he
has mortgaged to meet his gambling debts. He almost ruins
Mark Robarts by getting him to guarantee loans to help his
unsuccessful attempts to marry the heiress Martha Dunstable.
*Mr Sowerby was one of those men who are known to be very
poor – as poor as debt can make a man – but who, nevertheless,
enjoy all the luxuries which money can give ... Such companions
are very dangerous. There is no cholera, no yellow-fever, no small-
pox, more contagious than debt. If one lives habitually among
embarrassed men, one catches it to a certainty. No one had injured
the community in this way more fatally than Mr Sowerby. But
still he carried on the game himself. (Framley Parsonage)*

SPARKES, MRS CONWAY: A literary lady in Palliser circles. She
appears in *Can You Forgive Her?, Phineas Finn* and *Miss
Mackenzie.*

SPOONER, THOMAS PLATTER: Owner of Spoon Hall, near the
Chilterns' estate. Adelaide Palliser refuses to marry him, and
he later marries a Miss Leatherside. *He was still a young man,
only just turned forty, and was his own master in everything. He
could read, and he always looked at the country newspaper; but a
book was a thing that he couldn't bear to handle. (Phineas Redux.)*
He also appears in *The Duke's Children.*

SQUERCUM, MR: Adolphus Longestaffe's lawyer, of whom his
father stands in much awe. *He had established himself, without
any predecessors and without a partner, and we may add without
capital, at a little office in Fetter Lane, and had there made a
character for getting things done after a marvellous and new fashion ...
He did sharp things no doubt, and had no hesitation in supporting the
interests of sons against those of their fathers. (The Way We Live
Now)*

STANBURY, DOROTHY: Hugh Stanbury's younger sister. Refusing to be married off by her aunt to a clergyman, she insists on her own choice, Brooke Burgess, whose uncle had left Jemima Stanbury his fortune. (*He Knew He Was Right*)

STANBURY, HUGH: Jemima Stanbury's journalist nephew and brother of Dorothy Stanbury. He is the successful rival of Charles Glascock for Nora Rowley. *Reputed to be somewhat hot in spirit and manner. He would be very sage in argument, pounding down his ideas on politics, religion, or social life with his fist as well as his voice. He was quick, perhaps, at making antipathies, and quick, too, in making friendships; impressionable, demonstrative, eager, rapid in his movements, – sometimes to the great detriment of his shins and knuckles; and he possessed the sweetest temper that was ever given to a man for the blessing of a woman.* (*He Knew He Was Right*)

STANBURY, JEMIMA ('AUNT STANBURY'): Spinster aunt of Hugh and Dorothy. She cuts off Hugh for becoming a journalist and endeavours to prevent the marriage of Dorothy to Brooke Burgess, the son of her own former lover. *She was a little woman, now nearly sixty years of age, with bright grey eyes, and a strong Roman nose, and thin lips, and a sharp-cut chin. She wore a head-gear that almost amounted to a mob-cap, and beneath it her grey hair was always frizzled with the greatest care. Her dress was invariably of black silk, and she had five gowns, – one for church, one for evening parties, one for driving out, and one for evenings at home and one for mornings. The dress, when new, always went to church. Nothing, she was wont to say, was too good for the Lord's house.* (*He Knew He Was Right*)

STANDISH, LADY LAURA: Daughter of the Earl of Brentford and sister of Lord Chiltern. She assists Phineas Finn in his political rise, but, though she loves him, will not marry him since neither of them has a fortune. She makes an unhappy marriage with Robert Kennedy and after his death hopes in vain that Phineas Finn will now marry her, becoming an embittered recluse when he does not. *Phineas had declared at Killaloe that Lady Laura was six feet high, that she had red hair, that her figure was straggling, and that her hands and feet were large. She was in fact about five feet seven in height, and she carried her height well. There was something of nobility in her gait, and she seemed thus to be taller than her inches. Her hair was in truth red, – of a deep thorough redness . . . She never straggled when she stood or walked; but she would lean forward when sitting, as a man does, and would use her arms in talking, and would put her hand over her face, and pass her fingers through her hair, – after the fashion of men rather than of women; – and she seemed to despise that soft quiescence of her sex in which are generally found so many charms. (Phineas Finn.)* She also appears in *Phineas Redux.*

STANHOPE, CHARLOTTE: Dr Stanhope's elder daughter. *The influence which she had in her family, though it had been used to a certain extent for their worldly well-being, had not been used to their real benefit, as it might have been. She had aided her father in his indifference to his professional duties . . . She had encouraged her mother in her idleness in order that she herself might be mistress and manager of the Stanhope household. She had encouraged and fostered the follies of her sister, though she was always willing, and often able, to protect her from their probable result. She had done her best, and had thoroughly succeeded in spoiling her brother, and turning him loose upon the world an idle man without a profession, and without a shilling that he could call his own. (Barchester Towers)*

STANHOPE, ETHELBERT ('BERTIE'): Dr Stanhope's son. He proposes in vain to Eleanor Harding. *He was certainly very handsome . . . He was habitually addicted to making love to ladies, and did so without any scruple of conscience, or any idea that such a practice was amiss. He had no heart to touch himself, and was literally unaware that humanity was subject to such an infliction . . . All people were nearly alike to him. He was above, or rather below, all prejudices. No virtue could charm him, no vice shock him. He had about him a natural good manner, which seemed to qualify him for the highest circles, and yet he was never out of place in the lowest. He had no principle, no regard for others, no self-respect, no desire to be other than a drone in the hive, if only he could, as a drone, get what honey was sufficient for him. (Barchester Towers)*

STANHOPE, MADELINE. See NERONI, MADELINE.

STANHOPE, MRS: Dr Stanhope's wife, mother of Ethelbert, Charlotte and Madeline (Neroni). *The far niente of her Italian life had entered into her very soul, and brought her to regard a state of inactivity as the only earthly good . . . When we have said that Mrs Stanhope knew how to dress, and used her knowledge daily, we have said all. Other purpose in life she had none. (Barchester Towers)*

STANHOPE, REVD VESEY, D.D.: Absentee rector of Crabtree Canonicorum and of Stoke Pinquium, living in Italy. Father of Ethelbert, Charlotte and Madeline (Neroni). *He was a good looking rather plethoric gentleman of about sixty years of age . . . His reading seldom went beyond romances and poetry of the lightest and not always most moral description. He was thoroughly a* bon vivant; *an accomplished judge of wine, though he never drank to excess; and a most inexorable critic in all affairs touching the kitchen. He had had much to forgive in his own family, since a family had grown up around him, and had forgiven everything – except inattention to his dinner. His weakness in that respect was now fully understood, and his temper was but seldom tried. As Dr Stanhope was a clergyman, it may be supposed that his religious convictions made up a considerable part of his character; but this was not so. That he had religious convictions must be believed; but he rarely obtruded them, even on his children. (Barchester Towers.)* He also appears in *Doctor Thorne* and *Framley Parsonage.*

STANTILOUP, HON. MRS JULIANA: Smarting from losing a lawsuit with Dr Wortle, she spreads scandal about the Peacockes which comes close to ruining the school. *A lady who liked all the best things which the world could supply, but hardly liked paying the best price. Dr Wortle's school was the best thing the world could supply of that kind, but then the price was certainly the very best. Young Stantiloup was only eleven, and as there were boys at Bowick as old as seventeen – for the school had not altogether maintained its old character as being merely preparatory – Mrs Stantiloup had thought that her boy should be admitted at a lower fee. (Dr Wortle's School)*

STAPLEDEAN, MARQUIS OF: Of Bowes Lodge, Westmorland,

he is patron of the living of Hurst Staple, Somerset, to which
he appoints Arthur Wilkinson on conditions which preclude
him from marrying Adela Gauntlet. *He was, in fact, about
fifty; but he looked to be at least fifteen years older. It was evident
from his face that he was a discontented, moody, unhappy man. He
was one who had not used the world over well; but who was quite
self-assured that the world had used him shamefully. He was not
without good instincts, and had been just and honest in his dealings –
except in those with his wife and children. But he believed in the
justness and honesty of no one else, and regarded all men as his
enemies – especially those of his own flesh and blood. (The Bertrams)*

STAUBACH, MADAME CHARLOTTE: Linda Tressel's aunt with
whom she lives in Nuremberg and who tries to arrange her
unwanted marriage with Peter Steinmarc. (*Linda Tressel*)

STAVELEY, AUGUSTUS: Brother of Madeline and Isabella
(Arbuthnot). Friend of Felix Graham and one of Sophia
Furnival's suitors. *A handsome clever fellow, who had nearly
succeeded in getting the Newdegate, and who was now a member of
the Middle Temple. He was destined to follow the steps of his father,
and become a light at the Common Law bar; but hitherto he had not
made much essential progress ... His chambers were luxuriously
furnished, he had his horse in Piccadilly, his father's house at
Noningsby was always open to him, and the society of London
spread out for him all its allurements. Under such circumstances how
could it be expected that he should work? Nevertheless he did talk
of working, and had some idea in his head of the manner in which
he would do so. (Orley Farm)*

STAVELEY, JUDGE and LADY ISABELLA: Parents of Augustus,
who briefly woos Sophia Furnival; of Isabella Arbuthnot,
whose daughter Marion admires Felix Grahan; and of Madeline Staveley. *One of the best men in the world, revered on the
bench, and loved by all men; but he had not sufficient parental
sternness to admit of his driving his son well into harness. He himself
had begun the world with little or nothing, and had therefore succeeded; but his son was already possessed of almost everything that he
could want, and therefore his success seemed doubtful. (Orley Farm)*

STAVELEY, MADELINE: The Judge's daughter, wooed by Peregrine Orme and Felix Graham, to whom she becomes engaged.
*She smiled with her whole face. There was at such moments a
peculiar laughing light in her gray eyes, which inspired one with an
earnest desire to be in her confidence; she smiled with her soft cheek,
the light tints of which would become a shade more pink from the
excitement, as they softly rippled into dimples; she smiled with her
forehead which would catch the light from her eyes and arch itself
in its glory; but above all she smiled with her mouth, just showing,
but hardly showing, the beauty of the pearls within. I never saw
the face of a woman whose mouth was equal in pure beauty, in
beauty that was expressive of feeling, to that of Madeline Staveley.*
(*Orley Farm*)

STEINMARC, PETER: Elderly Nuremberg clerk who refuses to
marry Linda Tressel after her elopement with Ludovic Valcarm. (*Linda Tressel*)

STUBBS, COLONEL JONATHAN: An army officer, in appearance
an unlikely candidate for Ayala Dormer's 'Angel of Light',
but whom she marries at last, partly through the efforts of his
cousins, the Marchesa Baldoni, and her sister, Lady Albury.
(*Ayala's Angel*)

SUPPLEHOUSE, MR, M.P.: Journalist member of the Chaldicotes
set, on the staff of the *Jupiter* newspaper and ambitious for
political power. *Had been extolled during the early days of that
Russian war by some portion of the metropolitan daily presss, as
the only man who could save the country. Let him be in the ministry,
the* Jupiter *had said, and there would be some hope of reform, some
chance that England's ancient glory would not be allowed in these
perilous times to go headlong to oblivion. And upon this the ministry,
not anticipating much salvation from Mr Supplehouse, but willing,
as they usually are, to have the* Jupiter *at their back, did send for
that gentleman, and gave him some footing among them. But how
can a man born to save a nation, and to lead a people, be content to
fill the chair of an under-secretary? Supplehouse was not content.*
(*Framley Parsonage*)

TAPPITT, THOMAS: Surviving partner of Bungall and Tappitt,

o

Baslehurst brewers, forced into reluctant partnership with Luke Rowan. His wife is named Margaret and they have three spinster daughters, Augusta, Martha and Cherry. *It was a very bitter time for the poor brewer. He was one of those men whose spirit is not wanting to them while the noise and tumult of contest are around them, but who cannot hold on by their own convictions in the quiet hours. He could storm, and talk loud, and insist in his own way while men stood around him, listening and perhaps admiring; but he was cowed when left by himself to think of things which seemed to be adverse.* (*Rachel Ray*)

TEMPEST, REVD MORTIMER, D.D.: Rector of Silverbridge and chairman of the ecclesiastical commission to examine Josiah Crawley. His refusal to be influenced by Mrs Proudie finally breaks her will. *Dr Tempest was well known among his parishioners to be hard and unsympathetic; some said unfeeling also, and cruel; but it was admitted by those who disliked him most that he was both practical and just, and that he cared for the welfare of many, though he was rarely touched by the misery of one.* (*The Last Chronicle of Barset*.) He also appears in *The Duke's Children*.

TEWETT, SIR GRIFFIN: Young baronet to whom Jane Carbuncle arranges to marry Lucinda Roanoke. (*The Eustace Diamonds*)

THORNE, DR THOMAS: Greshambury doctor who brings up his brother Henry's illegitimate daughter Mary and is the catalyst in the affairs of the Greshams and Scatcherds. He marries Martha Dunstable. *He was brusque, authoritative, given to contradiction, rough though never dirty in his personal belongings, and inclined to indulge in a sort of quiet raillery, which sometimes was not thoroughly understood. People did not always know whether he was laughing at them or with them; and some people were, perhaps, inclined to think that a doctor should not laugh at all when called in to act doctorially. When he was known, indeed, when the core of the fruit had been reached, when the huge proportions of that loving, trusting heart had been learned, and understood, and appreciated, when that honesty had been recognised, that manly, and almost womanly tenderness had been felt, then, indeed, the doctor was acknowledged to be adequate to his profession. To trifling ailments he was too often brusque. Seeing that he accepted money for the cure of such, he should, we may say, have cured them without an offensive manner. So far he is without defence. But to real suffering no one found him brusque; no patient lying painfully on a bed of sickness ever thought him rough.* (*Doctor Thorne.*) He also appears in *Framley Parsonage* and *The Last Chronicle of Barset.*

THORNE, HENRY: Dr Thorne's dissolute brother. He seduces Mary Scatcherd, which results in the birth of her daughter Mary (Thorne) and is killlled by her brother Roger before the story proper begins. (*Doctor Thorne*)

THORNE, MARY: Henry Thorne's illegitimate daughter by Mary Scatcherd, brought up by Dr Thorne as his own daughter. She inherits the Scatcherd fortunes and marries Frank Gresham. *I know that she was far from being tall, and far from being showy; that her feet and hands were small and delicate; that her eyes were bright when looked at, but not brilliant so as to make their brilliancy palpably visible to all around her; her hair was dark brown, and worn very plainly brushed from her forehead; her lips were thin, and her mouth, perhaps, in general inexpressive, but when she was eager in conversation it would show itself to be animated with curves of wondrous energy; and, quiet as she was in manner, sober and demure as was her usual settled appearance, she could talk, when the fit came on her, with an energy which in truth surprised those who did not know her; ay, and sometimes those who did.* (*Doctor Thorne.*) She also appears in *Framley Parsonage.*

THORNE, MONICA: Wilfred Thorne's spinster sister; proud, snobbish and ten years his senior, she lives with him at Ullathorne Court. *To her all modern English names were equally insignificant: Hengist, Horsa, and such like, had for her ears the only true savour of nobility. She was not contented unless she could go beyond the Saxons; and would certainly have christened her children, had she had children, by the names of the ancient Britons.* (*Barchester Towers.*) She also appears in *Doctor Thorne* and *The Last Chronicle of Barset.*

THORNE, WILFRED: High Tory bachelor squire of St Ewold's, living at Ullathorne Court with his sister Monica. He is cousin to Dr Thorne and Henry Thorne, until the latter's behaviour causes an estrangement. *It would be unjust to say that he looked down on men whose families were of recent date. He did not do so. He frequently consorted with such, and had chosen many of his friends from among them. But he looked on them as great millionaires are apt to look on those who have small incomes; as men who have Sophocles at their fingers' ends regard those who know nothing of Greek.* (*Barchester Towers.*) He also appears in *Doctor Thorne, Framley Parsonage* and *The Last Chronicle of Barset.*

THOROUGHBUNG, MATILDA: Spinster member of the Buston brewing family, courted by Peter Prosper. *Miss Thoroughbung was fat, fair, and forty to the letter, and she had a just measure of her own good looks, of which she was not unconscious. But she was specially conscious of twenty-five thousand pounds, the possession of which had hitherto stood in the way of her search for a husband. It was said commonly about Buntingford that she looked too high, seeing that she was only a Thoroughbung.* (*Mr Scarborough's Family*)

THUMBLE, REVD CALEB: Sycophant to Mrs Proudie, hoping, through her influence, to replace Josiah Crawley as perpetual curate of Hogglestock. *A little man, about forty years of age, who had a wife and children living in Barchester, and who existed on such chance clerical crumbs as might fall from the bishop's patronage.* (*The Last Chronicle of Barset.*) He is a schoolmaster, with the same rôle, in the play *Did He Steal It?*

THWAITE, DANIEL: Tailor, and son of a tailor, Thomas Thwaite, who had befriended Countess Lovel after her rejection by the Earl. Enraged by her daughter, Lady Anna's, preference for Daniel over Frederick Lovel, the Countess tries to murder him; but the couple marry and emigrate to Australia. (*Lady Anna*)

TODD, SALLY: A wealthy, pleasure-loving friend of Mary Baker, courted in vain, for her money, by Sir Lionel Bertram. *A maiden lady, fat, fair, and perhaps almost forty; a jolly jovial lady, intent on seeing the world, and indifferent to many of its prejudices and formal restraints . . . She did not much care what she said of others, but dearly liked to have mischief spoken of herself. Someone once had said – or very likely no one had said it, but a* soupçon *of a hint had in some way reached her own ears – that she had left Torquay without paying her bill. It was at any rate untrue, but she had sedulously spread the report; and now wherever she ordered goods, she would mysteriously tell the tradesman that he had better inquire about her in Devonshire. She had been seen walking one moonlight night with a young lad at Bangor: the lad was her nephew; but some one had perhaps jested about Miss Todd and her beau, and since that time she was always talking of eloping with her own flesh and blood.* (*The Bertrams.*) She also appears in *Miss Mackenzie.*

TOOGOOD, THOMAS: London lawyer and cousin of Mrs Mary Crawley, he clears Josiah Crawley's name by discovering the real thief of the cheque. (*The Last Chronicle of Barset.*) He also figures in the play *Did He Steal It?*

TOWERS, TOM: Journalist whose articles in the *Jupiter* help to precipitate the investigation into the Hiram's Hospital accounts. *It is probable that Tom Towers considered himself the most powerful man in Europe; and so he walked on from day to day, studiously striving to look a man, but knowing within his breast that he was a god.* (*The Warden.*) He also appears in *Barchester Towers* and *Framley Parsonage.*

TOZER, TOM (alias AUSTEN): Jewish moneylender, who, with his brother John, has possession of the promissory notes signed by Mark Robarts for Sowerby. *Tom Tozer was a bull-necked, beetle-browed fellow, the expression of whose face was eloquent with acknowledged roguery. 'I am a rogue,' it seemed to say. 'I know it; all the world knows it: but you're another. All the world don't know that, but I do. Men are all rogues, pretty nigh. Some are soft rogues, and some are 'cute rogues. I am a 'cute one; so mind your eye.'* (*Framley Parsonage*)

TRAFFORD, LADY FRANCES: Daughter of the Marquis of Kingsbury and sister of Lord Hampstead, whose friend, George Roden, she persists in loving, despite family opposition because he is a clerk. (*Marion Fay*)

TREFOIL, ARABELLA: John Morton's unscrupulous fiancée, daughter of Lord and Lady Augustus Trefoil. She tries unsuccessfully to secure the greater advantage of a marriage with Lord Rufford, but John still leaves her a fortune at his death and she marries Mounser Green. *Did not care much for pleasure. But she did care to be a great lady, – one who would be allowed to swim out of rooms before others, one who could snub others, one who could show real diamonds when others wore paste, one who might be sure to be asked everywhere even by the people who hated her. She rather liked being hated by women and did not want any man to be in love with her, – except as far as might be sufficient for the purpose of marriage.* (*The American Senator*)

TREGEAR, FRANCIS OLIPHANT (FRANK): Fellow Oxonian of Lord Silverbridge, whose sister, Lady Mary Palliser, he marries. *He had taught himself to regard himself as a young English gentleman of the first water, qualified by his birth and position to live with all that was most noble and most elegant; and he could have lived in that sphere naturally and gracefully were it not that the part of the "sphere" which he specially affected requires wealth as well as birth and intellect. Wealth he had not . . . He was dark, with hair that was almost black, but yet was not black; with clear brown eyes, a nose as regular as Apollo's, and a mouth in which was ever to be found that expression of manliness, which of all characteristics is the one which women love the best.* (*The Duke's Children*)

TRENDELLSOHN, ANTON: Jewish sweetheart of the Christian Nina Balatka. Despite his family's efforts to discredit her in his eyes they eventually marry. (*Nina Balatka*)

TRESSEL, LINDA: Central figure of the story, who runs away with her sweetheart to avoid marriage to an old man, but is parted from her lover in the end. (*Linda Tressel*)

TREVELYAN, LOUIS: Orphaned, wealthy son of a noted barrister, he marries Emily Rowley, quickly becoming jealous of the attentions paid her by Colonel Osborne. He abducts his and Emily's child, Louey, to Italy, but becomes insane and dies. *Well spoken of at the clubs by those who had known him during his university career, as a man popular as well as wise, not a book-worm, or a dry philosopher, or a prig. He could talk on all subjects, was very generous, a man sure to be honoured and respected; and then such a handsome, manly fellow, with short brown hair, a nose divinely chiselled, an Apollo's mouth, six feet high, with shoulders and legs and arms in proportion – a pearl of pearls! Only, as Lady Rowley was the first to find out, he liked to have his own way.* (*He Knew He Was Right*)

TRINGLE, SIR THOMAS and LADY EMMELINE: Parents of Tom, Augusta and Gertrude. They provide a home for Ayala and Lucy Dormer after their father's death, and Tom becomes one of Ayala's unsuccessful suitors, involving him in many troubles. (*Ayala's Angel*)

TROWBRIDGE, MARQUIS OF: Principal landowner of Bull-hampton, at feud with the Vicar. *A silly, weak, ignorant man, whose own capacity would hardly have procured bread for him in any trade or profession.* (*The Vicar of Bullhampton*)

TRUMBULL, FARMER: Victim of murder, presumed committed by Sam Brattle. (*The Vicar of Bullhampton*)

TUDOR, ALARIC: Cousin of Charley Tudor. He marries Gertrude Woodward, rises from junior clerk in the Weights and Meas-ures to Civil Service Commissioner, but is imprisoned for embezzlement and then emigrates to Australia. *Tudor wore no whiskers, and his light-brown hair was usually cut so short as to give him something of the appearance of a clean Puritan. But in manners he was no Puritan; nor yet in his mode of life. He was fond of society, and at an early period of his age strove hard to shine in it.* (*The Three Clerks*)

TUDOR, CHARLEY: Cousin of Alaric Tudor. Bored by his dull job in the Internal Navigation Office, he solaces himself with undesirable habits in his spare time, is nearly entrapped into marrying a barmaid, Norah Geraghty, when forbidden to court Katie Woodward, but reforms and marries Katie in the end. *He was a gay-hearted, thoughtless, rollicking young lad, when he came up to town; and it may therefore be imagined that he easily fell into the peculiar ways and habits of the office. A short bargee's pilot-coat, and a pipe of tobacco, were soon familiar to him; and he had not been six months in London before he had his house-of-call in a cross lane running between Essex Street and Norfolk Street. 'Mary, my dear, a screw of bird's eye!' came quite habitually to his lips; and before his first year was out, he had volunteered a song at the Buckingham Shades.* (*The Three Clerks*)

TWENTYMAN, LAWRENCE: Sporting gentleman wishing to marry Mary Masters. She refuses and he marries her younger sister Kate. (*The American Senator*.) He also appears in *Ayala's Angel*.

UNDERWOOD, SIR THOMAS: Guardian of Ralph and *littérateur*. His daughters are Patience and Clarissa, the latter marrying the Revd Gregory Newton after many years' belief that she was in love with Ralph (the heir) Newton. (*Ralph the Heir*)

USBECH, MIRIAM: Daughter of the lawyer who drew up Sir Joseph Mason's will; rewarded by Lady Mason for witnessing the forged codicil. She marries Samuel Dockwrath. *Hers was a nature in which softness would ever prevail; – softness, and that tenderness of heart, always leaning, and sometimes almost crouching, of which a mild eye is the outward sign. But her comeliness and prettiness were gone. Female beauty of the sterner, grander sort may support the burden of sixteen children, all living, – and still survive. I have known it to do so, and to survive with much of its youthful glory. But that mild-eyed, soft, round, plump prettiness gives way beneath such a weight as that: years alone tell on it quickly; but children and limited means combined with years leave to it hardly a chance.* (*Orley Farm*)

USHANT, LADY MARGARET: Widowed aunt of John and Reginald Morton who brings up Mary Masters at Bragton Hall and then makes her her companion. (*The American Senator*)

USSHER, CAPTAIN MYLES: British police officer who seduced Feemy Macdermot and is killed by her brother Thady. *Good looking, strongly made, and possessed that kind of courage, which arises more from animal spirits, and from not having yet experienced the evil effects of danger, than from real capabilities of enduring its consequences.* (*The Macdermots of Ballycloran*)

VALCARM, LUDOVIC: Linda Tressel's sweetheart, with whom she elopes to avoid marriage to Peter Steinmarc. (*Linda Tressel*)

VAN SIEVER, CLARA: Mrs van Siever's daughter. Her portrait is painted by Conway Dalrymple, and she later marries him. (*The Last Chronicle of Barset*)

VAN SIEVER, MRS: Wealthy widow of a Dutch merchant and mother of Clara, she is associated with the dubious financial activities of Broughton and Musselboro. *She was a ghastly thing to look at, as well from the quantity as from the nature of the wiggeries which she wore. She had not only a false front, but long false curls, as to which it cannot be conceived that she would suppose that anyone would be ignorant as to their falseness. She was very thin, too, and very small, and putting aside her wiggeries, you would think her to be all eyes. She was a ghastly old woman to the sight, and not altogether pleasant in her mode of talking.* (*The Last Chronicle of Barset*)

VAVASOR, ALICE: John Vavasor's daughter, and cousin and confidante of Lady Glencora Palliser. She is engaged twice to John Grey and twice to her cousin George Vavasor, before finally marrying the former. *There was nothing that was girlish in her manners. Her demeanour was as staid, and her voice as self-possessed as though she had already been ten years married. In person she was tall and well made, rather large in her neck and shoulders, but as were all the Vavasors, but by no means fat. Her hair was brown, but very dark, and she wore it rather lower upon her forehead than is customary at the present day. Her eyes, too, were dark, though they were not black, and her complexion, though not quite that of a brunette, was far away from being fair ... I beg you, in taking her for all in all, to admit that she was a fine, handsome, high-spirited young woman.* (*Can You Forgive Her?*) She also appears in *The Eustace Diamonds*. She is Margaret de Wynter in the play *The Noble Jilt*.

VAVASOR, GEORGE: A stockbroker, brother of Kate and cousin of Alice. Wayward but fascinating, he wins the latter temporarily over from John Grey, aided by Kate, then tries to kill Grey after losing his seat in Parliament. He emigrates to

America. *He had lived in open defiance of decency. He had spent much money and had apparently made none, and had been, as all his friends declared, on the high road to ruin. Aunt Macleod had taken her judgement from this period of his life when she had spoken of him as a man who never did anything. But he had come forth again suddenly as a working man ... In fact, he stood well on 'Change ... He would not generally have been called ugly by women, had not one side of his face been dreadfully scarred by a cicatrice, which in healing, had left a dark indented line down from his left eye to his lower jaw. That black ravine running through his cheek was certainly ugly. On some occasions, when he was angry or disappointed, it was very hideous; for he would so contort his face that the scar would, as it were, stretch itself out, revealing all its horrors, and his countenance would become all scar.* (*Can You Forgive Her?*) He is Mark Steinmark in *The Noble Jilt*.

VAVASOR, JOHN: Alice's father, bored with his Government post, but reliant upon the income to keep him in indolence. He shares his house with Alice, but they live quite independent of one another. *They who have seen him scanning the steward's list of dishes, and giving the necessary orders for his own and his friend's dinner, at about half-past four in the afternoon, have seen John Vavasor at the only moment of the day at which he is ever much in earnest. All other things are light and easy to him, – to be taken easily and to be dismissed easily. Even the eating of the dinner calls forth from him no special sign of energy. Sometimes a frown will gather on his brow as he tastes the first half glass from his bottle of claret; but as a rule that which he has prepared for himself with so much elaborate care, is consumed with only pleasant enjoyment. Now and again it will happen that the cook is treacherous even to him, and then he can hit hard; but in hitting he is quiet, and strikes with a smile on his face.* (*Can You Forgive Her?*) He is M. de Wynter in the play *The Noble Jilt*

VAVASOR, KATE: George's sister, devoted to his interests. It is through her scheming that Alice puts up the money for George to stand for Parliament and becomes engaged to him. *To give Kate Vavasor her due, she was, at any rate, unselfish in her intrigues. She was obstinately persistent, and she was moreover unscrupulous, but she was not selfish.* (*Can You Forgive Her?*) She is Helen Steinmark in *The Noble Jilt*.

VAVASOR, SQUIRE: Grandfather of Alice, Kate and George Vavasor; Kate lives with him at Vavasor Hall. (*Can You Forgive Her?*)

VOSS, MICHEL: Landlord, with his second wife, Josephine, of the Lion d'Or hotel in Granpère, Lorraine. He opposes the marriage of his son, George, to his niece, Marie Bromar, but relents in the end. (*The Golden Lion of Granpère*)

WADDINGTON, CAROLINE: Granddaughter of George Bertram snr, she is brought up by her aunt, Mary Baker. She breaks her engagement with George Bertram jnr and marries Sir Henry Harcourt, but after his suicide she marries George. *She was a girl of twenty, and hardly knew her own power; but the time was to come when she would know it and should use it. She was possessed of a stubborn, enduring, manly will; capable of conquering much, and not to be conquered easily. She had a mind which, if rightly directed, might achieve great and good things, but of which it might be predicted that it would certainly achieve something, and that if not directed for good, it might not improbably direct itself for evil. It was impossible that she should ever grow into a piece of domestic furniture, contented to adapt itself to such uses as a marital tyrant might think fit to require of it. If destined to fall into good hands, she might become a happy, loving wife; but it was quite as possible that she should be neither happy nor loving.* (*The Bertrams*)

WALKER, GEORGE: Senior partner of the Silverbridge attorneys, Walker and Winthrop, who act for the Duke of Omnium and are much involved in the Crawley case. George Walker appears in *The Last Chronicle of Barset* and *The Duke's Children*.

WESTERN, GEORGE: He marries Cecilia Holt, admitting that he had jilted a girl in the past. When he learns eventually that Cecilia had once jilted a man, but has never confided it to him, he leaves her, but they are reconciled with the help of his sister, Lady Grant. (*Kept in the Dark*)

WHARTON, ABEL: Wealthy London lawyer, father of Everett

and Emily. Everett marries Mary, daughter of his father's brother, Sir Alured Wharton. *A spare, thin, strongly made man, with spare light brown hair, hardly yet grizzled, with small grey whiskers, clear eyes, bushy eyebrows, with a long ugly nose, on which young barristers had been heard to declare you might hang a small kettle, and with considerable vehemence of talk when he was opposed in argument . . . certainly a man of whom men were generally afraid. At the whist-table no one would venture to scold him. In court no one ever contradicted him.* (*The Prime Minister*)

WHARTON, SIR ALURED: Head of the Wharton family and father of Mary. (*The Prime Minister*)

WHARTON, EMILY: Daughter of Abel Wharton and sister of Everett. She marries Ferdinand Lopez but after his suicide is thankful to marry her childhood sweetheart, Arthur Fletcher. *Emily Wharton was a tall, fair girl, with grey eyes, rather exceeding the average proportions as well as height of women . . . Those who knew her well, and had become attached to her, were apt to endow her with all virtues, and to give her credit for a loveliness which strangers did not find on her face. But as we do not light up our houses with our brightest lamps for all comers, so neither did she emit from her eyes their lightest sparks till special occasion for such shining had arisen.* (*The Prime Minister*)

WHARTON, EVERETT: Son of Abel, he marries his cousin Mary Wharton. (*The Prime Minister*)

WHITTLESTAFF, WILLIAM: A middle-aged bachelor friend of Mary Lawrie's father, he takes her into his home after her stepmother's death and falls in love with her. She accepts his proposal, but when her young sweetheart, John Gordon, returns from abroad and proposes at last, the old man releases her. (*An Old Man's Love*)

WILKINSON, REVD ARTHUR: Oxonian friend of George Bertram, he succeeds his father, also the Revd Arthur, as vicar of Hurst Staple, Somerset. He finally marries Adela Gauntlet. *He was just older than young Bertram – by three months or so; just sufficiently to give to Wilkinson a feeling of seniority when they first met, and a consciousness that as he was the senior in age, he* should be the senior in scholastic lore. *But this consciousness Wilkinson was not able to attain; and during all the early years of his life, he was making a vain struggle to be as good a man as his cousin; that is, as good in scholarship, as good in fighting, as good in play, and as good in spirit.* (*The Bertrams.*) He also appears in *Miss Mackenzie.*

WINTERFIELD, MRS: Clara Amedroz's wealthy aunt, who leaves her nephew Capt. Aylmer her fortune on condition that he marries his cousin Clara. *An excellent lady – unselfish, given to self-restraint, generous, pious, looking to find in her religion a safe path through life – a path as safe as the facts of Adam's fall would allow her feet to find . . . To fight the devil was her work, – was the appointed work of every living soul, if only living souls could be made to acknowledge the necessity of the task. Now an aunt of that kind, when she assumes her duties towards a motherless niece, is apt to make life serious.* (*The Belton Estate*)

WOODWARD, MRS BESSIE: Widowed mother of Gertrude, Linda and Katie, and cousin of Harry Norman. *She was a quick little body, full of good-humour, slightly given to repartee, and perhaps rather too impatient of a fool. But, though averse to a fool, she could sympathise with folly. A great poet has said that all women are rakes at heart; and there was something of the rake at heart about Mrs Woodward. She never could be got to express adequate horror at fast young men, and was apt to have her own sly little joke at women who prided themselves on being punctilious. She could, perhaps, the more safely indulge in this, as scandal had never even whispered a word against her.* (*The Three Clerks*)

WOODWARD, GERTRUDE and LINDA: Mrs Woodward's elder daughters and sisters of Katie. They marry, respectively, Alaric Tudor and Harry Norman. *Gertrude carried by far the greater air of command. She was the handsomer of the two, and the cleverer. She could write French and nearly speak it, while her sister could only read it. She could play difficult pieces from sight, which it took her sister a morning's pains to practise. She could fill in and finish a drawing, while her sister was still struggling, and struggling in vain, with the first principles of the art. But there was a softness about*

Linda, for such was the name of the second Miss Woodward, which in the eyes of many men made up both for the superior beauty and superior talent of Gertrude. (The Three Clerks)

WOODWARD, KATIE: Youngest of the Woodward sisters. Forbidden by her mother to encourage Charley Tudor's attentions, she persuades him to mend his ways and is enabled to marry him after her near-fatal illness. *Katie, with all her juvenile spirit, was delightfully feminine; every notion of hers was easy, and every form into which she could twist her young limbs was graceful. She had all the nice ideas and ways which a girl acquires when she grows from childhood to woman's stature, under the eye of a mother who is a lady. Katie could only be untidy on occasions; but her very untidiness was inviting. All her belongings were nice; she had no hidden secrets, the chance revealing of which would disgrace her. (The Three Clerks)*

WORTLE, REVD JEFFREY, D.D.: Owner and headmaster of Bowick School, a preparatory school for Eton. He employs the Peacockes and stands by them when they admit their unwitting bigamy. *The Rev. Jeffrey Wortle, D.D., was a man much esteemed by others – and by himself . . . He liked to be master, and always was. He was just, and liked his justice to be recognised. He was generous also, and liked that, too, to be known. He kept a carriage for his wife, who had been the daughter of a poor clergyman at Windsor, and was proud to see her as well dressed as the wife of any country squire. But he was a domineering husband. His wife worshipped him, and regarded him as a Jupiter on earth from whose nod there could be and should be no appeal, but little harm came from this. If a tyrant, he was an affectionate tyrant. His wife felt him to be so. His servants, his parish, and his school all felt him to be so. They obeyed him, loved him, and believed in him. (Dr Wortle's School)*

WORTLE, MARY: The Wortles' only child, engaged to Lord Carstairs, whom she marries. *She was at the present time of the age in which fathers are apt to look upon their children as still children, while other men regard them as being grown-up young ladies. It was now June, and in the approaching August she would be eighteen. It was said of her that of the girls all round she was the prettiest; and indeed it would be hard to find a sweeter-favoured girl than Mary Wortle.* (*Dr Wortle's School*)

WORTLE, MRS: Dr Wortle's wife and mother of Mary. *Probably as happy a woman as you shall be likely to meet on a summer's day. She had good health, easy temper, pleasant friends, abundant means, and no ambition. She went nowhere without the Doctor, and wherever he went she enjoyed her share of the respect which was always shown to him.* (*Dr Wortle's School*)

WYNDHAM, FANNY: Niece and ward of the Earl of Cashel, despite whose opposition she eventually marries Lord Ballindine, having rejected Cashel's son, Lord Kilcullen. *Fanny Wyndham's light burned with so warm a flame, that butterflies were afraid to trust their wings within its reach.* (*The Kellys and the O'Kellys*)